THE NATIONAL CURRICULUM AND ITS EFFECTS

The National Curriculum and its Effects

Edited by

CEDRIC CULLINGFORD and PAUL OLIVER
University of Huddersfield, UK

LONDON AND NEW YORK

First published 2001 by Ashgate Publishing

Reissued 2018 by Routledge
2 Park Square, Milton Park, Abingdon, Oxon OX14 4RN
711 Third Avenue, New York, NY 10017, USA

Routledge is an imprint of the Taylor & Francis Group, an informa business

Copyright © Cedric Cullingford, Paul Oliver and the contributors 2001

All rights reserved. No part of this book may be reprinted or reproduced or utilised in any form or by any electronic, mechanical, or other means, now known or hereafter invented, including photocopying and recording, or in any information storage or retrieval system, without permission in writing from the publishers.

Notice:
Product or corporate names may be trademarks or registered trademarks, and are used only for identification and explanation without intent to infringe.

Publisher's Note
The publisher has gone to great lengths to ensure the quality of this reprint but points out that some imperfections in the original copies may be apparent.

Disclaimer
The publisher has made every effort to trace copyright holders and welcomes correspondence from those they have been unable to contact.

A Library of Congress record exists under LC control number: 2001086237

ISBN 13: 978-1-138-72441-9 (hbk)
ISBN 13: 978-1-138-72440-2 (pbk)
ISBN 13: 978-1-315-19247-5 (ebk)

Contents

Notes on Contributors   vii

Preface   viii

Acknowledgement   x

1. Introduction: Can a Curriculum be National?   1
   Cedric Cullingford

2. Conceptual Issues in a Centralised Curriculum   19
   Paul Oliver

3. The Crumbling Shrine: the National Curriculum and the Proposals to Amend it   33
   John Elliott

4. Secondary School Pupils' Experience of the National Curriculum   45
   Cedric Cullingford

5. Pupil Perceptions of the National Curriculum   63
   Leroy McDonald

6. Secondary Subject Teaching and the Development of Pupil Values   79
   Bob Butroyd

7. Excluded or Empowered: The National Curriculum and Exclusions   103
   Robert Berkeley

8. Exploring the Policy Influence of England's National Curriculum on School Exclusion: A Dilemma of Intended Entitlement and Unintended Exclusion?   121
   E. Rustique-Forrester

9	Horse Before the Cart: Developing an Evidence-Based Approach to Educational Policy *Fay Smith and Frank Hardman*	151
10	National Curriculum Subjects are Repositories of Values that are Under-Explored *Bob Butroyd*	173
11	ICT in the National Curriculum - Revised but not Resolved *Matthew Pearson*	193
12	Conclusion: Logic, Rationality and the Curriculum *Paul Oliver*	207

Notes on Contributors

Cedric Cullingford is Professor of Education in the School of Education and Professional Development at the University of Huddersfield.

Dr Paul Oliver is Principal lecturer in the School of Education and Professional Development at the University of Huddersfield.

John Elliott is Professor of Education within the Centre for Applied Research in Education (CARE) at the University of East Anglia, Norwich.

Leroy McDonald is a doctoral research student in the School of Education and Professional Development at the University of Huddersfield.

Bob Butroyd is Senior lecturer in the School of Education and Professional Development at the University of Huddersfield.

Robert Berkeley is a researcher in the Department of Educational Studies at the University of Oxford.

E. Rustique-Forrester is a researcher at the Centre for Educational Management, at the University of Surrey, Roehampton.

Dr Fay Smith is lecturer in the Department of Education at the University of Newcastle-upon-Tyne.

Dr Frank Hardman is Senior lecturer in the Department of Education at the University of Newcastle-upon-Tyne.

Dr Matthew Pearson is Senior lecturer in the Department of Education and Professional Development at the University of Huddersfield.

Preface

It has been over ten years since the Education Reform Act. As its title implies, this was introduced as making a radical change to the education system. The battery of tests, the provision for opting out, and Local Financial Management, together with the concomitant League Tables and changes to Inspection, all gave evidence of principles that were at one moment founded on the concept of market forces, and at another on clear centralised control. The most central example of the latter was the National Curriculum which, for all the subsequent tinkering, has remained intact.

During the last ten years there have been many people who have doubted the wisdom of imposing a 'broad and balanced' curriculum, supported by tests, on the whole population. The doubts have centred on whether this 'de-professionalising' of teachers enhances or devalues standards, and on whether pupils are making better or worse progress. This book is based on seeking out the evidence that would suggest whether the experiment has been successful or not. It has explored empirical data, rather than opinion. It is, of course, difficult in such a complex human endeavour such as education to single out a particular variable, like the curriculum. Correlation, like the rise of exclusions and truancy, should not be mistaken for causes. Nevertheless there is a consistency in the findings that should give more than a pause for thought.

There is not only consistency but positive intellectual overlaps between the chapters. Any doubts they display about pupil standards, motivations and welfare are the result of a close and fair scrutiny of the evidence. The first three chapters give a theoretical as well as factual framework to the rest of the book, summarising evidence from the earliest debates to the more recent changes. The next three chapters from four to six explore pupils' experience and perceptions of the National Curriculum: what is it really like for them? Has the 'entitlement' of the curriculum enhanced their learning, or burdened them with fact?

Chapters seven and eight explore the relationship between the National Curriculum and the experience of disaffected pupils. The rise in exclusions is well documented, but can this be attributed to the results of the Education Reform Act? Chapter nine takes this look at the actual effects of the National Curriculum somewhat further through an analysis of literacy hours in particular. Chapters ten and eleven explore not only teachers' perceptions of the national curriculum but their experience of it.

Between the different chapters and the evidence that is presented there is a great deal of consistency. The respect for valid evidence means that the judgements and conclusions are not lightly made. If the National Curriculum delivered exactly what Kenneth Baker promised on its introduction then that should be a matter to be celebrated. If it has, in fact, the opposite effect to that intended, then that should be made known.

Acknowledgement

The editors are very grateful for the help and expertise of Susan Smith of the Academic Typing Services unit at the University of Huddersfield.

1 Introduction: Can a Curriculum be National?

CEDRIC CULLINGFORD

Everyone has their own curriculum. As in a curriculum vitae it is like a loose fitting set of cultural clothes, an idiosyncratic texture of knowledge that is unique. There are as many hidden or overt curricula as there are people. The word curriculum is therefore a Humpty-Dumpty word: "When I use a word it means exactly what I want it to mean, neither more nor less". "The question is" says Alice, "whether one can use a word like that?" "The question is" replies Humpty-Dumpty, "who is to be master, that's all".

The great irony about such a lubricious term is that it has become redolent with its association of a firmly imposed, inflexible will. The National Curriculum as in the curricula imposed on communist countries rests on the supposition that there is a clear collective whole appropriate to everyone. The very concept of 'entitlement' is that all should feast at the same table. The 'broadness' and the 'balance' is all inclusive. All the tests must be 'standard'. That we meet with the collective experience of submitting to one agreed centralised plan, where, in the words of one child at the official opening of a new school building, 'all of us sang the National Curriculum'.

There are many layers of meaning attached to the curriculum from the personal to the collective. This is why there has always been debate about what kinds of knowledge are most appropriate. Since Plato the debates about what 'subjects' were appropriate were as much to do with politics and society, the way in which individuals not only saw the world but their places in it, as with fitness for purpose or different types of pleasure. The history of this debate is fascinating and could have been useful as a corrective to the rather superficial arguments that were developed since Mr Callaghan's much invoked 'Ruskin' speech that was taken as a starting point, as if nothing of the kind had been addressed before. Indeed the National Curriculum, in the way it is enshrined, is noteworthy for its eschewing of philosophical principles.

Debates about the curriculum have always been about underlying tensions, which are still with us. Some are to do with the distinctions between knowledge and the acquisition of useful facts, since 'knowledge is power', and the need for 'manners', for the development of such understanding as improves the character and strengthens the morals. There is also a tension between the discipline of thinking - the word 'discipline' here chosen deliberately - and the practical application of knowledge. There are some subjects, associated with the academic, not only deemed to be useful for their own sake but empowering those who study them with such strength of thought that their critical skills can be applied to almost anything. Against this is placed the formidable amounts of practical knowledge and accumulated understanding on which we tend to rely, or trust, in surgeons and engineers.

The curriculum is not just a matter of facts. It involves skills which are transferable and personal development. There are some who suggest that it does not matter which subject is studied as long as it is done with adequate depth and conviction. There are, for example, some private institutions in the United States whose curriculum consists of nothing more or less than a selection of one hundred books, its own 'Great Tradition'. The curriculum in the broadest sense is inclusive and unavoidable. The moment it is subject to control and choice it tends to be exclusive. Nearly all formal curricula, again from Plato onwards, tend to be for some kind of 'elite', however that is defined. Most of the debates about the curriculum are about exclusion; how many people are capable of entering the inner sanctum of T.S. Eliot's cultural aristocracy, or S.T. Coleridge's 'Clerisy'.

One of the tensions about the curriculum is the extent to which it should be 'relevant' to the modern world, or should be above such immediacy. Trilling (1966) lamented the "unargued assumption ... that the true purpose of all study is to lead the young person to be at home in, and in control of, the modern world" (p.4), long before the idea of a 'core' curriculum was thought of. Bantock (1980) makes a distinction between the banal 'truth' of physical actuality and the higher truth of moral and aesthetic spheres, "in touch with the historical nature of their consciousness, which has hitherto largely been ignored" (p.137).

Technical and vocational education have never gained that intellectual prestige accorded to the academic. This is a conclusion which is reached in many different parts of the world. A sense that the most able or gifted are those who aspire to that which is least useful is an atavistic instinct which runs deep even in anti-intellectual cultures like the British. Advanced levels are the natural standard entrance requirements to prestigious universities;

vocational qualifications tend to be associated with those who are, how shall we put it, less 'fitted' in that direction. Even in subjects like accountancy, useful, practical and lucrative, where one would have assumed that prior knowledge required at university would make for well qualified entrants to the profession, there are latent academic snobberies. The large accountancy firms in the City of London recruit at least three quarters of their staff from the ancient universities, who continue to eschew such mundanely practical subjects. To have read classics remains respectable.

Such distinctions in prestige have long been with us. There is a resistance to new subjects, such as rural studies or environmental studies, even in schools (Goodson, 1982). This is not just a result of clinging to the familiar, or even of despising the potentially utilitarian. It is a result of a sense of the curriculum as something that can be controlled and be imposed. The complexities of real practice mean that there can never be a sense of the coherent whole. As Schoen (1987) so often pointed out, the contamination of actual problems can lead to deeper reflection about practice, but it often develops into the protection of established academic hegemonies.

This idea of a perfect curriculum in terms of coherence, theory and testable outcomes is not only deep-seated in the National Curriculum, but closely linked to the assumption of traditional values and beliefs. One of the results of the lack of philosophical debate about the National Curriculum is that many traditional assumptions are left unexamined. Whether it is for better or worse, the State's curriculum is not geared towards inclusiveness, towards addressing the needs of the deprived or disadvantaged. Nor does it deal with either new ways of studying or new ways of being assessed. The very idea of league tables and of set targets would anyway undermine genuine notions of 'inclusiveness' as opposed to 'entitlement'. There is something both traditional and elitist in the National Curriculum.

Goodson (1994) compares the secondary regulations of 1904 with the National Curriculum and concludes that the curriculum remains a process of social privitising. He sees it as a form of social control, with subjects of high status resisting new intrusions. As in the 1970s and 80s subjects that are new, like environmental studies, social studies or political education, are rejected or marginalised against the established core. Perhaps they are too technical, or too subversive. The given curriculum in its traditional monumentality prevails.

It could be argued that the National Curriculum is properly elitist and divisive in its intentions, for all the desire for uniformity. Those who do not meet the standards can always be 'disapplied' either formally or psychologically. But the purpose of the National Curriculum has rarely been debated. There are different models for the curriculum (Ahier and Ross, 1995). There are those which see the curriculum as a form of cultural transmission, passing on a received body of knowledge - the 'academic'. The curriculum can be alternatively understood as a means of developing social, economic and technically desirable skills - a utilitarian approach. Or the curriculum can be a means of developing social understanding of the world, including inculcating values and good behaviour. The National Curriculum is an uneasy turning away from all three. It could easily have been thought of as a troubled combination, but any concern with personal social education or with citizenship, or with high levels of communication and information technology are marginal.

Those who witnessed and commented on the introduction of the National Curriculum all point out that it was never really thought through. When one compares the way in which some countries approach the curriculum with the 1988 Educational Reform Act, we see some interesting contrasts. The Act has perhaps half-a-page on the purpose of the curriculum, and one thousand pages on the content. Other counties put all their energies into debating the tensions between the needs of society and those of the individual, and then have perhaps one page on the content. This is one result of what all who were involved saw as indecent haste.

It is ironic that after a number of years in which the curriculum was subject to contemporary debate, with a number of pamphlets produced by HMI and focus groups, long before the idea became a political mantra led by one Secretary of State, the actual National Curriculum was introduced in a great deal of hurry. This is a result of the politics involved. The Education Reform Act was a symbol of the will of politicians. It signaled the desire to interfere with the education system in a way unprecedented for at least one hundred years, since the imposition of payment by results. This use of education as a sign of political will set up in the Education Reform Act has been continued ever since (Hunter, 1997). Humpty-Dumpty's rhetorical question about who is to be master has a more sardonic ring.

The haste behind the reforms was apparent to all involved. Even at the time some of the results of political interference were anticipated and warned against (Graham and Tytler, 1993). There are many inadvertent signals, as well as prescience, about what might happen next. Even supporters of the Act, including those who made a living from it, could anticipate the dangers.

> Narrowing it to the basics could be superficially appealing, easy, testable and cheap, but that is the route of the Philistines ... (Graham and Tytler, p.147)

The many subsequent clashes between the government and those involved in education stem from the very concept of whether political actions give the results that are intended. Here we can only hint at what is a real debate: on the one hand the research evidence which shows that good educational results occur when there is a sense of ownership by those involved - (stakeholders?) - and the political expediency of wanting to make things happen.

This tension between freedom and control is real, but it tends, like the debate about the curriculum itself, to be reduced to analysis of a fairly simple kind, with inspection seen as purely punitive (Cullingford, 1995) and any hint of opposition dismissed as part of the entrenched educational establishment. The problem is that 'control', an imposed system, never can operate as intended. There are too many factors, let alone people, involved. The Holy Grail of all politicians is an Act which makes a clear difference, for which the instigator is remembered. Whether the results are beneficial or not are of secondary concern.

Nothing demonstrates the desire to impose reform through set structures better than the way in which the National Curriculum was developed. At the heart of the reform was the complete system of tests. The Task Group on Assessment and Testing was set up to create a structure into which the National Curriculum would fit. The argument then focused not on purposes, or the reasons for choosing subjects, but simply on the battles within and between subjects, for space within the overall framework. The Chair of TGAT is one of many who felt himself to be deceived; to be manipulated and used for purposes which were nefarious, essentially political rather than educational (Black, 1997).

From the start the National Curriculum was viewed with suspicion, not only because of the speed, or the political inferences but because of its lack of a theoretical basis. There were many warnings made of its dangers and unforeseen consequences, warnings that were so weighty that they were assumed to be persuasive (Haviland, 1988). They were ignored, and continue to be so. The set, conservative idea that there should be three core subjects, and seven 'foundation' subjects, prevailed. The amount of time given to each was not specified. Nor were the teaching methods, the timetable or textbooks. The early assumption was that only seventy percent of the time would be spent on the National Curriculum. It is telling to note how more and more rigid has become the control. Literacy hours and numeracy hours, and regulations including personal and social education, as well as ever increasing inspectorial powers, all demonstrate that the experiment in imposing a will, especially through target setting, continues not only unabated but with ever fierce and tighter determination.

The imposition of this political will contains a deep-seated irony. The rhetoric behind the National Curriculum was that of the importance of market forces (Tomlinson, 1988). Nothing could be more contradictory. Local management of schools, parental choice, and grant maintained schools are all manifestations of the significance of the social market. Against this is a curriculum seen as a 'safety net', a control system for all of those not in the independent system. The social divisions which are growing rapidly according to the government's own figures have some of their origins here. The Institute of Economic Affairs pointed out that the centrally imposed curriculum was wrong. "The most effective national curriculum is that set by the market" (Haviland, 1988, p.28).

The National Curriculum in its introduction and continuance was never really thought through. It was seen to be pragmatic. The consequences of its imposition have rarely been explored, not only because of the difficulty in isolating one set of variables in such a complex area but because the political will is there that it should be left unexamined. There are, however, many questions which were raised at the time the National Curriculum was being introduced, and these still deserve some answers. Many public bodies expressed grave doubts about the reforms. The RSA suggested that there was too much emphasis on knowledge. The Roman Catholic Bishops called it 'utilitarian', a "National curriculum which effectively ignores beliefs and values" (p.16). The NAS/UWT was against a prescriptive curriculum and national tests. The Association of Secondary Heads felt that the "prescriptive proposals will severely limit pupils' opportunities".

These are just some examples of the doubts which were expressed by professional bodies at the time. To what extent do they remain unallayed? Perhaps the most telling worry, which goes to the heart of the matter, is that expressed by one of the Local Education Authorities, Derbyshire, at a time when they still had a significant role to play. Their doubts, however, were not about their own position, nor about the details of the curriculum, but about the fundamental assumption on which the National Curriculum was and is based.

> The general tone of the document is one of disbelief in the teaching profession, a disbelief that the teacher can be anything more than a conveyor of given information.
> It presents a quality control system based on a model already rejected by industry; top-down with no trust displayed in the work force. (p.39)

Who is to be master? One hundred years ago the centralised curriculum, with set targets to be attained, against which individual teachers were to be measured, was found to have two unforeseen consequences. The first was to diminish the self-esteem and the enterprise of the teacher. Payments by result meant the acceptance of the mechanical routine; what was to be learned was what was given. There was no room for personal manoeuvre. The second consequence was even more significant. The pupils were the ones who suffered most. They knew they had to submit to what was imposed on them. They knew that the teachers were like mechanics carrying out other people's orders. The weight of sheer fact wore them down.

Some cynics suggested that this might have been the idea. The independent schools went entirely their own way. It was, however, a system that was soon abandoned, and those who wonder why have all their answers clearly expressed in a series of royal commissions on education which more truly reflect the possibility of engaging not only in philosophical debate but considering the empirical evidence.

It is the evidence, and a critical scrutiny of the evidence, that lies at the heart of this book. But evidence, as opposed to opinions, anecdotes and perceptions is difficult to come by. The whole educational experience is complex. It depends less on schools than other factors, like the home, the socio-economic influences, the subtleties of peer pressure and the chances of personal motivation. The mythology of instant effect, whether of a policy or of a particular medium, has long been disproved, even if myths remain influential. The National Curriculum might have been enshrined in legislation, but the way in which it has been enacted is quite another matter. Habits and assumptions do not change overnight. Some of the policies might have done good and some terrible damage, but it is very hard to pick out that particular variable that makes all the difference.

The National Curriculum might be monumentally prescriptive but it depends on the ways in which teachers interpret it. Whilst its ethos is that of rejecting teachers' expertise, it relies on teachers' professionalism to deliver it. This irony actually reveals a great deal about the strength of teachers. Whatever their misgivings about the policy they implemented it, however difficult. They submitted to the preparing of tests, and to a whole new battery of demands. Some have suggested that over the subsequent years teachers have learned how to adapt to the conditions and to these impositions in a way that accepts the limitations of their role. What is certain is that teachers have adapted to the circumstances in their own individual ways (Hargreaves, 1994).

Some teachers have reacted to the National Curriculum in a minimalist way (Helsby and McCulloch, 1997). They have continued to carry out their professional duties, attempting to teach not only critical thinking but those aspects of the general curriculum that they believe to be most relevant. They have used opportunities to explore a topic just as they used to do. They have allowed inspiration rather than prescription to flourish. Deeply held beliefs about what it is to teach and to learn are persistent, and remain despite the ethos of the reforms. Roberts (1995), for example, found that despite the clear mandate of the National Curriculum any three schools were teaching not only in different ways but with quite different materials. Older teachers might be accused of being slow to adapt, or unwilling to adapt to change. This could be as much a sign of their professional experience as of their inflexibility. It is younger teachers who make the greatest attempts to use the written curriculum. But even these tend to go their own way as they get older and more experienced (Kosunen, 1994).

One assumption about the implementation of the National Curriculum is that any falling away of standards is not so much due to the National Curriculum itself as to the resistance to it by teachers. Either teachers are a pure conduit for a central curriculum or they are the curriculum makers themselves (Clandinin and Connelly, 1992). Teachers live out the curriculum. They know it is far more complex than what is prescribed. This is one reason why some countries, like Finland, see teachers' ownership of what they are presenting, and their styles, as of far greater significance than anything written. Teachers have a subtle and iterative relationship with their pupils which influences what as well as how they teach. It is not all one way delivery. As teachers become more experienced what they teach becomes less important than the learning processes of their pupils (Pye, 1989).

There are, of course, many different types of teacher and there always have been. Studies like the Oracle project (Galton, 1980 and since revisited) have demonstrated certain habits of organisation that mean that no-one teaches the whole of the curriculum in the same way. There have always been some who are classic text-book followers, conveying what is there according to a syllabus or the given exegesis. There are those who follow distinct objectives, however they arrive there. There are those who respond to different student needs, according to the pace and interests of individuals. And there are those who follow their inner convictions and their conceptions of what should take place according to previous experience (Schmidt et al., 1987). To all of these an imposed curriculum will mean different things.

It is impossible to make the kind of sweeping generalisations about effects that the National Curriculum itself makes. Entitlement to the prevailing subjects, access to so many hours of teaching, exposure to particular methods of instruction and the experience of the same skills and attitudes does not mean that all pupils' experience will be the same. Some attitudes are deep-seated. One of these is that the curriculum, whatever the school imposes, will be found boring (Raven, 1979). Another is that the given curriculum will be thought of as irrelevant and without purpose (White with Brockington, 1983). And another is that the curriculum is whatever the teacher demands; it has little personal connection to the pupil beyond trying to guess what is wanted. Alienation from the set, given curriculum was always a prevailing attitude, whatever the individual exceptions. The question is whether a greater prescription causes greater disengagement, firstly with the teachers and then with the pupils. The research that predates the National Curriculum suggests that the dangers of greater imposition are clear. Rather than be more flexible or subtle, and rather than match it to the needs of pupils, the curriculum has become ever more a matter of imposition.

The curriculum has always been unproblematic for those who have the power to impose it. Those who choose what others should learn have only limited power in fact, since the learning process is so much more complicated than the receiving of wisdom or the imbibing of subjects. Choosing what should be taught - leaving the learning aside - can become a kind of game. It always depends upon personal experience, but it is always a temptation to discuss what should be in a curriculum as a way of interpreting the world as collectively, or personal experience. Debates about what history should consist of, let alone whether history should be part of the National Curriculum, reflect passionate views of history as a series of great events, or history as the lived experience of individuals in society, and history as that of the British, of conversely, that of the Scots, the Welsh and other more limited ethnicities (Philips, 1998). Subjects reflect experience and ways of marking out the cultural significance of this experience. They are therefore both personal, full of specialisms, of territories not to be invaded by outsiders, and hugely complex, the result of collective experience.

The complexity of any curriculum comes about because it is impossible to impose it satisfactorily or completely on anyone else, and yet there is an almost atavistic desire to do so. No-one wants to let go of control. The subjects that people are taught are supposed to make them what they are. How can one therefore be so careless, in every sense, about their being free? All debates about the curriculum are ostensibly about the tension between personal satisfaction, curiosity and fulfilment, and the needs of society, for skills, for those matters of the greatest utility. This tension seems real, but the question is whether one should continue to debate the curriculum at this level, in terms of 'subjects'; an array of facts bound together by a common language and forms of thought.

There are some underlying truths about the curriculum that would suggest that the focus on a 'given' or established curriculum might be misplaced. There is more than a little irony in the government campaigns to recruit more people to the teaching profession. The fact that their policies might have made it less attractive passes them by, but so does the way in which they couch their appeals. Despite the National Curriculum they ask people to remember the best teacher they ever had. Inevitably what is evoked are memories of inspiration, of personalities full of curiosity, of an interest in the aptitudes of individual pupils of a kind that rubs sorely against the grain of the National Curriculum. The greatest lessons all people remember were those that went into their own direction, away from the syllabus, regardless of statutes and indifferent about whether anything could be tested. Against those moments of excitement the rest seems at best routine, at worst absurd.

Introduction: Can a Curriculum be National? 11

It can be argued, as it is inevitably remembered, that the most clearly remembered, the most inspired lessons were out of the central control of the set curriculum (Cullingford, 1996). In that case does it matter which subject is studied? The greatest minds are motivated by their specialist curiosity. Should they be encumbered by the limitations of the broad and the balanced? The word 'entitlement' suggests that pupils can receive what they demand. It actually means they are given what they are told. Any subject can inspire and make a personal connection with the purpose of learning. Indeed, any subject can be the basis for learning many others. Learning how to learn, how to develop the confidence to satisfy ones own curiosity, is far more powerful than learning to be indifferent to a whole range of subjects.

Even the disenfranchised, the excluded, remember particular lessons and particular subjects, associated with their teachers (Cullingford, 1999). Despite what they *ought* to learn they can recall what they did learn, with relish. It could be said that this distinction between what is supposed to be learned and what is actually learned is exaggerated. It is the 'relish' of the distinction which might be cavilled at. The actual distinction is at the heart of all knowledge of learning. This is usually termed 'learning theory', but the latter word is the kind most quickly reacted against by those who put together the most comprehensively theoretical model of learning ever practically thrown together.

In the approaches to the National Curriculum, in all those signs that something might happen - the HMI documents, like *A View of the Curriculum*, the papers like the Department of Education and Science's, "A Framework for the Curriculum" and the *Primary Survey* - there were some consistencies that are, with hindsight, telling. There were concerns not so much with subjects as specific forms of experience. There were recognitions of the lack of consistency of need from class to class, and the ability to recognise that each should be catered for differently (Alexander, 1992). The distinction was clearly drawn between those decisions which look so easy intellectually and those which were in fact difficult politically (Stenhouse, 1980). The tragedy is that politically easy decisions often have terrible intellectual consequences.

Many of the consequences of the Educational Reform Act and the development of the National Curriculum are hard to isolate. Effects take a long time. They come about because of changes in tone, in motivation and expectancy. To rely solely on measures of testing width of knowledge is not to prove any worthwhile long-term change. Those who cast doubt on the imposition of a centralised curriculum cannot point to that kind of instant empirical evidence that would prove their case. Their case is more subtle and long-term, and therefore the more easily dismissed as reactionary, as being against inevitable reform rather than positive about alternatives. The National Curriculum is concerned with testable results, not attitudes. It depends on the continuing goodwill of teachers for its implementation. If targets are not met, is it then the fault of the teachers?

Teachers are the creative mediators who have to respond to and implement change (Croll, 1996). They submit to their duties. There is, however, a real sense of loss, detected by parents as well. The pleasure of teaching, the excitement in children's learning seem to be eroded. Instead of the creative endeavour of free exploration the primary duty of a teacher appears to be to protect themselves, and to a lesser extent, their pupils, from failure. Targets and inspections imply a defensiveness that does not fit easily into the taking of any intellectual risk. Teacher accountability is, after all, dependent on the key areas dominated by the core. English, maths and science become even more powerful as there are attempts to scale down the sheer amount to be learned. A return to the 'core curriculum' is almost inevitable, but it will be backed with a renewed emphasis on instrumentalism, on certain key skills that must be imposed and must be tested.

The National Curriculum is powerful not only in its detail but in the shift of emphasis. To understand its effects is to explore the subtle and complex experience of schools from the participant's point of view; the teachers and the pupils rather than the inspectors. The locus of power is no longer in individuals, or even in the small institutions which contain them, but outside. The voice of authority is not that of the teacher, but that of the Secretary of State, or the Chief Inspector of Schools. The impulse of learning is replaced by the prerogative of being tested. Pupils observe teachers anxious of the test results and fearful of being inspected. Any encouragement to learn is then interpreted as a cajoling to do well for the teacher's sake. A central trust is lost. Those who are allowed to 'disapply' the National Curriculum, even at the margins, are deemed to be the failures, the socially and academically inept (Cullingford, 2000).

What evidence do we find about the effects of the National Curriculum? On the one hand there is the School Effectiveness industry; with emphasis on the power of the 'super' head teachers, on accountability and tight control, supported by results against set targets. On the other hand there is the growing social divide, with greatly increased truancy and exclusion. Could the two possibly be connected? Those who are trying to draw the evidence together, like those in this book, appear to think so.

For some pupils schools were always somewhat alienating institutions. The underlying ideology suggested that they do little to foster the development and the learning of individuals (Salmon, 1998). The National Curriculum must enforce this impression where pupils are valued as statistics, as performance targets met or failed. The mass of fact and reliance on testing is an imposition of will that can cause significant subordination. Those schools which have the highest truancy rates tend to be those which emphasise the ritualistic and traditional exchanges exemplified in the National Curriculum (Collins, 1998). Those schools which manage to develop more sophisticated types of exchange of information where the autonomy of the individual still counts, which indeed, by-pass the official requirements of the National Curriculum, have far greater retention rates. Those schools which retain community involvement, which does not fit easily into the National Curriculum, have far more beneficial long-term effects (Ball, 1998).

There are many reasons for estrangement from school. Individual pathology and defective parenting have a part to play. There is a new element that commentators need to add beyond meeting the needs of children (Hoyle, 1998). This is the 'blaming system' of the National Curriculum, where schools are encouraged to be sites of deliberate brutality, of failure to meet targets. This primitive culture is wonderfully exemplified in the law that punishes parents as well as teachers for pupil failure (Blacktop and Blyth, 1999). Student disaffection with school can be interpreted therefore not only in terms of personality traits or social deviance but also as a rational choice when school experience is increasingly disconnected from the students' personal experience (Elliott, 1998).

The passive acquisition of subject knowledge is not the same as active engagement in understanding one's place in a complex society. Indeed, society is presented as a series of demands, of control, of inspection, of blame and of inevitable failure, for a large number. Is this a society anyone would wish to join? Every day the pupils appear to witness the domination of the National Curriculum. Teachers cut down on pupil participation in order to get through the demands (Galton and Fogelman, 1996). There is less time to listen. Whilst teachers try to be creative this is despite the bureaucratic, technical view of teaching in the National Curriculum (Helsby and McCulloch, 1997). In the experience of children all that counts is their success or lack of it at SATs. Self-esteem and school achievement are significantly linked (Mortimore et al., 1988). Self-esteem amongst children has dropped significantly over the years. Some see this as a direct link with the imposition of so many tests (Davies and Brember, 1997).

Here is a shift of emphasis from the curriculum to tests. Just as the concept of 'targets' has replaced that of 'education', so 'standards' have become the centre of policy, with greater control over the details of pedagogy (Davies and Edwards, 1999). The question is whether this greater control creates higher standards. The school curriculum is increasingly more a sense of failure than one of enlightenment for many (Kinder, 1997). The opposite effect to that intended seems to prevail. In certain subjects standards appear to be lower. This is so in science (Hacker and Rowe, 1998), and mathematics (Ridout and Ruddock, 1998). Even in its own terms, it appears, the National Curriculum is having exactly the opposite effect to that intended. That is true, at least, of a significant number of pupils. Not all. There are some that succeed, as they would in any system. This counters that shibboleth of 'entitlement' that was supposed to enable all, and not just that percentage (sic) of pupils that would probably succeed anyway (Willan, 1998).

The gap between the rhetoric that the National Curriculum raises standards, and the reality appears ever widening (Evans et al., 1999). The blunt oppressive instrument appears to ignore the individual needs of those whom it is supposed to serve (Mitchell and Brumfitt, 1997). So it appears. But can this be proved?

On a philosophical level, given the accumulated wisdom of the past, one would have thought that the National Curriculum might be a great mistake. On a pedagogical level - thinking about the actual experiences of pupils - it is clearly not thought out. On a practical level, which, to an extent, is the subject of this book, the National Curriculum has all kinds of effects which are negative. In a country which has a far more flexible approach to the curriculum, with less rigidity and less prescription, there appears to be more professional development and better student-teacher relationships (Cowley and Williamson, 1998). Most countries have long found that the means of educational improvement are the opposite to the kinds of measures embodied in the National Curriculum. In this great and unthought-out experiment, not tried for over one hundred years, communist countries apart, what can be learned?

References

Alexander, R. (1992) *Policy and Practice in Primary Education*, London, Routledge.

Ahier, J. and Ross, A. (1995) *The Social Subjects Within the Curriculum: Children's Social Learning in the National Curriculum*, London, Falmer.

Ball, M. (1998) *School Inclusion: The School, the Family and the Community*, York, Joseph Rowntree Foundation.

Bantock, G. (1980) *Dilemmas of the Curriculum*, Oxford, Martin Robertson.

Black, P. (1997) Whatever happened to TGAT? in Cullingford, C. *Assessment versus Evaluation*, London, Cassell, pp.24-50.

Blacktop, J. and Blyth, E. (1999) School Attendance and the Role of Law in England and Wales, in Blyth, J. and Milner, J. *Improving School Attendance*, Routledge, London.

Clandinin, D. and Connelly, F. (1992) The Teacher as Curriculum Maker, in Jackson, P. (ed) *Handbook of Research on the Curriculum*, New York, Macmillan.

Collins, D. (1998) *Managing Truancy in Schools*, London, Cassell.

Cowley, T. and Williamson, J. (1998) A Recipe for Success? Localised Implementation of a (flexible) National Curriculum, *The Curriculum Journal*, Vol.9, No.1, pp.78-94.

Croll, P. (1996) *Teachers, Pupils and Primary Schooling: Continuity and Change*, London, Cassell.

Cullingford, C. (1996) *Parents, Education and the State*, Aldershot, Ashgate.

Cullingford, C. (1997) *Assessment versus Evaluation*, London, Cassell.

Cullingford, C. (1999) *The Causes of Exclusion: Home, School and the Development of Young Criminals*, London, Kogan Page.

Cullingford, C. (2000) Research on Disapplication in Secondary Schools, forthcoming.

Davies, J. and Brember, I. (1997) Did the SAT's lower Year 2 Children's Self-esteem? A four year Cross-sectional Study, *Research in Education*, No.57, pp.1-11.

Davies, M. and Edwards, G. (1999) Will the Curriculum Caterpiller Ever Learn to Fly? *Cambridge Journal of Education*, Vol.29, No.2, pp.265-275.

Elliott, J. (1998) *The Curriculum Experiment: Meeting the Challenge of Social Change*, Buckingham, Open University Press.

Galton, M., Simon, B. and Croll, P. (1980) *Inside the Primary Classroom*, London, Routledge and Kegan Paul.

Galton, M. and Fogelman, K. (1998) The Use of Discretionary Time in the Primary School, *Research Papers in Education*, No.13, pp.113-119.

Goodson, I. (1982) *School Subjects and Curriculum Change*, London, Croom Helm, 1982.

Goodson, I. (1994) *Studying Curriculum: Cases and Methods*, Buckingham, Open University Press.

Graham, D. with Tytler, D. (1993) *A Lesson for Us All: The Making of the National Curriculum*, London, Routledge.

Hacker, R. and Rowe, M. (1998) A Longitudinal study of the effects of implementing a National Curriculum project upon classroom processes, *Curriculum Journal*, Vol.9, No.5, pp.95-103.

Hargreaves, A. (1994) *Changing Teachers, Changing Times: Teachers' work and culture in the Post Modern Age*, London, Cassell.

Haviland, J. (1988) *Take Care, Mr Baker!* London, Fourth Estate.

Helsby, G. and McCulloch, G. (1997) (eds) *Teachers and the National Curriculum*, London, Cassell.

Hoyle, D. (1998) Constructions of Pupil Absence in the British Education Service, *Child and Family Social Work*, Vol.3.

Hunter, P. (1997) The Market Experiment, in Cullingford, C. (ed) *The Politics of Primary Education*, Buckingham, Open University Press.

Kinder, K. (1997) Causes of Disaffection: The views of pupils and Education Professionals, EERA Bulletin, Vol.3, No.1, pp.3-11.

Kosunen, T. (1994) Making Sense of the Curriculum: Experienced Teachers as Curriculum Makers and Implementers, in Carlgren, I. et al. *Teachers Minds and Actions: Research on Teachers' Thinking and Practice*, London, Falmer.

Mitchell, R. and Brumfitt, C. (1997) The National Curriculum Experience of Bilingual Pupils, *Educational Review*, Vol.49, No.2, pp.159-180.

Mortimore, P. et al. (1988) *School Matters: The Junior Years*, Wells, Open Books.
Philips, R. (1988) *History, Teaching, Nationhood and the State*, London, Cassell.
Pye, J. (1989) *Invisible Children: who are the real losers at school?* Oxford University Press.
Raven, J. (1979) School Rejection and its Amelioration, *Education Research*, Vol.20, pp.3-9.
Ridout, M. and Ruddock, G. (1998) *Mathematics Attainment in Primary Schools*, Slough, NFER.
Roberts, M. (1995) Interpretations of the Geography National Curriculum: A Common Curriculum for all? *Journal of Curriculum Studies*, Vol.27, No.2, pp.187-205.
Salmon, P. (1998) *Life at School: Education and Psychology*, London, Constable.
Schmidt, W., Porter, A., Floden, R., Freeman, D. and Schwille, J. (1987) Four patterns of teacher content decision making, *Journal of Curriculum Studies*, Vol.19, No.5, pp.439-455.
Schoen, D. (1987) *Educating the Reflective Practitioner*, San Francisco, Jossey-Bass.
Stenhouse, L. (1980) *Curriculum Research and Development in Action*, London, Heinemann.
Tomlinson, J. (1988) Curriculum and Market: Are they compatible?, in Haviland, J. (ed) *Take Care, Mr Baker!* London, Fourth Estate, pp.9-13.
Trilling, L. (1966) *Beyond Culture*, London, Secker and Warburg.
White, R. and Brockington, D. (1983) *Tales Out of School: Consumer's Views of British Education*, London, Routledge.
Willan, P. (1998) Whatever Happened to Entitlement in the National Curriculum? *Curriculum Journal*, Vol.9, No.3, pp.269-283.

2 Conceptual Issues in a Centralised Curriculum

PAUL OLIVER

The writers of the official documents for the National Curriculum in England, are very keen to enunciate a set of principles, very often ethical principles, which have informed and continue to inform, the development of this initiative. In order to be brought to life however, principles require concepts to be used in ways which can convey to people the underlying ideas of those principles. An example of such a principle which recurs throughout the National Curriculum literature, is that all pupils should experience an education with certain shared, or indeed minimal, characteristics. The word 'should' is very important here, because it indicates that there is an ethical content to this argument. The National Curriculum documents prescribe an education of a certain kind. The concept which is used over and over again to delineate this notion is 'entitlement'. This is however a complex idea and bears further examination. An example of its use by the School Curriculum and Assessment Authority (SCAA) is as follows:

> The National Curriculum was established by the Education Reform Act 1988 to provide the minimum educational entitlement for pupils of compulsory school age. It aims to raise educational standards by setting demanding but achievable targets for pupils' learning. (SCAA, 1996, p.3)

Now in general terms an entitlement is something like a 'right'. It is an experience to which we should have access, by virtue of a shared understanding of what it means to be a human being. From an ethical point of view we are not entitled for example, to trample all over the flower beds in the city park, because it is an infringement of the rights of our fellow citizens to enjoy looking at the flowers, and fundamentally because society places limitations upon our freedoms in the general public interest. Hence we do not have an entitlement to behave exactly as we would wish. On the other hand society does prescribe certain entitlements which are seen as being functional to the social system in which we live. In a democratic system, citizens have an entitlement to vote for the political party which will govern the country. This entitlement is set within the parameters of a particular type of political system, and would not exist in an autocracy or a military dictatorship. In other words, these types of entitlement either exist or do not exist, within a form of social system. They are entitlements which are created because of a particular type of social or political system. We might think of a variety of similar entitlements such as the entitlement to live where we wish; to work where we wish; and to travel where we wish. However, although we may think of one society where there are few restrictions in these areas, we may very well be able to think of other societies where there are considerable restrictions. In other words we begin to envisage a class of entitlements which are socially constructed because they are functional within, and supportive of, a particular socio-political system.

The other aspect of such entitlements is that they are relative rather than absolute. It would perhaps be difficult to argue that one particular form of selecting political rulers was absolutely superior to the wide range of other possible systems. Even within a broadly democratic system there are very many different systems for selecting representatives to the legislature. Some people may argue for one system, others will argue for another. This of course does not even take into account the great variety of other political systems. Hence we see that entitlements of this nature are not absolute, but created first of all by individual social systems, and are relative to other such entitlements. We may prefer one kind of system to another, but there are other people who would no doubt feel differently. In order to decide which was the most valuable of such entitlements one would have to establish criteria and weigh different entitlements against such criteria. Now, if we accept that there is a class of entitlements which are socially constructed and are relative to each other, one is left wondering if there is a separate class of entitlements which exist *a priori*, and which are true in an absolute sense.

For example, we may consider that we are entitled to sustain our own religious beliefs; to express those beliefs to others provided that there is no attempt necessarily to convert them to one's own belief system; and to worship the Divine as we conceive Her/Him as long as this imposes no constraints upon others. We may believe this to be an *a priori* entitlement since we may consider that the individual human being should be able to place himself or herself within a particular religious and cosmological framework, and give expression to that feeling. Furthermore, we may consider that this is an entitlement which cannot be given to us by other human beings. We possess this entitlement already. Indeed we are born with it. The entitlement to possess a religious understanding of the world, is a part of being a sentient and thinking human being. Not only can this entitlement not be given to us, but nor can it be removed. No social or political system; no human being; no ruler may take this from us. They may wish to impose limitations upon the way in which we give expression to our religious feelings, but they may not take away the entitlement to believe as we do.

Equally well we may wish to argue that all human beings have an intrinsic entitlement not to be attacked and killed by an aggressor. We have the entitlement to live out our natural lives until the end, without having our lives cut short by the deliberate act of another human. In short, we have an entitlement to the natural span of our life. We acquire this entitlement when we are born. We do not need to be told that we have an entitlement to our own lives. We know that already. Equally well, we are aware that unpleasant things happen in the world, and some individuals do not behave in a manner which we would normally classify as 'human'. Society also takes measures to protect people and to exert constraints upon the behaviour of the few, by a variety of well-publicised sanctions and punishments. But whether or not society is successful in protecting us from the unpleasant actions of the minority, we nevertheless retain our entitlement to life and to being free from assault from an aggressor.

In summary then, it begins to appear that there may be two main categories of entitlements. There are those which are relative to a particular society or culture, are socially-constructed, and are given to us as members of that society. Alternatively, there are those *a priori* entitlements which accrue to us by virtue of our being human.

Now to return to the National Curriculum it is interesting to examine some of the language which is employed in relation to the concept of entitlement. In explaining the principles of the National Curriculum, the Department for Education and Employment (DfEE) and Qualifications and Curriculum Authority (QCA) wrote:

> It sets out a clear, full and statutory entitlement to learning for all pupils. It determines the content of what will be taught, and sets attainment targets for learning. (DfEE and QCA, 1999, p.3)

The notion that this is a form of entitlement conditioned by society is emphasised by the use of the word 'statutory'. This entitlement is clearly enshrined in legislation created by human beings, and hence is presumably an entitlement which is specific to a particular society and culture at a given time. As has been argued earlier, we cannot claim that such an entitlement is in any way absolute. Bearing this in mind, it is interesting that the word statutory is juxtaposed with the concept 'full'. This concept clearly carries connotations of 'complete' and 'sufficient in itself'. In what other sense could the National curriculum be regarded as full. And yet, there is a contradiction here. The concept of a relative curriculum, of one specific to a certain society, is regarded also as complete. The only way to reconcile these apparent contradictions is to assume that the curriculum is full in relation to the needs of English society at this time. In other words, one might wish to infer that while there is the slightest of suggestions that other curricula are at least possible, the present National Curriculum meets the needs of English pupils to the full. It is all that they will need in the foreseeable future. However, in another sentence it is said of the National Curriculum:

> It must be robust enough to define and defend the core of knowledge and cultural experience which is the entitlement of every pupil, and at the same time flexible enough to give teachers the scope to build their teaching around it in ways which will enhance its delivery to their pupils.
> (DfEE and QCA, 1999, p.3)

It is really unclear what is meant by the second part of this sentence. However, by the use of the concept 'flexible' and the phrase 'build their teaching around it' there is the clear implication that this curriculum is not quite as full as we might have thought. Indeed, later in the same document we gain an insight into exactly how flexible the National Curriculum is:

> While these four purposes do not change over time, the curriculum itself cannot remain static. It must be responsive to changes in society and the economy, and changes in the nature of schooling itself.
> (DfEE and QCA, 1999, p.13)

Hence it becomes clear that the National Curriculum is not conceived as a curriculum which is merely relative to that of other societies, but is in fact in a state of dynamic equilibrium with society, the economy and with the 'nature of schooling'. This is quite a remarkable statement, for it establishes the principle that the National Curriculum, far from being an absolute entity, is in fact highly relative. It is intended to reflect the state of society, which is clearly subject to continual change. It is intended to reflect the state of the economy, which is also in continual change. It is also intended to reflect the state of schooling which presumably incorporates the attitudes of parents, pupils and teachers and other interested members of society, and also to reflect the processes and procedures in schools. Presumably, these attitudes also are in a state of constant flux.

Therefore we begin to build up a picture of a curriculum which is far from being 'full' in the sense of complete. As soon as we regard it as complete, it will require modification. And yet in the very notion of a National Curriculum, of a centrally-administered body of official knowledge there is a sense in which such a curriculum is absolute and for all time. One certainly wonders how many parents and members of the public view it in this way. Clearly however, no curriculum can be of this type, unless it is constructed in a rigid authoritarian society. Arguably, not only should the curriculum itself be flexible, but it should enable pupils themselves to be flexible, and to be adaptable to the wide range of choices available in society. This certainly seems to be what is advocated by Letwin (1994, p.241):

> If we care at all about living in a liberal democracy, in which people are permitted to make choices for themselves, then we are duty-bound to provide everybody with tools which enable them to make and express such choices, on the basis of understanding what is being chosen, rather than as mere arbitrary leaps in the dark.

And so the concept of 'entitlement' is clearly an important one within the 'National Curriculum'. Indeed so important is it apparently, that one suspects at times that it is a little over-used, as in the following sentence:

> An entitlement to learning must be an entitlement for all pupils.
> (DfEE and QCA, 1999, p.3)

However, there are other concepts which appear to be important in the National Curriculum and one such example is that of inclusivity. As an example of its use, there is the following sentence for a discussion on the development of a more inclusive curriculum:

> In carrying out the review, QCA has sought to ensure that all recommendations contribute to a more inclusive curriculum framework for all pupils.
> (QCA, 1999a, p.14)

Now one normally understands by the word 'include', the notion of certain boundaries or parameters, and that certain entities are within those boundaries ie. included, and certain entities are without, ie. excluded. In the above extract, the word inclusive is an adjective applied to 'curriculum framework'. One assumes therefore that the issue under discussion is the range of different subjects or disciplines which are to be included within the said boundaries. The notion that this should be 'more' inclusive suggests apparently that there is the intention of extending the boundaries in order to embrace more curricular elements within. The extract does specify all pupils, and hence it is a reasonable assumption that the extent of the inclusivity relates to the curriculum and not to the pupils. After all, if we are talking about 'all' pupils, then this phrase suggests the maximum possible inclusivity.

We thus have the notion of the National Curriculum expanding (and presumably contracting) as external forces demand. Yet, if we return to the very first extract in this chapter, we remember that the National Curriculum is defined as the 'minimum educational entitlement' of pupils. The concept of 'minimum' in this context is extremely interesting. The term minimum is generally employed when we wish to specify a lower limit to a continuum. The minimum is usually a level which is susceptible to being quantified precisely. Thus we may speak of the minimum recorded temperature during the last week. Alternatively, we may speak of the minimum force required to move a particular mass under specified conditions, or the minimum speed required to reach a particular place in a certain period of time. In other words, a minimum is not a vague and general term. It specifies a level precisely. It is an entity which we normally consider to be quantifiable. In educational terms then we perhaps assume that a minimum educational entitlement, is a specified body of knowledge to which all pupils should have access. It does not say, for example, that pupils in category X should have a particular 'minimum' entitlement and that those in category Y should have a different entitlement. In other words, we can perhaps envisage the minimum entitlement as being a kind of lowest common denominator in curriculum terms. It is what everyone should experience irrespective of their abilities or aptitudes. Yet is this really what the

National Curriculum purports to provide? This concept is firstly very much at odds with the idea of a 'more inclusive' curriculum carrying the implications of a curriculum which is changing and in a state of dynamic equilibrium. The concept of a minimum, is of an entity which is fixed. Hence there is a fundamental conflict in the manner in which the National Curriculum is described. We are uncertain whether it is conceived as something which is changing, or whether it has a fixed composition which is the same for all pupils.

Some light on these philosophical problems is shed by another QCA document published in the same year as the last extract.

> There is a need to move from simply providing a statement on access to the National Curriculum, to more supportive guidance on the inclusion of all pupils. (QCA, 1999b, p.2)

It does seem a little strange that it is apparently necessary to provide a statement on access, when the National Curriculum is avowedly for all pupils in England. Does this mean that some schools which should be teaching the National Curriculum are failing to do so? One assumes that this is not the case. However, we do notice that in the last phrase of the extract there is a clear application of the term 'inclusion' to pupils. In some ways this is a strange use of language. The term inclusion has apparently moved from being applied to the curriculum to being applied to pupils. One wonders however whether there is any ambiguity here about whether indeed some pupils are being excluded from the National Curriculum. This seems rather unlikely, and yet it is a strange use of the word 'inclusion'. Further light is shed on the use of this term in an extract from QCA (1999a, p.15):

> However, there are continuing concerns about whether the current arrangements for access and participation are resulting in a full entitlement to educational opportunity, particularly for pupils with special educational needs, gifted and talented pupils and pupils from ethnic minority groups.

This at least gives us a few further insights into the planning behind the curriculum. If we try to analyse the language here it seems that certain types of pupils are identified who, it is apparently asserted, possess certain characteristics. It is then suggested that these categories of pupils are perhaps not having the same educational opportunities as other pupils (as presumably the majority of pupils). Of course, in a special sense, no two pupils have an identical educational experience, if we regard the latter not simply as the body of knowledge studied, but as the sum total of the learning experiences undergone. Once a teacher says something to pupil X in class, and fails to say this to pupil Y at the other side of the room, then their learning experiences are, in a very subtle way, different. What it is possible to say however, is that in principle, the official statement of the body of knowledge and skills to be acquired is the same for all pupils across the country. Now the delineation of a body of knowledge and skills is one matter, and in principle this is capable of being expressed fairly precisely. However, if we assume that we have defined the body of knowledge (curriculum) and also that there is a network of schools in which the curriculum will be delivered, then assuming that pupils attend the schools, issues of participation are largely issues of pedagogy. It may be that some pupils do not participate fully in lessons; that they do less homework than they perhaps should; and fail to acquire parts of the stipulated body of knowledge. However, failure to participate is this sense is an issue of pedagogic style on the part of teachers and of motivation and application on the part of pupils. It is not a question of curriculum.

What we see here then is an apparent use of terminology, which read superficially appears to have some coherence, but when analysed, is at best somewhat perplexing. We sadly fare little better when we examine some of the ethical statements about the National Curriculum. Consider the following statement about the curriculum:

> It should pass on the enduring values of society, develop pupils' integrity and autonomy and help them to be responsible and caring citizens capable of contributing to the development of a just society.   (QCA, 1999c, p.5)

First of all, the phrase 'enduring values' is relatively imprecise, simply because it is rather difficult to say which values are 'enduring'. It is easy to think of values, but some of them may not exactly appear to be enduring. It also depends to some extent on what we mean by values. We may decide to have recourse to values such as truth-telling for instance. It would certainly be difficult to argue that truth-telling is not an enduring value, but if we consider many other apparently 'basic' values, we get into some difficulty in terms of establishing whether or not they are enduring. For example, we may propose that being peaceful and non-violent in our dealings with our fellow human beings is an enduring value, and yet there are facets of our society which are indeed violent. We may propose the value of sustaining family life, and yet we live in a society where the conventional notion of the family is being challenged. In fact, one could easily argue that one of the characteristic features of English society is that values are in fact regularly challenged, and in reality are in a state of flux. If someone could unequivocally establish the enduring values of society, then no doubt teachers via the curriculum, would take their fair share of the responsibility for transmitting them.

To move on in the extract to the concept of autonomy, this raises again a slight conflict in one's mind between a compulsory curriculum and the notion of independently-motivated freedom of choice. Are we to say to pupils that they must attend school, and must study a specified curriculum, and must take specified tests and must also be autonomous? There seems to be something a little strange here. Is it really possible to be autonomous within a closed, constrained system? Autonomy presupposes that there are some freedoms inherent in a system, and that there is the possibility of some freedom of choice. A pupil may decide to study P rather than Q. There is also an argument that autonomy is something that one must be capable of practising before one can be regarded as autonomous. In other words, it may be arguably nonsensical to describe a person who is constrained from acting autonomously, as in principle autonomous. 'They would be autonomous, if only they had the freedom'. Autonomy is arguably something a little like a skill. One must practise it; practise making decisions and finding out later whether they were sound ones, before one can have a sense of ones own autonomy.

Finally, in the extract there would seem to be some difficulty in encouraging pupils to contribute to the development of a just society, when society is in many respects so unjust. Pupils are only too aware of the unjust features of society. As they turn on the television they learn that access to health care appears to depend at least partly upon the area of the country in which you live; they learn that employment rates and house prices differ enormously from region to region; they learn that some children are born into unbelievable wealth, while others live in poverty; moreover they learn that such accidental factors as the wealth of the family into which one is born will probably affect ones life expectancy. It seems slightly unrealistic that pupils studying the National Curriculum can be persuaded that their studies will assist in the creation of a just society.

So far then, we might sum up this discussion by suggesting that the language employed in the principles which underpin the National Curriculum is confused. It has an apparent coherence when read rapidly and superficially, but closer analysis reveals fairly extensive conceptual confusion. The essential problem is that the entire approach to the discussion of the National Curriculum principles tends to overlook the notion that the curriculum is socially constructed. Goodson (1994, p.16) expresses this very clearly:

> The school curriculum is a social artifact, conceived of and made for deliberate human purposes. It is therefore a supreme paradox that in many accounts of schoolings the written curriculum, this most manifest of social constructions, has been treated as a 'given'.

With any entity which is constructed through social dialogue one should be very careful about the problem of reification. This is the, at times, almost imperceptible process whereby individuals come to speak of and write of, something which is clearly relative to a variety of social contexts, as if it were in reality a fixed and rigid system. The danger is that insufficient attention is given to ways in which the curriculum, even a 'centralised' curriculum could be varied and adapted to specific circumstances. Hand in hand, with the tendency to think of the curriculum as being relatively fixed, can sometimes arise a type of authoritarianism which sees the curriculum in its 'agreed' form as something to be imposed. Once an entity is seen as being fixed, then it is a fairly short step to assume that everyone ought to see the wisdom of this and to conform.

There appears to be a sense in much of what is written about the National curriculum that it is over-ambitious in what it is seeking to achieve. There are broad statements about the supposed change in attitudes and values which will occur in children. For example, in QCA (1999c, p.5) there is the following statement about the school curriculum:

> It should develop their awareness, understanding, and respect for the environments in which they live, and secure their commitment to sustainable development at a personal, local, national and global level.

It seems reasonable and perhaps achievable that pupils can be made more aware of the environment in which they live. Empirical evidence can be presented to them showing the effects of pollution, and they are able to corroborate much of this by observing the world around them. One might even argue (although this is stretching the point much further) that the curriculum can develop respect for the environment. The concept of a development suggests a change for the better of some type, yet that change need not be of a particular magnitude. In other words it is not perhaps unreasonable to expect teachers to enhance, in however small a manner, the respect which pupils feel towards the environment. In some pupils, this may not be achieved, since one cannot be certain that teachers alone can inculcate respect for the environment. The pupil has to be reasonably receptive to such ideas, and of course other influences such as parents, the family, and the media must contribute to engender this respect. Perhaps a more satisfactory wording would be 'attempt to develop'. It seems reasonable that teachers should certainly try to develop respect, although the extent to which this is expected to be achieved, is a debatable issue.

However, the wording of the second part of the extract is much less satisfactory. The extract is concerned with creating a change in moral outlook in pupils. It is concerned with encouraging them to be more sensitive to the environment. However, it is simply impossible for teachers or the curriculum to 'secure' a commitment to a moral position. One can 'encourage', 'attempt to develop', 'inform', pupils in relation to a moral position, but one cannot guarantee that one is able to 'secure' a commitment to a cause. The language appears to be far too definite and all-embracing. One is also left wondering about the nature of the word 'commitment'. I may say, for example, that I am committed to the idea of getting regular exercise every day from now on. This would not seem a very extreme statement. It is a perfectly reasonable goal to have. Equally well, one might say that one is committed to raising money for the local hospice. This again seems a perfectly reasonable commitment, partly because it is a moral thing to do, but also because it is very achievable - at least in principle. However, if I suddenly announced to my friends that I was unshakeably committed to the prevention of the pollution of the arctic with plastic and metal waste, and was also committed to preventing the gradual melting of the south polar ice pack, they may think these claims a little extreme. In the normal use of the world 'commitment' we tend to reserve it for areas where we potentially can do something practical to demonstrate our commitment. Are we really saying that it is reasonable to expect the National Curriculum to result in a commitment to sustainable development at a global level? Let us stretch our imaginations for a moment, and suppose that the National Curriculum is able to secure such a thing. In this case how would we test that the commitment had actually been secured. Perhaps we could ask all pupils. "Having studied such and such aspects of the National curriculum, do you now have a commitment to sustainable development?" The answer to this issue is that one cannot normally establish 'commitment' except by watching the behaviour of people often over a considerable period of time. Commitment is a characteristic which is to be demonstrated and not simply asserted.

This chapter has attempted to analyse some of the official language used to describe the National Curriculum. The language appears to be on some occasions imprecise and indeed it is extremely difficult to understand exactly what is being claimed. There appears particularly to be a confusion in conceptual terms between an attempt to establish an absolute body of knowledge which will be the accepted curriculum for all children; and the acknowledgement that any curriculum must adapt and evolve under external constraints. There certainly does tend to appear to be an absolutist trend in many of the writings on the National Curriculum:

> Accordingly it seemed essential that all pupils should be guaranteed a curriculum of a distinctive breadth and depth to which they should be entitled irrespective of the type of school they attended, or their level of ability or their social circumstances and that failure to provide such a curriculum is unacceptable. (HMI, 1994, p.232)

There would seem in general terms to be two possible ways in which the issues raised in this chapter may be resolved. One would be to address these issues and try to clarify the ways in which concepts are employed in the National Curriculum dialogue. The other strategy would be to accept the relativism inherent in any curriculum, and to attempt to adapt the curriculum itself, its delivery and the mechanisms for periodic revision to reflect this relativism.

References

DfEE and QCA (1999) *The National Curriculum: Handbook for Secondary Teachers in England*, London, DfEE and QCA.

Goodson, I.F. (1994) *Studying Curriculum*, Buckingham, Open University Press.

HMI (1994) The entitlement curriculum, in Moon, B. and Mayes, A.S. (eds) *Teaching and Learning in the Secondary School*, London, Routledge.

Letwin, O. (1994) Grounding comes first, in Moon, B. and Mayes, A.S. (eds) *Teaching and Learning in the Secondary School*, London, Routledge.

QCA (1999a) *National Curriculum Review: Developing the School Curriculum*, London, Qualifications and Curriculum Authority.

QCA (1999b) *The Review of the National Curriculum in England: The Secretary of State's proposals*, London, Qualifications and Curriculum Authority.

QCA (1999c) *The Review of the National Curriculum in England: The Consultation Materials*, London, Qualifications and Curriculum Authority.

School Curriculum and Assessment Authority (1996) *A Guide to the National Curriculum*, London, HMSO.

3 The Crumbling Shrine: the National Curriculum and the Proposals to Amend it

JOHN ELLIOTT

Introduction

The consultation process that was carried out by the Qualifications and Curriculum Authority (QCA) at the end of the last millennium involved a large number of teachers as well as organisations. It elicits views about the character and shape of the National Curriculum and whether changes should be made to it. The advice presented to the Secretary of State as a result of this was consistent and clear. The general consensus was that the original orders of the National Curriculum were a straitjacket, both constricting and controlling, and that any future progress would depend on some degree of liberalisation, with greater professional autonomy for teachers.

The modifications which were indicated in the proposals in *Achieving Excellence through the National Curriculum* which are the focus for this chapter were revealing not only as yet another proposal for 'excellence' to be achieved, but of the limitations of the existing framework which they unwittingly revealed. If the proper pattern for a National Curriculum were to be more flexible and less prescriptive, then what did it say about the effects of the original Act, with its very precise statements on what should be learned and how it should be measured? Could there have been a sense that not all the results of the National curriculum were those which were intended? Could there have been some notice taken of student disaffection?

The Proposals Viewed as a Response to Pupil Disaffection from Learning

The Secretary of State's proposals for a less prescriptive and more flexible national curriculum framework were broadly welcomed by teachers. They are intended to give teachers greater scope for selecting and organising content in ways which match the learning needs of their particular pupils.

Much of the early opposition to the national curriculum framework was based on the view that it would put teachers in a straitjacket and replace their professional judgement with a large amount of prescriptive detail. I was particularly opposed at the time to a framework that, in spite of its espoused aims, appeared to neglect 'the inner being' of pupils and their personal and social development in a rapidly changing and increasingly complex world. I predicted, albeit over-dramatically, that 'the proposed national curriculum will unwittingly alienate young people from their own natural powers, which will nevertheless manifest themselves on a massive scale in ever new and sophisticated forms of human destructiveness' (Elliott, 1988).

After ten years of the National Curriculum we are increasingly aware that the growing number of young people who turn to crime as a persistent way of life tend to be those whom schools have failed to engage in personally meaningful learning. This is not to argue that the national curriculum is *the* cause of it all, only that it failed as an appropriate response to the major challenges that social and economic change in advanced modern societies presents for education.

The Secretary of State's proposals commendably acknowledge that the national curriculum 'was failing to engage a significant minority of 14-16 year olds, who were as a consequence becoming disaffected from learning'. The reductions proposed for most subjects, in the level of detailed prescription and the introduction of more curricular flexibility, together with the new opportunities for school initiatives at key stages 3 & 4 (in the areas of Personal, Social and Health Education [PSHE] and Citizenship Education [CE]) are clearly intended to give teachers more 'space' to experiment with ways of preventing and overcoming disaffection. The proposals offer teachers opportunities to engage all pupils with learning experiences that are personally meaningful for their lives in an advanced modern society. Moreover, they do so without sacrificing the principle of giving pupils' *equal access* to a common curriculum. They avoid succumbing to the temptation of placing pupils on separate curriculum tracks, which convey differing levels of expectation about their academic capabilities. There is, however, a telling addition to the legislation which allows some pupils to be 'disapplied' from certain parts of the National

Curriculum, a freedom which tends to be associated with the least able and the most disaffected.

The national curriculum framework tended to confuse giving pupils equality of access to key concepts and skills with the rigid standardisation of illustrative content. The newer proposals make a significant contribution to ending this confusion, by acknowledging that raising standards for all pupils does not necessarily entail they always have to develop their knowledge, understanding and skills in relation to the same things. This is not to deny that there are some things all pupils ought to learn about in our society and which need to be prescribed in the national curriculum. The proposed revisions construct a better balance between *prescription* and *flexibility* in these respects.

There is increasing evidence that disaffection from learning in schools exists on a much larger scale than the traditional behavioural indicators of 'disruption' and 'truancy' suggest (See Rudduck et al., 1996; Elliott, 1998 and Rickenson, 1999). In our classrooms there are many pupils who are passively compliant with what is required of them. They 'go through the motions of learning' without achieving their full potential. These include pupils who, as headteachers of 'successful schools' will often acknowledge, are achieving 'the standard' C grade in their GCSEs. If disaffection from learning can be attributed to far more than a 'significant minority', then we should ask whether the latest revisions are flexible and radical enough to meet the sheer diversity of pupils' learning needs in a rapidly changing society. In order to answer this question we need to evaluate the proposed revisions in the light of the challenges social and economic change is posing for schools in the new millennium. It appears that the QCA review of the national curriculum was not grounded in any systematic analysis of such challenges, even though they exist (eg. Posch, 1994 and Elliott, 1998). Such analysis as there was tended to be piecemeal and intuitively derived.

We should also ask whether, given the scale of the disaffection problem, the revised curriculum framework needs to be further developed to incorporate more explicit guidance to teachers on matters of pedagogy? My answer to this question would be 'yes'. Studies of curriculum change have shown that it is over-optimistic to presume that significant pedagogical change will automatically follow from simply giving teachers more freedom to select relevant curriculum content. It is clear that the Secretary of State's proposals are driven by a concern to engage all pupils in meaningful and challenging learning experiences at school. Selecting appropriate content is important in this respect, but so are the ways in which teachers structure pupils' experience of the content; the kinds of learning tasks they set pupils and the strategies they use to engage pupils in them. As I shall argue, the proposed revisions imply pedagogical criteria for structuring pupils' curriculum experiences. Why not make them explicit to teachers?

I will now explore the implications of the current proposals for the processes of teaching and learning in schools, and how the national curriculum framework might be re-designed to accommodate them. In the final section of the paper I will briefly review these implications in the light of four particular challenges that social and economic changes were posing for schools at the end of the last millennium.

Breaking Through the 'Straitjacket' Towards a More Pedagogically-Driven Curriculum

The 'new framework' document was a breakthrough in at least two respects. First, it acknowledged that further progress in *raising standards* depends on finding ways of engaging *all pupils* in some form of personally meaningful learning, and therefore signalled to teachers that excluding the disaffected from classrooms and schools is inconsistent with the government's *standards agenda*. Secondly, it acknowledged that this agenda cannot be accomplished without reinstating *trust* in teachers to develop, within a supportive rather than restricting national curriculum framework, their own pedagogical solutions to the problems of engaging all pupils in learning experiences which are meaningful for them. It is a pity that these two points are not more clearly highlighted in the proposals. They clarify the basis for a future educational partnership between the government and teachers and the responsibilities of each partner. The challenge for teachers is to develop more *socially inclusive pedagogies* in their classrooms and the challenge for government is to design a curriculum framework which supports such development.

The proposals indicate a shift of concern; away from a concern with over-detailed specifications of content, towards a greater concern with the quality of the learning processes in which pupils are engaged. This shift towards a more *pedagogically-driven curriculum* is reflected in a number of specific revisions to existing national curriculum subjects, as well as in the proposals for PSHE and CE.

Embedded in these proposals are a range of criteria which function as *procedural principles* for defining what is to count as a worthwhile learning process. They include the following.

- To contextualise the knowledge and skills to be learned by linking them to their practical applications in society and every-day life.
- To integrate the processes of acquiring knowledge and learning to use and apply it.
- To select topics and themes in terms of their relevance to pupils' lives in contemporary society.
- To select specific topics and themes to study with the aim of ensuring that pupils' learning experiences are personally meaningful and engage them at 'deeper' levels of their being than mere 'surface' learning.
- To engage pupils in an active rather than passive learning process, where they have opportunities to develop 'dynamic qualities' by engaging in problem-based inquiry learning, discussion and debate, and action learning through community involvement.

Such *procedural criteria* provide teachers with guidance for structuring pupils' engagement with curriculum content. They define the form learning should take in classrooms and schools, some in relation to particular kinds of content, and others more generically across the whole curriculum. It is a pity that the 'new framework' document does not systematically develop an explicit criterial framework for developing teaching and learning within the national curriculum, as an expression of its concern about the quality of pupils' engagement with learning.

The reason for this may in part stem from a fear of appearing to be over-prescriptive at the level of classroom processes. The attraction of an outcomes-based curriculum framework is that it appears to give teachers freedom to decide how the specified outcomes are to be achieved at the classroom level. However, teachers will feel that, since they are only judged by results, outcomes alone justify the means. It is a scenario which fosters surface learning at the sacrifice of a deep engagement on the part of many pupils, who consequently under-achieve when this is judged against their actual potential.

Raising standards, as the document acknowledges, depends on deepening pupils' levels of engagement with learning. Guidance on how this can be done is not adequately provided by a national curriculum framework which is based on the assumption that educational outcomes can be defined independently of the kind of learning process pupils are engaged in.

Outcomes and Processes

There are many worthwhile educational outcomes that cannot be adequately described independently of the processes through which they are achieved. For example, it is inconceivable that a teacher could develop pupils' thinking skills through a learning process that required them to be continually guessing the answers s(he) had in mind by answering leading questions. In which case why not explicitly remind teachers that the development of pupils' thinking skills pedagogically requires them to aim at fostering independence of thought in their classrooms by adopting the principle of asking 'open-ended' rather than 'leading questions'. Implementing this principle leaves plenty of scope for teachers to experiment with different questioning strategies and to form a judgement about how 'open-ended' they are. As a principle it does not prescribe specific teaching behaviours but provides a criterion for reflecting about the intentions and aims which underpin them.

Good examples of curriculum frameworks already exist (see Bruner's curriculum for teaching social science concepts in elementary schools in Hanley et al., 1970; Stenhouse's curriculum for teaching controversial issues, 1975, and the OECD's curriculum to support school initiatives in environmental education in Posch, 1991 and Elliott, 1998). These include clarifications of procedural aims and principles for the teaching and learning of particular kinds of content, and are not simply confined to outcome specifications. They have provided demonstrable support for the development of teachers as 'reflective practitioners' and 'researchers', and their capacity to enhance rather than diminish the quality of their classroom judgements and decisions is well documented.

Although such procedural frameworks are internationally recognised as examples of a *process model* of curriculum design, little awareness of them is displayed in the 'new framework' document. Nevertheless, the latter provides a reasonable basis for the further development of a national curriculum framework to incorporate criteria for what are to count as high quality teaching and learning processes.

Interestingly, the *process model* is currently influencing the re-design of national curriculum frameworks in some of the Pacific Rim countries, against which we have been encouraged to benchmark the performance of our teachers and schools. They include Taiwan, Japan and Hong Kong, where there is a growing concern that purely outcomes-driven processes are failing to deal with the competitive pressures social and economic changes are putting young people under, and may even be reinforcing them. Increasing boredom, disaffection, bullying and suicide rates are seen as challenges which need to be addressed through new kinds of curriculum frameworks. The development of such frameworks is more explicitly aimed at improving the quality of educational processes in classrooms and seeing the introduction of greater curricular flexibility and responsiveness as an integral part of this endeavour.

The Design Fault in the Frameworks for PSHE and CE

The production of separate curriculum proposals for 'citizenship' and 'personal, social and health' education at key stages 3 and 4, and the proposals to integrate them at key stages 1 and 2, raises questions about *coherence*. One can infer a possible reason for this separation; namely, that historically PSHE has not systematically covered areas of knowledge and understanding that are central to informed citizenship in a democratic society. However, this could be handled by fundamentally re-thinking the PSHE curriculum as a form of Citizenship Education, rather than simply bringing together existing elements and treating CE as a discrete subject.

The stated PSHE aims of 'promoting the personal and social well-being of pupils', and 'enabling them to deal with the difficult moral and social questions they face', and CE's stated aim of 'developing capacities for active citizenship in a modern democracy', imply a unified learning process in which discussion and debate are core activities. What constitutes personal and social well-being in particular human situations involve controversial value-judgements which cannot be resolved entirely be resorting to the facts, since the relevance or significance of certain facts depends upon the evaluative perspective from which they are viewed.

Moreover, a mature pluralistic democracy is characterised by the existence of procedures, at different levels of civil society, which enable citizens to have a say in what constitutes their personal and social well-being and to play an active role in bringing such conditions about. Educating pupils for democratic citizenship is a matter of inducting them into such procedures, and inasmuch as such a process involves pupils coming to accept responsibility for their own personal and social well-being, it also constitutes a process of personal and social development. The aims of 'personal and social development' and 'education for active citizenship' simply highlight two aspects of a single educational process of induction into democratic procedures, which enable people to shape the conditions of their existence in society.

There is a 'design fault' in the key stage 3 and 4 proposals for PSHE and CE. It is based on the assumption that their aims refer to categories of learning outcomes, which can be described independently of the procedural values that define a worthwhile teaching and learning process. Such categories are then used as a basis for constructing discrete curriculum frameworks which obscure rather than clarify the relationship between high quality educational outcomes and pedagogical processes. These frameworks misleadingly convey the impression that teachers are entirely free to devise their own approaches to teaching and learning.

The central aims of PSHE and CE are best understood in terms of outcomes which cannot be defined independently of the procedural values which ought to shape pupils' engagement in learning. Hence, 'developing capacities for active citizenship' implies that pupils are *actively engaged* in shaping the conditions of their lives, while 'personal and social development' implies that such engagement involves *accepting responsibility* for what constitutes their personal and social well-being. Moreover, such procedural values (sometimes referred to as 'pedagogical aims') can be further analysed into more specific principles governing pupils' engagement in learning, eg. understanding what is at stake in deciding upon a course of action from other people's points of view, or respect for evidence and facts in determining what constitutes one's personal and social well-being.

The frameworks proposed for both PSHE and Citizenship Education are somewhat lacking in clarity. This is because they use outcomes to articulate aims, which cannot be articulated independently of the learning processes involved in realising them. Specific knowledge objectives tend to get mixed up with aims that imply certain teaching and learning processes. Elements in these frameworks appear to be inconsistent with the claim that teachers are entirely free to decide on their own approaches. For example, the aim of *learning to discuss and debate topical issues and events* says a great deal about the learning processes involved. The pursuit of this aim would involve a significant pedagogical shift for many teachers from an instructionally-based classroom to a discussion-based one. As an aim it is very different in kind to a specification of content objectives like 'learning the basic facts and laws – about illegal substances'. How such facts and laws are best learned is an open matter. Less confusing and more coherent frameworks need to be developed. They should not only provide guidance on the specific knowledge to be acquired, but provide teachers with procedural criteria for judging what is to count as a worthwhile way of engaging pupils with issues and questions that cannot be resolved on the basis of factual knowledge alone.

It is interesting at this point to note that New Labour is at least going some way towards addressing the need to embed procedural values in school cultures, through its recently announced Healthy Schools Standard. Although this initiative relates to school ethos, it does have implications for classroom ethos, particularly with respect to giving pupils a voice on matters relating to their experience as learners. In particular, there is a need to clarify the relationship between this national initiative and the proposals for PSHE and Citizenship Education.

Four Challenges for the National Curriculum to Address

Earlier it was argued that the national curriculum framework for the next century needs to be further developed in relation to a more systematic analysis of the challenges which profound social and economic changes are posing for education. Let us conclude with Posch's (1994) attempt to describe these challenges. They can be summarised as:

1. The irreversible decline of traditional social ties and bonds maintained by obedience to norms and conventions of behaviour, based on deference to authority. This implies that new forms of social affiliation have to be established on the basis of discussion and negotiation. In schools a curriculum which in its detail represents 'a culture of

predefined demands' and is therefore not open to very much 'negotiation' and 'discussion' with pupils is unlikely to match this challenge.
2. The loss of 'continuity in social relationships' from which people increasingly defect for the sake of short-term gains. The price is that people lose their capacity to trust each other and to exercise 'social responsibility'. In this context the relationship between teachers and pupils becomes increasingly instrumental. If pupils cannot discern short-term gains from their experience in classrooms and schools, more and more of them are likely to 'defect' from engaging with learning. The results of such an outlook is that pupils decreasingly trust teachers to take care of their futures, or see themselves to be in any way responsible for the well-being of their peers in the way they conduct themselves in classrooms and schools. The challenge for teachers is to create learning situations which provide new conditions for trust to emerge in their relationships with pupils, and a new basis for the latter to exercise responsibility for each others well-being. Such situations will need to involve forms of collaborative learning which foster mutual respect and a sense of community, and are valued because they engage and challenge pupils at deeper levels of their personal and social being than simply a desire for short-term satisfaction and gain.
3. The growing complexity of the economic and social conditions which impinge on people's lives, and the inability of centralized agencies to control their impact. In this context the latter depend on individual citizens to exercise more control over these conditions at the point of impact, ie. at the 'grass-roots' level. The challenge for teachers is to develop in their pupils those abilities, which will enable them, as future citizens, to cope with the 'unstructured situations' of every-day living. This will entail a learning process which engages pupils in making sense of the practical problems and issues such situations present, in making decisions about appropriate courses of action, and accepting responsibility for them.
4. An increasing consciousness on the part of citizens that they live in a 'risk society' where the consequences of technological innovation for human well-being are ambiguous, context-bound, and beyond the power of science to predict with certainty. In 'the risk society' scepticism and doubt about the uses of science grow with increasing dependence upon it. In this paradoxical situation definitions of what

constitutes useful scientific knowledge can no longer be left to 'central authorities' and scientific experts if public confidence in science is to be maintained. They need to be negotiated with those whose well-being may be affected in particular localities. Social processes for establishing 'local truth' within our risk society will need to be established in ways which can handle differences and conflicts of perspective among citizens at the local level. The challenge the 'risk society' presents for teachers is to 'develop both an appreciative and critical stance towards scientific knowledge', through inducting pupils into social processes within their own localities and communities aimed at establishing 'local knowledge' about the impact of technology on their own and others well-being.

All four challenges suggest that a national curriculum framework should support the development of new pedagogical processes in schools. They also suggest that the principles which underlie the original framework of the National Curriculum were a long way removed from the social challenges facing pupils in schools. The National Curriculum has been concerned with the fine details of what should be known and when. Its message of 'entitlement' was of access to vast tracts of knowledge, with some commensurate genuflection towards skills. It was, however, a curriculum which failed to acknowledge the complexities of a changing society and the demands on the individuals within it. The admission of its limitations, the acknowledgement of the need for the pedagogical flexibility that allows for critical dialogue, and the at least tacit acceptance of a whole range of concerns outside the traditional core curriculum, are to be welcomed.

The desire to control the achievement of 'excellence' remains. The fundamental question to be asked about the proposed revisions to the national curriculum is whether they are flexible enough to support the pedagogical innovations indicated by these challenges. Looked at in this light, and in the absence of a well-defined and coherent set of procedural values to orientate pedagogical change in schools, this is a difficult question to answer. All one can say is that they appear, at the very least, to be a move in the right direction. Whether the move is radical enough remains an open question.

Acknowledgement

I am grateful to Geoff Whitty and Ted Wragg for their helpful comments on a draft of this paper. I have done my best to revise it in the light of these. However, they should not be held responsible for the views expressed.

References

Department for Education and Employment (1999) *Learning to succeed: a new framework for post-16 learning*, London, Stationery Office, Cm 4392.

Elliott, J. (1988) The State v Education: 'The Challenge for Teachers', in *The National Curriculum*, British Educational Research Association.

Elliott, J. (1998) *The Curriculum Experiment*, Milton Keynes, Open University Press, Ch.7.

Hanley, J., Whitla, D., Moo, V. and Walter, A. (1970) *Curiosity, Competence, Community: Man: a course of study, an Evaluation*, 2 vols. Cambridge, Mass., Educational Development Centre.

Posch, P. (1991) Environment and School Initiatives: background and basic premises of the project in *Environment, Schools and Active Learning, Part 1*, Paris, OECD (CERI).

Posch, P. (1994) 'Changes in the culture of teaching and learning' in *Educational Action Research: an international journal*, 2(2), pp.153-61.

Qualifications and Curriculum Authority (1999) *Developing the school curriculum*, London, QCA Publications.

Rickinson, M. (1999) *The Teaching and Learning of Environmental Issues through Geography*, Unpublished DPhil Thesis, University of Oxford.

Rudduck, J., Chaplain, R. and Wallace, G. (1996) *School Improvement. What can Pupils Tell Us?* London, David Fulton Publishers.

Stenhouse, L. (1975) *An Introduction to Curriculum Research and Development*, London, Heinemann Educational.

4 Secondary School Pupils' Experience of the National Curriculum

CEDRIC CULLINGFORD

The National Curriculum is a monument to central planning and control. This much is agreed by both those who advocate it and those who decry it. Since the collapse of most communist education systems there has been no other attempt to prescribe exactly what children should learn, and when, and no such battery of tests to regulate the outcome. Even the styles of teaching and the length of lessons are dictated by national requirements, and an inspection system in place which monitors whether teachers are obeying their instructions. The argument that bolsters the National Curriculum is that it gives all pupils a broad and balanced curriculum, with due attention to key skills and knowledge. They can only be certain that they have their true entitlement if every lesson and every teacher is in some way monitored. Only if there is specific assessment can success against targets be properly measured.

Those who doubt whether such a centralised curriculum delivers the intended outcomes see the very monument as a redundant monolith, a symbol of itself rather than an attempt to have an affect on others. The weight is seen to reside in facts, the accumulation of knowledge that can easily be tested, rather than the ability to think, understand or even be original. By telling teachers what to do it is argued that they are made into artisans, semi-skilled workers who have little professional autonomy.

Given these fundamentally opposed views it is perhaps surprising that many of the debates about the curriculum are about the margins. After the Dearing report has the load been lightened? What is the place for Personal and Social Education? Is Citizenship education a necessary extra? Should health education and parenting education find a place in the face of the dominance of maths and language? What emphasis should be placed on the core curriculum? These marginal debates, debates politically allowed and even encouraged, rarely ask the fundamental questions about what a curriculum is for, in terms of purpose and outcomes. That matter is assumed to be self-evident as if 'broad and balanced' were axiomatic of keen skilled operatives, numerate, computer friendly and willing. And yet it is at this fundamental level that the real debate should be taking place.

Occasionally there are glimpses into a deeper set of concerns about the effects of the National Curriculum, from unexpected sources. Teachers might not be allowed to question the central thrust of the National Curriculum, or they might fight for their particular subject, or their approach, but parents have the ultimate well-being of their own children as their fundamental concern, and this leads then to question some of what they see taking place. The fascination with qualifications and with league tables might be the media's idea of what concerns parents, but there are many more complex attitudes expressed. The impact of the national curriculum might be clear on those who are in successful schools but they might be even more fundamental on those pupils who are less successful. The rate of truancy and the number of exclusions are rising inexorably, and parents, especially those not normally given a voice, are concerned about this.

Parents are assumed to welcome the National Curriculum. They know what their children are supposed to learn. They are told that teachers are now accountable, and they receive reports detailing exactly what their children have achieved. And yet the irony is that this very system seems to disenfranchise them; parents feel alienated from it (Cullingford, 1996). Instead they voice their concerns about what they perceive is happening to their children. They worry about the levels of stress that are the result of so much testing.

> Stress starts to build up and I think it's unnecessary, unnecessary stress and I don't think we should be doing it to our children. (in Cullingford, 1996, p.62)

The pressure on children to do well seems to them to have the opposite effect, certainly on those to whom examinations do not come easily.

The National Curriculum is also perceived by parents as causing stress to teachers. The sheer amount of work, the demands of accountability and the need to demonstrate outcomes are all seen to making them not only work harder but to less effect, and with less time either for individual pupils or parents.

> dashing around like a National Curriculum fiddler-abouter ... really inspired teachers ... engendered an excitement, and interest. I should think there is less of that and more hassle now. (in Cullingford, 1996, p.76)

The effects of delivering the National Curriculum are perceived to be not only on the levels of stress, but are assumed to be lowering standards. There is less inspired teaching. Pupils, like teachers, are constrained. In fact as more than one study has demonstrated, parents are very suspicious of the National Curriculum despite all the efforts of the government to present it as part of the Parents' Charter (Hughes et al., 1994). Their views are negative.

> It can have an adverse effect on children ... it takes the individuality out of the teacher.
>
> I don't think it has improved standards.
>
> One day they're doing that, the next day they're doing this, that and the other ... they're messing about with the future.
>
> The dreadful National Curriculum. (in Cullingford, 1996, p.68)

There is therefore a debate about the long term *effects* of the National Curriculum that is rarely publicly aired. It is at this level, in terms of effects on emotions and attitudes, on motivations and purposes, that the debate should be encouraged, rather than the question of a 'balance' between similar types of input in various branches of the core curriculum. Those targets that are set can be easily measured. That is what they are for. But what are these targets? Do they include more subtle aspects of learning? Do they in fact have an adverse effect? Do they, again, have the opposite result to that intended? Parents suggest that this is so in so far as they are allowed to reflect on the matter an compare the experience of their children to their own days in school.

Parents' perception of the effects of the National Curriculum is that it constrains opportunities for pupils to think for themselves, to become immersed in an enthusiasm or develop an excitement for learning. Teachers are perceived to be most concerned with delivering what pupils are entitled to. They are even told what to do during the literacy hour, one of the core aspects of the curriculum in primary schools. This means there is little time for pupil participation. This result has been observed over a number of years. Pupils have less time to listen. Traditional teaching methods prevail. The constraint of 'getting through' the demands of the curriculum means that pupils cannot be fully engaged (Galton, M. et al., 1999; Galton and Fogelman, 1998; Croll, 1996). There is therefore perceived to be a level of effect that is fundamental. If active learning is replaced by a passive acquisition of subject knowledge, what does this mean to the future of the school population?

Some would argue that such approaches lead to long term student disaffection; that the rise of exclusions is directly linked, in a causal way, with the way in which the curriculum is presented (Elliott, 1998). Instead of rational questions about purpose and outcome, the experience of learning is centred on meeting other people's intended outcomes, outcomes on which *they* are being measured through their pupils. But then some would argue that even talking about the curriculum itself is becoming out of date, that the concept of 'standards' or 'targets, targets, targets' is at the centre of policy (Davies and Edwards, 1999). Even the old shibboleth or the 'broad and the balanced' is eroded. Government policy share ever greater control over not only the curriculum but pedagogy.

The problem with 'effects' is that they are never simple. Despite the policymakers' best intentions teachers might still go on encouraging their pupils to think. They might have to adapt to the National Curriculum and submit to targets but they still do so in their own way. Some would argue that teachers are still being creative *despite* government policy (Helsby and McCulloch, 1997; Woods, 1995). The central control might be based on a bureaucratic or technical/rational view of teaching but teachers have to adapt, and therefore acknowledge their exciting values and beliefs. Nevertheless there is a strong case that there is a powerful tension between teacher's attempts to retain their standards, and the demands of the curriculum. They try to accept and respond to change, but there is a real sense of loss, and the erosion of the pleasure of seeing children learn (Croll, 1996). It is as if teachers were attempting to protect their pupils against the National curriculum.

The curriculum has been characterised in a number of research studies as a 'blunt instrument' that fails to recognise or respond to the needs of pupils (Mitchell and Brumfit, 1997). It is based on the notion that only through clear central control can people be certain that teachers are delivering what they should, and what can be measured. That this has a clear effect on teachers is clear. Whilst some adapt to the fact, and indeed even welcome it, if this is the way they see their own job, most feel deprofessionalised and disheartened. Those who argue for the National Curriculum would assert that teachers could not be trusted, that standards were too low and that was the teachers fault. The sense of beleaguerment in teachers is therefore no surprise to anyone, or their sense of stress, and pressure.

The question is whether this shared outlook directly or indirectly affects pupils. The government could argue that such pressure on teachers is a necessary concomitant to the raising of standards. A few suicides and heart failures is a 'price worth paying' for the meeting of targets. And the question therefore is inevitably that about the experience of learning. Do pupils learn from their teachers and their teachers' attitudes, or are teachers merely the instruments through which knowledge is acquired? If teachers are disaffected, what of their pupils? Do pupils feel that entitlement is a privilege or is it meaningless, and merely the meeting of current, and ever-changing, requirements (Willan, P., 1998). Are teachers so busy assessing and delivering an overloaded curriculum that standards are actually falling, through *less* talk, and fewer types of interaction? (Hacker and Rowe, 1998). In fact, is the effect of the National Curriculum, for many pupils, that of alienation and failure, especially in later years and in inner cities? (Kinder, 1997).

It is easier to describe that it is to prove effects. Each school is complex, let alone the education system. There are all kinds of inadvertent outcomes and it needs no citing of all the research or scientific realism and chaos theory to demonstrate this. And yet the present policy on the curriculum and testing is posited on the belief that one can manage and control outcomes provided one is precise enough. The way that the curriculum, and its targets, operates is clear, but what effect does this have on the outlook of pupils?

In order to explore these issues a qualitative study was carried out in which 260 secondary pupils in years 10 and 11 took part in semi-structured interviews. These interviews were lengthy and tape-recorded. In the usual approaches to semi-structured interviews, the 'structure' is the certainty that all the respondents have covered the same topics in order to preserve the validity and reliability of the conclusions. The order in which the questions are asked is not important since extensions of ideas arise according to the direction of thought of the interviewee. It is impossible to predict when the opportunity to ask 'why?' may arise. The very open starting point might be either creating the right atmosphere, the certainty of respect for the integrity of what the individual is saying, or it might be a natural chance to home in on one of the main concerns of the interviewee.

In these interviews a slightly more formal approach was taken in that they generally followed the same order. Open questions about how they were enjoying school and probing questions that asked them to elaborate were interspersed with questions that followed a consistent pattern, asking about their experience of the curriculum, which subjects they considered the most important, the extent to which these or other subjects might be useful in their subsequent careers and who gave them the best advice. These questions were followed by others that explored the relationship they saw between schooling and future employment. But these wider questions are not of immediate concern here, where we will be focusing on their views of the curriculum as presented to them rather than issues about which subjects they like and why, and how they related to different teachers.

The sample of pupils was taken from several secondary schools representing variations in socio-economic intake, and in minority ethnic representation. Inner city schools, suburban schools and rural schools were all represented, and all schools were very cooperative. The deputy heads or heads selected what they considered to be a typical spread of pupils, allowing for a balance of gender and equal representation of years 10 and 11. The interviews were carried out at a time of year when there was no particular exam pressure, and the pupils appreciated the opportunity to talk confidentially, anonymously and informally in a private room which each school provided. Indeed, as word spread that the interviews had taken place there were many other pupils who would have liked to have taken part and had to be disappointed.

In addition to the schools a smaller sample of 35 interviews were carried out at a Careers Service Office; these were with pupils representing the same schools who had left and were either seeking jobs or seeking advice. The majority of these (the exception being three over 20) had recently left school, either to seek employment or planning to go on to further study elsewhere.

What is reported here is representative of the sample as a whole. Whilst the circumstances of each individual was noted, always amply embellished by their frank descriptions of themselves and their own circumstances, and any differences between gender or socio-economic status sought out, the data did not prove to fall into any particular clusters. At the level of analysis on which understanding the findings depend there is a degree of homogeneity and consistency that is telling and important. This is true both of the surface level of content and at the deeper conceptual levels where the interviewees give indications of their more personal feelings and insights.

One of the central tenets of the National Curriculum ever since the great debates of the late 1970s has been the importance of a central core. Sometimes this has been expressed in terms of core subjects, especially Maths and English. Sometimes it has been described in terms of core skills, especially numeracy and literacy. But the debates about balance, and about what other parts of the curriculum should be left out, and which have to be included, all centre on the question of the relationship between the core and the periphery. Indeed it has been argued that English and Maths are more powerful than ever since the ostensible scaling down (Coulby and Ward, 1996). The key areas remain the same for statutory tests and for teacher accountability. To this core has been added science so that in the present description of the National Curriculum there is a triumvirate at the core. What makes science somewhat different in fact, if not in theory, is the fact that it depends much more on teacher interaction through experiments and the resources have not been put into it to make the subject generally as successful as hoped (Hacker and Rowe, 1998).

The message about the significance of the core curriculum is duly recorded by the pupils. After so many years of being told about the importance of English, Maths and Science, they automatically reiterate that they are the most important subjects in the curriculum.

> I think the main ones are English, Maths and Science, because a lot of people look at those ...The teacher that we have tells us we've got to do like A levels, the GSCE work. It feels a bit worrying ... (male, year 11)

> If you pass English, Maths and Science, they will let you in ... (male, year 11)

> Maths and English mostly. Because when you get a job you mostly have to add things and stuff. English you have to spell right and put your words in the right places and stuff. Well, Maths and English mostly. (female, year 10)

> Maths and English ... I don't know if you want to go to college and I think you need them most and you can have like sciences on the side and things like

that but Maths and English I think you need for nearly everything.
(female, year 10)

It is clear that the core curriculum is embedded in their minds as central. They have clearly been told this often. The subjects are usually not the ones that actually interest them, but they are nevertheless deemed important. "A lot of people look at those", and teachers stress the importance of the central skills. Those who cite the subjects often go on to say that they hate them, but that does not diminish their perceived significance. Pupils have clearly been told that these are the subjects you need to get into college or to get jobs. These are the subjects they 'need'.

Beyond the taken for granted obviousness that the core curriculum is important, pupils find it more difficult to say why. Perhaps all jobs demand levels of numeracy and science that GCSE's are meant to provide, but further probing normally elicits a reiteration of the main point.

> I find that pretty boring, the maths. I don't find it very interesting or anything. English and Maths ... well, because ... well, obviously they are the most important. (female, year 11)

The catechism that is often repeated is that the purpose of these subjects is to prepare them for employment. This is no surprise. From an early age the one purpose of school that is presented to them, in the absence of any other, is to acquire a job (Cullingford, 1991). Sometimes, on further reflection, and on being closer to actual employment, some of the relevances of particular subjects are far more questioned, especially science. As they begin to think of a particular job they know far more clearly which subjects will be useful to them. Nevertheless they still bow to the message of the curriculum.

> Maths, English, Science ... and Home Economics, Food. Because Maths, Science and English are the major GCSE ones and Home Economics Food because I want to be a Chef. (male, year 10)

These citations of the 'major' subjects is a result of years of experience of seeing how the central core dominates, especially in terms both of time and placement during the school day. Even before the advent of the sacrosanct literacy and numeracy laws pupils experienced the way that the timetable was divided and delivered (Burgess, 1989). The central message was that there were certain subjects that were of great importance and therefore others of peripheral concern. The idea that all kinds of different skills could be learned through different subjects was never pursued. The idea of a 'subject' and subject boundaries was embedded at an early stage, and this was true before the National Curriculum enshrined the concept. What seems to have changed is that the National Curriculum has strengthened the idea of the curriculum as a body of knowledge that has to be learned for its own sake. The role of the teacher might have been diminished but the role of the teacher as the conveyor or guardian of knowledge - even if imposed by someone else - is hammered home. There might be a sense of alienation that arises from this. What is certain is that the perception of school as being for the sake of teachers, and their assessments, is strengthened.

As is so often the case, pupils have to guess the purpose of what is going on in school. The curriculum is as much a 'given' as the arrangements of classroom and corridors. The reasons for doing many things are, it appears, rarely explained, since the role of pupils is to submit to what is given. Some would say that the role of teachers is also, increasingly, to submit to what is given them. What is certain is that the National Curriculum is not a symbol of ownership or cooperation. It is not only given to people, but a given. Its real purpose, beyond being broad and balanced, remains obscure.

One of the underlying perceptions that pupils share is that no-one has ever explained to them the purpose of what they are doing. This might be because the purpose of schooling is so obvious - getting a job, giving pupils skills, and passing exams - that it does not need elaboration. Of course any educational thinker will point out that such assumptions are at best problematic and at worst questionable. Indeed, in other countries the whole purpose of the curriculum is the main thrust of policy, with few if any words on the content. Teachers are not to be blamed for not pursuing the purpose of the curriculum. There is pressure on them not to question, as if that were undermining. Besides, they haven't the time.

But pupils subsequently resent the fact that no-one took them into their confidence enough to explain *why* they were in school. The disaffected and the unemployed have long resented the irrelevance of the curriculum as presented to them and the lack of any sense of purpose in their schooling (White and Brockington, 1983). They wished that it could have been different. Whilst some would dismiss this as the inevitable consequence of failure, the same sense of a lack of perceived or shared purpose is felt by those in school and, indeed, those who are ostensibly successful.

The reason why the question about the significance of the curriculum receives such a bland or blank answer is that no-one, in their experience, has bothered to explore the reasoning behind it. When it comes to skills that pupils find useful, little mention is forthcoming about the given curriculum. Skills are peripheral. So why do they take for granted the shrine of the Core Curriculum except that it is never questioned? They reiterate the fact that whatever the personal experience, there are subjects that they have to undergo -

> English: It's alright sometimes. To me it's just a bit boring, that's all. The teacher's alright. It's just boring. I don't like it. It's too hard as well ... Maths, English, Science ... Modern Languages. I can't remember the others ... Because I'm told by the teachers. Maths and Science and English and Modern Languages. (male, year 10)

"Because I'm told by the teachers." What pupils are told is to submit to the experience of the curriculum without questioning it. All these pupils were asked if anyone ever talked to them about the purpose of the curriculum. Having raised the subject themselves, the possible relevance to their subsequent lives and the sense that they wanted to understand better, all had to say 'no'. No-one talked about purposes, to their regret. It was a complete lack, one which they would have loved to overcome. Indeed, one of their regrets on leaving school was that they had never realised how important it could be, since no-one ever talked about it.

The Pupils pointed out that teachers did not have time to talk to them individually.

> No, not really. I don't think they tend to spend a lot of time with people who just get on with it and do whatever they want. You know it's like the people who don't tend to behave. They're the ones who get talking to all the time, so. If you do what they want you to do they don't bother talking to you really, so. (female, 17)

This might encapsulate the conclusions of many studies of teacher-pupil dialogue, the attention seekers and the difficult disciplinary cases dominating the proceedings. But it is also a symbol of the absence, of dialogue, of explanation, of the language of communication rather than instruction. If teachers are so busy, so beleaguered by delivery then it is no surprise that it is in their interests to ignore those who "just get on with it and do whatever they want" (Pye, 1989). Do teachers talk about purposes?

> No, not really, no. To learn, I think. To get your certificates, your exam certificates and get your good grades and you've got something behind you when you leave. (male, 17, unemployed)

It is the absence of any other kind of dialogue, that regretted absence of shared purpose and meaning that leads inevitably to the common conclusion. Schools are only there to prepare for jobs.

The one aspect of the curriculum that begins to make any sense to them is in the immediate relevance of a subject that might have some bearing on their work. Placed against this pragmatic interest, the given significance of the curriculum as a whole, especially the core, begins to fade. What they are told is not the same as what they find:

> I can't see what learning about the structure of a molecule is going to do for me when I leave. I can't see myself going round the supermarket and saying 'well that's made up of it'. I don't know. Unless you're going into that field when you leave I can't see it doing anything for me.

In the absence of the sense of shared curiosity two kinds of pragmatism set in. One is the recognition of qualifications, the passing of the barriers of terminal tests; the other is the immediate utility of a subject to a particular end.

> I think English, Maths and maybe CDT. Well, I'm thinking about either going into Law or Accountancy so law is the English and Maths is the Accountancy, but if I can't get into those two I'd like to do something in Design and Communication. (male, year 10)

Some think directly of their possible careers - food and catering. Others try to work out for themselves the utility of the subjects they are studying; so that English and Maths are given their own relevance. Others just accept that all subjects, especially the core ones, have an intrinsic purpose in equipping pupils for jobs. Qualifications are passports. It is often with hindsight that those who have left school either lament the missed opportunities or try to reconstruct what the curriculum was for.

> I don't think any of it prepared me for what ... really for ... jobs and that. 'Cos they say that there's jobs out there and everything but when I've been going to the Job Centre and sitting there and the woman's gone through and there's been nothing ... [purpose of school?] They ... It was to give you all your qualifications to get a job with basically. (female, 17)

Qualifications, especially in Maths and English, are enshrined as the explicit purpose of schooling, in order to acquire jobs. But nothing has really prepared them. The reality of life outside school does not seem to connect to their experience within it. This does not help them even at the time, for they are conscious of the disjunction. They nevertheless try to make a connection.

> English, in case you get a job that you need to write, you know. Science could be useful if you're working in a chemical factory. That sort of thing. And home economics, like I'm looking for a job like a chef or something like that at the moment so Home Economics would come in handy. (male, 17)

There is sometimes almost a sense of desperation in trying to make sense of things, in drawing connections. It is possible to argue that any explanation of the curriculum is philosophically demanding and that it would be a challenge for any pupil to articulate anything more than pragmatism. But the absence of any dialogue or discussion of the subject is clear, and the reasons for it - teachers so busy delivering - equally consistent. On reflection the pupils regret this lack of purpose.

They also regret the lack of time teachers have for individuals. Talking, including open questions, is perceived as rare. Teachers are too busy, and too grateful for pupils getting on quietly with their work. They also save their energy for dealing with troubles or challenges. The question is whether, given the demands of the curriculum set against targets, teachers could ever really have time.

> I didn't really speak much to the teacher. I normally just got on with my work and stuff. I'll be honest, I didn't really communicate well with teachers because like I communicate better with my fellow pupils ... (male, 17)

Afterwards, such lack of dialogue is often a matter of regret but it does suggest this is a habit. If teachers are busy with the curriculum it is no wonder that real communication takes place with other pupils. The pupils, the 'good' ones are supposed to 'get on with their work'. That is what they are for.

The perception of teachers as very busy people who are there to deliver a given curriculum leads to the impression that teachers do not care, which is the most damning, if unfair, one of all. Pupils perceive caring as having time to talk with them, to show a personal interest, to share a private joke. They can all think of moments when this happened. But generally they see this personal connection taken away from them partly because teachers are so busy and partly because teachers are most concerned for their own accountability. Pupils are aware of league tables and SAT results. They realise that teachers are judged by their performance. Whilst it is always easy to criticise teachers, (and the government policy appears to be based on this) the pupils' sense of alienation must be partly attributable to the demands both on teachers' time and on the accountability to deliver a set of facts so that the assessments are satisfactory.

Exam systems test the teachers as much as the pupils.

> I mean they just sit there and they give you all these equations and you know you just look at them and you can't figure them out and the difficult part is that all three of the teachers explain it in a different way. I mean you can't understand it. I mean you get into an exam and you know I don't understand what they are saying ... Some of the teachers they tend to give you text books ... make it from there, but if they told be verbally and showed it properly step by step I may have understood it that way. (female, year 11)

There are many of them and a lot of material to get through. Do teachers have time for patient explanation? There will, after all, be no extra help in an exam. But the perception that teachers do not have time is universal and pointed up by the occasional exception. "Just sitting there" could be a signal of laziness or indifference. It could also be a symptom of the circumstances being so out of joint that only the most creative and determined and optimistic person could overcome them. Whatever the explanation the pupils are talking about the situation they find themselves in, not in a spirit of blaming others, but regretting what is happening.

The pervasive sense amongst the pupils in a variety of different schools is that the teachers do not have time; that perception is shared with the parents. The result is that at an individual level the teachers are concerned with their own problems.

> Most of them at my school just never really bothered. They concentrated more on just getting the lesson over and done with - getting one lesson after another all the way really, instead of trying to get in with you. (male, 17)

The central emphasis is on the curriculum, rather than the pupils. That is the nature of the National Curriculum, of targets and outcomes. It might be successful in its own terms but it does not appear to pupils to be in their personal interests. "Getting things done" is not the same as "getting on with you" but it is more easily measured.

If teachers are distracted then pupils will be left more to their own devices. They will turn to their peer groups and they will be the more easily bored. The emphasis is more and more on 'delivery', on the conveying of information.

> Maths ... it's a bit boring when it gets going on ... teachers just go on and on. I suppose they just want to get it into your head, don't they? (female, year 11)

Less and less time is spent on the underlying matters to be learned.

> Maths. It's alright, but some of the stuff I don't see any point in doing. I know that you need to add, subtract and stuff like that but some things I don't really see the need in ... it's boring and pointless. (female, year 10)

Tasks to be done because you have 'got' to do them are never as successful as those undertaken because there is an understanding of what they are for. The National Curriculum sets itself up, in the minds of pupils, as a task that has to be carried out, as something enormous and monumental that has to be achieved. The problem is that it is difficult to imagine a personal sense of anything but failure. How can anyone be successful at all that? The notion of failure is deeply embedded, even if it is at a subconscious level.

Pupils therefore either play lip service to the received wisdom as embodied in the general system, or they try to make their own sense of what is happening to them. There must be explanations for what they are undergoing. They clutch at the straws of relevance to their future careers or, failing that, relevance to their personal skills. They were asked what particular skills they had learned were useful to them. It is telling that at this point literacy and numeracy disappeared from their minds. Pupils were far more pragmatic. There were either those particular aspects of knowledge that helped them in their career or those more generalistic requisitions which were the results of chance.

> I think my Performing Arts will, because it shows how well I am at communicating with other people and it shows that I'm not scared to show my views and also help other people and people help me. (male, year 11)

Communicating is one of those 'skills' - extra curricular - that pupils esteem. It might have happened in or out of lessons. It might be a 'core' intention of the National Curriculum in English. But it happens inadvertently.

> Well, I don't think I've actually learnt many skills in the school apart from socialising 'cos I used to be very shy. But most of my skills, my social skills, were taught by my parents and are done out of school. (female, year 10)

The ability to communicate, to hold a dialogue, to interpret, to undergo a flexible, iterative process, is recognised as being at the heart of learning (Cullingford, 1990). The National Curriculum sets down what pupils must learn. Despite this they cite what is of more importance to them, the importance of social skills, of relationships and of complex understandings. It is the nature of the National Curriculum to insist on what can be measured. The outcomes are to be testable. Human relations are not.

And yet pupils talk of skills as 'social'. They might apply to particular jobs, and the refinement of language might be a skill. But when they talk of useful skills in the curriculum they think of the relevance of knowledge to particular jobs, but also those more invisible abilities, those more subtle attributes of the ability to communicate, as in the peripheral theatre studies. What pupils deem to be relevant depends on their own interpretations. They are trying to make sense of their own lives against the monumental curriculum. This is always a tension between the private, inner demands of understanding and the more public relevance of their skills. If the only relevance of the curriculum is a job, this becomes apparent:

> If they had offered me some of the stuff that they're taking now, I would probably have been alright. (female, 21)

> Not relevant, not really. Well some things you have to do, you know, in your heart of hearts that you know you're not going to do that. Like in physics you

know I'm not going to be a physicist. I know that for certain so I just ... not real life at all. (male, 17)

The way in which pupils are left to make their own sense of what is happening depends on two beliefs. The first is that there is a common assumption in what the curriculum is about, which needs no examination or explanation. The experience of pupils refutes this but from the point of view of the implementation this does not count. The second is that pupils will always question what is happening to them from their point of view, and that they will always have a tendency to do so. Clearly their views count even less. Turn this argument on its head and one wonders for whom the curriculum is intended. If pupils themselves are not the outcome then what is the underlying purpose? Control?

The finding that there is widespread disaffection, amongst the successful as well as the failures, is clear. This is a matter not often examined. Indeed, it is a matter more often ignored or dismissed. The evidence from this substantial body of representative pupils at least raises the question of whether the kind of experience that they are receiving in school is really attuned to their needs or the needs of their different communities, let alone society as a whole. At best we recognise a sense of normlessness, of 'alienation' from the unexpressed, inarticulated manifestations of society. At worst we see them trying to find their own way, alone, pragmatic and essentially disillusioned.

The question this research poses, in the limits of this particular report, is the extent to which any outcomes are attributable to the National Curriculum itself. The outcomes should be disturbing enough; pragmatism, restlessness, insecurity and a lack of belief in school. But are these inevitable? Was it always such, in all schooling systems? All changes, like all effects, are subtle. There are findings here that are true of years ago, and will remain so too long hereafter. But if the school is a monument to the unreasonable hegemony of the State and its purposes over communities and neighbourhoods, is this exacerbated by the centralised curriculum? The most modest conclusion must be that it is so.

References

Burgess, H. (1989) The Primary Curriculum: The Example of Mathematics, in Cullingford, C. *The Primary Teacher: The role of the Educator and the Purpose of Primary Education*, London, Cassell.

Coulby, D. and Ward, S. (1996) (eds) *The Primary Core National Curriculum: Policy into Practice*, London, Cassell.

Croll, P. (1996) (ed) *Teachers Pupils and Primary Schooling: Continuity and Change*, London, Cassell.

Cullingford, C. (1990) *The Nature of Learning*, London, Cassell.

Cullingford, C. (1991) *The Inner World of the School*, London, Cassell.

Cullingford, C. (1996) *Parents, Education and the State*, Aldershot, Ashgate.

Davies, M. and Edwards, G. (1999) Will the Curriculum Caterpillar Ever Learn to Fly? *Cambridge Journal of Education*, Vol.29, No.2, pp.265-275.

Elliott, J. (1998) *The Curriculum Experiment: Meeting the challenge of social change*, Buckingham. Open University Press.

Galton, M. and Fogelman, K. (1998) The Use of discretionary time in the Primary School, *Research Papers in Education*, No.13, pp.119-139.

Galton, M., Hargreaves, L., Comber, C., Wall, D. and Pell, T. (1999) Changes in Patterns of Teacher Interaction in Primary Classrooms 1976-96, *British Educational Research Journal*, Vol.25, No.1, pp.23-37.

Hacker, R. and Rowe, M. (1998) A Longitudinal study of the effects of Implementing a National Curriculum project upon classroom processes. *Curriculum Journal*, Vol.9, No.1, pp.95-103.

Helsby, G. and McCulloch, G. (1997) (eds) *Teachers and the National Curriculum*, London, Cassell.

Hughes, M., Wikeley, F. and Nash, T. (1994) *Parents and their Children's Schools*, Oxford, Blackwell.

Kinder, K. (1997) Causes of Disaffection: The Views of Pupils and Education Professionals, *EERA Bulletin*, Vol.3, No.1, pp.3-11.

Mitchell, R. and Brumfit, C. (1997), The National Curriculum Experience of Bilingual Pupils, *Educational Review*, Vol.49, No.2, pp.159-180.

Pye, J. (1989) *Invisible Children: Who are the real losers at school?* Oxford University Press.

White, R. and Brockington, D. (1983) *Tales Out of School: Consumer's Views of British Education*, London, Routledge.

Willan, P. (1998) Whatever happened to Entitlement in the National Curriculum? *Curriculum Journal*, Vol.9, No.3, pp.269-283.

Woods, P. (1995) *Creative Teachers in Primary Schools*, Buckingham, Open University Press.

5 Pupil Perceptions of the National Curriculum
LEROY MCDONALD

The National Context

The Education Reform Act 1988 heralded the beginning of a new era in compulsory education. The establishment of a National Curriculum was an ambitious undertaking to say the least, but as Crawford (1988) argues:

> The National Curriculum was a response to a nation at risk in two ways. First, in terms of the decline of the nation state in face of globalization, technological and economic change. Second, in terms of a cultural decline brought about by the claimed relativism of post-modernity. In both these senses, the economic and the cultural, the National Curriculum was a nation-building curriculum.
> (p.273)

The present Government is committed to the National Curriculum, as the DfEE and QCA argues:

> The National Curriculum lies at the heart of our policies to raise standards. It sets out a clear, full and statutory entitlement to learning for all pupils. It determines the content of what will be taught, and sets attainment targets for learning. It also determines how performance will be assessed and reported. An effective National Curriculum therefore gives teachers, pupils, parents, employers and their wider community a clear and shared understanding of the skills and knowledge that young people will gain at school.
> (DfEE and QCA, 1999, p.3)

Labour Party (1994), cited in Davies and Edwards (1999), suggests that New Labour are attempting to address the aforementioned economic and cultural issues through education:

> For New Labour 'education is the key to personal fulfilment for the individual, to economic success for the Nation, and to the creation of a more just and cohesive society' ...
> (p.271)

The purpose of this chapter is not to scrutinise the processes that led to the present version of the National Curriculum, but rather to examine how those at the receiving end perceive it - pupil perspectives.

Background

The author is currently employed as a teacher by a company that seeks to improve the educational outcomes of 20 year 11 pupils, who are at risk of underachieving, at a co-educational, comprehensive school in the north of England. Pupils are selected towards the end of year 10 based on their levels of educational achievement, attendance, punctuality, behaviour, gender, ethnicity and additional evidence obtained from the Pastoral Care Team. The aim is to form a group that is mixed in terms of the aforementioned. Having been selected, these pupils participate in a programme that replaces the school's year 11 PSHE (Personal, Social and Health Education) provision.

This arrangement places the author in a unique, perhaps even enviable, position in relation to the amount and type of contact that he has with pupils. It is his responsibility to produce and deliver a programme that enables pupils to make informed decisions about their futures. Given these circumstances, it is not surprising that it was decided to investigate how pupils perceive the National Curriculum, as it is felt that such understandings could contribute to the further development of the aforementioned programme and perhaps that of the school.

The Investigation

It was decided that a small number of pupils would be interviewed, individually. These interviews were partially structured, in that they were based on themes rather than a set of rigid, structured questions, and they were conducted in school. Interviews lasted between five and ten minutes and were tape-recorded. Pupils were invited, rather than required, to participate after permission had been obtained from senior members of staff. Pupils were asked to be as truthful as possible at the beginning of each interview and anonymity was assured. A sample of 11 students participated in this investigation and were chosen at random - four females and seven males - who come from a mixture of ethnic backgrounds and range from year 8 to year 11 pupils. A number of these pupils are involved in the aforementioned programme, but some represent individuals with whom the author has had contact in his capacity as individual mentor.

This investigation was never intended to produce data that could be described as conclusive or definitive, but it is hoped that it will liberate insights that may be helpful to practitioners and beneficial to pupils. The author will not focus on issues to do with gender, ethnicity or age, as his aim is to explore pupil perceptions of the National Curriculum in general terms. The themes that formed the bases of the interviews are:

- What is the National Curriculum?
- Why do you do all of this work at school?
- How do you feel about schoolwork?
- What do you think of the topics?
- What part do teachers play?
- Why are some pupils not interested in schoolwork?
- How could schoolwork be improved?

The interviews were conversations that revolved around these themes, but were not restricted by them, thereby giving pupils the opportunity to respond more authentically. What follows is a presentation of the data that was obtained.

What is the National Curriculum?

In general, pupils seemed to have a relatively limited understanding of what the National Curriculum is. There was one pupil in particular who didn't even feel able to hazard a guess. A number of pupils feel that the National Curriculum is compulsory:

> I think it's like to do with school and lessons and if you don't want to do it, you have to, because it's the National Curriculum.

> I think it's when you don't want to do something but you have to, because most of it's in the National Curriculum.

> I think the National Curriculum is about work and school, about your GCSE's and stuff like that, I don't know. Like, people give you these things about the National Curriculum and you have to do them. I don't know what it is really.

Some pupils indicate that the National Curriculum is what they are taught:

> Everything that the teachers teach is on the National Curriculum, the work.

> Like, the teachers set the work for the children.

Pupils also highlight subjects as being the National Curriculum:

> Education, coming to school and learning my lessons, English, Maths, Science, German, PE, Youth Award, Complimentary Studies, Social Education, DT ...

> What you have to learn in school, English, Science, Maths and Geography ...

> All the subjects in school.

These pupils also seem to be indicating that learning and education are significant, but restricted to specific subjects. One pupil feels that it is the achievement of targets that is central to the National Curriculum:

> You're supposed to achieve. Like, when you go through the Key Stages, like Key Stage 2. It means that, like, the average child is supposed to pass that level.

Another pupil feels that exams are what the National Curriculum is all about, but seems unsure:

> Exams, or something like that.

These responses seem to indicate that pupils may not be privy to the '...clear and shared understanding of the skills and knowledge that young people will gain at school' (DfEE and QCA, 1999, p.3). Individual pupils seem to emphasise a separate aspect of the National Curriculum in trying to explain what it means for them. In addition there is some lack of clarity in their apparent understandings.

Why Do You Do All of This Work at School?

Nearly all of the pupils feel that schoolwork is a preparation for the world of work, as indicated by the following responses:

> So you can get a job, so you can get a good education. So you can learn something about whatever you want to do.

> To get good GCSE marks so you can get a job when you leave school.

> To get a good job, to get good GCSE's, because like in English you wouldn't know how to spell and write and whatever and Maths, you wouldn't know how to add-up, so it's a good point for doing work I think. If you don't, you won't get a job.

> So you can learn and get a good career and get a good job.

> So when you leave school you've got an education and you know how to read and write and then you can get a job and your own house, married and stuff like that.

> So you learn subjects, so you know them in the future, so it can help you get different levels like GCSE's, A-Levels for whatever you want to become. So that you can get a good job in the future, so you can earn a good living, not just a poor one. Not a bad living but a good one.

> So it's easier to get a job.

One pupil, as well as some of those above, highlights the importance of basic skills:

> Like Maths, you wouldn't be able to add-up or anything and English, if you don't know anything about English you probably wouldn't be able to spell your name or write.

Another pupil believes that there is an ethical dimension to schooling:

> So that we get taught all of the right things that we need.

So it would appear that securing a good job or career, for some of these pupils, is linked to the qualifications that they gain at school. Learning the basic skills, or the more particular skills, related to a job or career and learning things that are 'right' and necessary are also perceived to be the purpose of the National Curriculum. Pupils seem clear that in order to secure a good job, and therefore the wealth to facilitate a 'good life', one must be educated. Labour Party (1994), cited in Davies and Edwards (1999), seems to fit with these pupils' perceptions, in terms of what could loosely be described as 'personal fulfilment', but what about:

> ... Economic success for the Nation, and to the creation of a more just and cohesive society ... (p.271)

These pupils seem to focus more on their own personal success, rather than that of the Nation. Perhaps they are not yet mature, or informed, enough to be able to see the link between personal and national success. They also seem unaware of the agenda that seeks to 'mend' our society through education.

Tate (1999) argues that:

> ... It is important to ensure that our National Curriculum guarantees to all our children access to all those things that as a society we have decided we value and which we wish to pass on to our successors. (p.10)

Perhaps the pupil who mentioned 'need' and 'the right things' comes closest to articulating the cultural-reproductive aspect of the National Curriculum. Arguably, for the majority of these pupils, the National Curriculum is about enabling the successful transition from school to work, perhaps with some additional education in between.

How Do You Feel About Schoolwork? And What Do You Think of the Topics?

Firstly, in relation to schoolwork, a number of pupils indicate that the level of difficulty and their understanding of schoolwork are important:

> It's hard and it's sometimes easy.

> It's all right, it can get a bit hard sometimes when you don't understand things, but most of it's all right though. Year 10's got hard. It's all right, you get used to it when you've been in year 10 for a while.

> I think it's all right, it's not easy and it's not hard, it's just normal if you listen and understand the work, but if you're messing about you won't understand it. When you listen it's easier. Like if it's English and you listen to the teacher, it feels so easy you can just do it, but if you don't listen you won't understand what you're supposed to be doing.

> If it's too easy it's boring, you can just skip through it.

Some pupils feel that the extent to which they find schoolwork interesting or boring is significant:

> Some of it's boring, some of it's all right and some of it's easy.

> It's the same old thing all the time.

> Some of it's good; some of it's boring.

> I think it's rubbish, because I don't learn anything, because I don't listen, because it's just boring listening to the teacher. They just blab on, you don't get a say or anything.

One student feels that activities and communication are important in relation to schoolwork:

> When you get to do like drawing and stuff, not too much writing ... Too much writing, no activities to talk to your friends.

Another student feels that pressure is an issue:

> I don't feel pressured, but when it comes to exams I feel a bit of pressure.

So, for these pupils, the level of difficulty, interest vs. boredom, variety of activities and pressure all play a part in their perceptions of schoolwork.

In relation to topics, some pupils mentioned difficulty again:

> They're all right but some of them are hard.

> They're good, but some of them are hard, but they're all right.

In a similar way, two pupils highlight interest vs. boredom:

> Some are all right, but some are just boring, like when you do just writing.

> I don't like Science or languages, because they're just not interesting.

Two pupils comment on progression in relation to topics:

> I think it's good the way that it's set out from year 7 and in year 9 we did Romeo and Juliet and now we're doing Macbeth. I think it's good the way that it's set out like that. If the teacher like gives you a load of work all at the same time, it can get really hard and you just don't have a clue.

> The work from year 7 up is like your understanding and learning. Like in year 7 we didn't do hard stuff, it's just like easy, but in year 8 you start maturing more and you start going into more detail in a book and in year 9 you start doing more and more and then year 10 you understand it then. Like in year 7 we never used to hear swearing in a book, but now we hear swearing in books, because you've matured more now. If you were in year 7 and you heard swearing in a book you'd probably start laughing, but in year 10 it's like you understand that now and we're more mature about it.

One pupil felt strongly that relevance was an issue:

> Some of them you don't like need to know. Like Algebra, well, where do you use it?

The pupils seem to be suggesting, in relation to both schoolwork, in general, and topics in particular, that the level of difficulty and interest vs. boredom are important considerations. Pupils also feel that the variety of activities and perhaps, to a lesser extent, pressure play a part, in relation to schoolwork. Progression from year 7 upwards is looked upon favourably, but one pupil argues that some topics are not relevant. Hailes et al. (1977), suggest that:

> We have identified three key dimensions to conceptualise these attitudes towards school activities - interest versus boredom, level of difficulty, and success versus failure. (p.607)

Although pupils did not explicitly mention success and failure, it is evident that these are intimately related to the level of difficulty of schoolwork. It would seem that these pupils are set at an appropriate level of difficulty, that incorporate a variety of activities and do not produce strong feelings of pressure are more desirable. Before we go any further with this discussion perhaps we should consider the role that teachers play, in relation to the delivery of the National Curriculum.

What Part Do Teachers Play?

The role that teachers play, in relation to the National Curriculum, is felt to be important by all of the pupils, as illustrated by the following response:

> Teachers are important because they're the ones that teach you. If they don't know it, they can't teach you.

Pupils describe a 'good' teacher as follows:

> You have to be strict but fair and easy to talk to.
>
> A good teacher listens to you.
>
> A good personality, like if you've got problems you can just tell them and that.
>
> Someone who's not too strict and talks to you like a friend, not like a teacher. Teachers just want to teach you, they don't want to know you.
>
> Someone who listens and helps you, a lot of teachers don't listen to you and expect you to listen.
>
> One that respects the pupil, like respects what position they're in.
>
> They laugh and joke with you and help you.
>
> Listening to the students and taking notice of what you're saying and caring for the students. Like listening to what they're saying, like some teachers just don't listen to you. Like you've got a problem, they just don't listen and they need to listen to know what your problem is.

> A good teacher makes a good lesson.
>
> When they're teaching you they're not boring and give you loads of work. They explain things in different kinds of ways. Some teachers just write a load of crap on the board and ask you to copy it down, that's boring, but if they stand there and tell you all about it and then say examples about stuff like that then it's good.
>
> Fair and honest, equal. They listen to both pupils. Someone who knows what they're on about.

Many pupils describe a 'bad' teacher as the opposite of the above, but some pupils describe a 'bad' teacher as follows:

> You can put your hand up for ages and they'll just look at you and turn away.
>
> Like we don't have any respect for him because he doesn't make an effort.
>
> Just laughs at you all the time, doesn't listen to what you've got to say. They won't let you talk: just get on with your work.
>
> Ratty, and they shout at you for something you haven't done and blame it on you.

It is evident from these quotations that some, if not all, of these pupils have encountered 'bad' teachers and 'good' teachers. Arguably, teachers make the National Curriculum happen. They are required to deliver the content of the National Curriculum in such a way as to make it possible for all pupils, parents, employers and the wider community to benefit from it. Hailes et al. (1997) argue that:

> It is clearly important for children to be given the opportunity to obtain or seek out information - from the teacher or other resources - to enable them to complete set activities and experience the pleasure of successful achievement as opposed to failure and the negative consequences that follow from this.
>
> (p.608)

If pupils feel that a particular teacher, for example, is unapproachable, doesn't listen, makes rash judgements, doesn't make the effort, doesn't explain things very well, doesn't respect pupils and so on and so forth, then it is more likely that the pupil will fail on one or a number of levels, in relation to their achievement, because they will not have felt able to seek the help or support that was necessary for them to be successful.

These pupils seem to be saying that they want to be taught by caring human beings and in such a way as to make the learning experience an interesting one. They want to be in a position to be successful; they also want to be respected.

Why Are Some Pupils Not Interested in Schoolwork? And How Could Schoolwork be Improved?

In relation to why some students are not interested in Schoolwork, pupils comment that, again, the level of difficulty is important:

> Because they don't know it and they find it hard.

> Maybe because they find it too hard, they might be under a lot of pressure from school, they might just not like going to school, they might find it too hard, they might have learning difficulties and stuff like that and just can't do the work.

> Because they find it hard so they don't bother or they don't like working, lazy.

One pupil feels that interest vs. boredom is an issue:

> Because of what they've got to do with the teachers. Lessons can be boring and teachers can be boring.

A number of pupils feel that the extent to which pupils consider schoolwork to be relevant is important:

> Because they think that they don't need to know, because of friends or they might know what they want to do and they might not do all like exams.

> Why do we have to take a language or RS [Religious Studies]. I've asked a teacher why we do it, he says in case you want to work abroad. I don't want to work abroad, so I don't think that I should have to do German. I could be doing something else that's going to be helping me. I don't think it's helping me much and I don't understand all this religious stuff that we do in RS. Like

in Soc. Ed. [Social Education] I'm doing stuff about what I want to do when I'm older, you can do all sorts. The teacher doesn't help you: you find stuff out yourself.

The majority of pupils feel that it is because many pupils just can't be bothered:

Because maybe they don't want to learn, because some people just aren't bothered, because if their family's not bothered then they won't come and they won't learn will they.

Because they just want to mess about, because they've got nothing else to do, because they can't be bothered to listen.

Because they don't want to learn, they're not bothered about work, they're not bothered about life really, or they'd do the work.

Because some people just don't want to get a job and don't want to have a life and they want to be unemployed and that and people who want good jobs, good educations, good grades and you can still have a social life and get an education, some people can.

One very articulate pupil feels that the home is central:

Because they don't want to put their mind to the work, well really I think it's from home, because if they're from different backgrounds at home, where you're seeing the life at home, you bring that into school with you, because if you had a good mum who says go to school, I want you to get a good education, then the kid would think well, I want my mum to be proud, I want to get a good job, but some parents don't care and they just sit down, don't care what time they come in at night and then they bring that to school and they think well, if my mum doesn't care then I don't need to do any work either, I just want to be like my mum or dad, whatever.

These pupils seem to be suggesting that the level of difficulty, interest vs. boredom, relevance, the attitude of the pupil and the home all play a part in the emergence of students who are not interested in schoolwork. These are observations made by pupils at a comprehensive school that is not particularly unique. The next logical step is to explore how pupils think that schoolwork could be improved.

A number of pupils feel that no improvements are necessary or could not think of any improvements. One pupil thinks that schoolwork should be easier. A number of students feel that communication is the key:

> Do a lot of communication work, like pairs and groups, but I'd still do individual work.

> I don't know. Some teachers explain it more and some teachers don't. Some teachers just talk for about ten minutes and just tell you to get on with it, but some teachers will explain for forty-five minutes, then the next time you come into class, you do a full hour of it, so you know what you're doing, but some teachers it's just ten or fifteen minutes and then you get stuck and then it's just hard.

> I think they're all right now, but I'd improve them by giving the students chance to talk one at a time, and listen to all the examples that they're saying.

One student feels that variety and choice can improve the situation:

> I'd do different things, like one week, say you have a Tuesday and a Thursday and on a Tuesday say it's a double [two hours], you can look through a book and then another day, say it's a single [one hour], you can do your own thing as long as it's something to do with Maths, like work through a textbook of your own choice.

These pupils, then, are suggesting that the level of difficulty, opportunities to communicate with their peers, teachers who communicate effectively, variety and choice are factors that need to be considered, in relation to improving schoolwork. Davies and Edwards (1999) comment that:

> Of particular concern to us is the degree of control learners have over the contents and/or methods of their learning and how these might relate to what are considered to be worthwhile areas and forms of inquiry.   (p.272)

Pupils are generally placed in situations over which they have little control. They are asked to work, to learn and participate. Teachers are perhaps in a situation where they feel unable to respond to the individual needs of students, because of curriculum and staffing constraints, but this does not mean that pupils stop having feelings about the whole thing. Gillard (1995) observes that:

> ... It worries me that it is so content-based. Who decides what the content will be? It certainly isn't the children - it isn't even the teachers: it's some government quango. (p.72)

> Don't forget the child is a living thing, with thoughts and beliefs, hopes and choices, feelings and wishes; helping him [her] with these must be what education is about, for there is nothing else to educate. (p.73)

Conclusion

Based on the responses of these pupils, it is possible to extract a number of issues that have implications for practitioners and the educational achievement of pupils. Firstly, pupils seem to have a limited understanding of what the National Curriculum is. If we consider how much time pupils spend in compulsory education, it seems a little odd that they are unable to articulate a sophisticated understanding of the foundations of our education system. To a slightly lesser extent, this could be argued to be the case in relation to their understandings of the purpose of the National Curriculum. The majority of pupils suggest that the purpose of schoolwork is to prepare them for the world of work, or perhaps further education, but they don't seem to be aware of the ideological constructs and the broader aims that underpin the National Curriculum, apart from perhaps one exception. The author would argue that there is a need for clarity. Would we expect a building firm to successfully construct a house without first granting them access to detailed information about the project - plans, surveys, customer preferences, aims - and yet this is exactly what we may be asking our children to do, in relation to their education.

Secondly, teachers as individuals play a not insignificant role in the education of children. It would seem that these pupils suggest that interesting schoolwork and topics, that are progressive and relevant, set at an appropriate level of difficulty, that incorporate a variety of activities and do not produce strong feelings of pressure, are more desirable. This situation can only occur if: a) the curriculum if flexible enough to allow teachers to be creative; and b) teachers are able to treat pupils with respect. These pupils highlight the importance of variety, progression, relevance, choice, level of difficulty, interest vs. boredom and communication, but what stands out is their desire to be treated as human beings. Unfortunately, many mainstream teachers are not able to make decisions about the organisation of the curriculum. They are not able to allow pupils to make choices about what they will learn. They do not have the time to 'get to know' pupils as individuals. The National Curriculum can be thought of as the plans that are given to our building firm, but it is through the builders on site that the job gets done. It becomes evident that the plans and their execution are not mutually exclusive:

> Research indicates that for a significant number of young people the school curriculum, in terms of both content and pedagogy, is not a pathway to enlightenment and empowerment but a source of alienation and failure, especially so in the later years of compulsory schooling and in inner city areas.
> (Davies and Edwards, 1999, p.271)

Teachers can only work within the confines of the National Curriculum, which is both demanding and perhaps demoralising. Teachers are human beings as well. They have feelings, aspirations, purposes for being in education, and dreams. The author can remember how inspired he felt when he realised that he would be able to make a real difference to the lives of others through education, but then he was released from the safe environment of the university campus into the real educational world.

As a practitioner, listening to students is always a high priority. This investigation has reinforced the belief that sometimes we look in the wrong direction for answers: we look away from those who we say we wish to help. The author argues that teachers must be given the power to be responsive to pupils in a new way. Thankfully, with the introduction of Disapplication and Citizenship in the National curriculum, we may be witnessing the continuation of the process of contextualisation in education, but the national context is changing rapidly and pupils do not wear blinkers all of the time:

> So, for the foreseeable future, schools will continue to work within the confines of a 'prescriptive', 'content-specific', 'over-assessed', 'conceptually arid' (Labour Party, 1993) National Curriculum that, arguably, serves neither the personal needs of pupils nor the social, political and economic needs of the society in which they live. (Davies and Edwards, 1999, p.268)

As a parent, it is difficult for the author to be complacent regarding the responses that these pupils have shared. As a practitioner, he considers it his duty to constantly strive to safeguard the interests of those for whom he is responsible. As a human being, he feels compelled to respond.

References

Crawford, K. (1998) The construction of the National Curriculum: an ideological and political analysis. *Research Papers in Education*, 13 (3), pp.261-276.

Davies, M. and Edwards, G. (1999) Will the curriculum caterpillar ever learn to fly? *Cambridge Journal of Education*, 29 (2), pp.265-275.

DfEE and QCA (1999) *The National Curriculum: Handbook for Secondary Teachers in England*, London, Department for Education and Employment and Qualifications and Curriculum Authority.

Gillard, D. (1995) Children's needs and interests and the National Curriculum, *Forum*, 37 (3), pp.71-73.

Hailes, J. et al. (1997) Children's attitudes to the National Curriculum at Key Stage 1, *British Educational Research Journal*, 23 (5), pp.597-613.

Tate, N. (1999) What is education for? *English in Education*, 33 (2), pp.5-18.

Willan, P. (1998) Whatever happened to entitlement in the National Curriculum? *Curriculum Journal*, 9 (3), pp.269-283.

6 Secondary Subject Teaching and the Development of Pupil Values

BOB BUTROYD

Why Look at Values

This chapter explores the relationship between the espoused values of teachers, and those enacted through practice. This is an important issue. The National Curriculum introduced in 1988 was unusual in that it was subject led. The values underlying the curriculum were never articulated beyond generalisations based upon a 'broad and balanced curriculum'. This left schools, and teachers in particular, open to charges that they were letting values drift. The focus of these accusations was moral values. Teachers were accused of not distinguishing between right and wrong. Tate (1996) whilst Chief Executive of the Schools Curriculum and Assessment Authority (SCAA), asserted that the essence of the teacher, the core values, are so inhibited by political correctness that our children are left to wander without guidance, without a shared vision for the future. He felt that schools were threatened by 'political correctness' and that they were afraid of instilling the difference between 'right and wrong'. SCAA (1996) responded to this perceived crisis through a consultation process, which sought to discover a level of agreement on the values that schools should promote on society's behalf. Subsequently, they commissioned a pilot project (QCA, 1997) to promote pupil's spiritual, moral, social and cultural development. These values eventually surfaced in the revised National Curriculum (QCA, 1999). However there was little research on the nature and impact of the teachers' values within the context of the Secondary classroom. This chapter addresses this deficiency.

During 1999 the Gordon Cook Foundation funded a project, Research into Values in Secondary Education (ReVISE), to explore the values of teachers and how these values either intentionally, or unintentionally influenced their pupils' values during the crucial period of mid-adolescence (13-16 year olds). This chapter explores how pupils reacted to the values encountered in National Curriculum English and Science, and considers whether pupils engaged with the values that teachers said were important in their classrooms.

What is a Useful Way of Looking at Values?

The New Oxford Dictionary of English (Pearsall, J., 1998) offers a useful definition of values for the purposes of this research:

> One's judgement of what is important in life.

This simple definition allowed the research to explore the values of the classroom, in all their forms. However, the whole area of values is a complex and demanding one. The focus of the research was to examine how teachers attempted to engage the pupils with the values evident in the classroom. In this context the work of Dewey (1944) was to prove illuminating. Dewey distinguished between intrinsic and instrumental values. An intrinsic value 'serves its own end, which cannot be supplied by a substitute'. In this sense intrinsic values emerged from the data as ends to be satisfied. Intrinsic values can be considered as preferences that we seek to satisfy; those things that we aim for, and we see as worthy of pursuit. These are values that have the potential for pleasure or satisfaction in themselves. Instrumental values emerged from the data as 'means' to an end. These are things or concepts that are valued, not necessarily for themselves, but because they can offer access to other things, including intrinsic values.

Whether an idea, or concept, is an instrumental or intrinsic value depends to a large degree upon whether they are means or ends in the context in which they are found. As we shall see later, what might in the normal course of events be considered instrumental values have in some instances become ends in themselves, but they fail to offer the satisfaction that an intrinsic value would offer.

Dewey makes this distinction between instrumental and intrinsic values because he sees that instrumental values are an important starting point for engaging youngsters in learning. The practical nature of instrumental values can enable youngsters to develop a broader appreciation of the pleasure and satisfaction to be gained from learning. In other words, instrumental values are important because they can lead to intrinsic values. The research suggested a similar process in the work of teachers. They often expressed their pleasure in their subject teaching in terms of intrinsic values, such as the 'satisfaction of curiosity' in Science, or a 'discovery of the inner person' in English, although what was observed in many of the classrooms was the use of instrumental values to engage youngsters. In the classroom that successfully engaged pupils in the values of their subject the teachers started with the instrumental nature of a value and used this to lead onto the intrinsic nature.

The distinction between the potentially more abstract and distant intrinsic values, and the more immediate and assessable instrumental values grounds this research in the life, work and experiences of teachers.

How Were Values Identified?

The research was designed to investigate a small number of classrooms in depth, in order to explore the difficult area of the mismatch between teachers' intentions and the actual outcomes in terms of young people's learning, their behaviour and their developing values. The data was drawn from seven English teachers, one Drama teacher and seven Science teachers across four secondary schools. Two of the Science teachers were female, as were five of the English and Drama teachers. The two subjects were chosen because they offered the possibility of exploring whether values development was possible through core subjects of the National Curriculum.

The nature of the research was necessarily intrusive, as it explored very personal values, attitudes and feelings. On a number of occasions teachers explained how they had never talked of such issues before, particularly in a professional context. These teachers were brave to allow a stranger to enter their classroom, to explore their feelings and the feelings of their pupils towards them. The research took place in the North of England and the names of the schools and the names of the participants have been changed to maintain the anonymity that has made this research possible.

The data collection was carefully sequenced as follows.

A Preliminary semi-structured interview with the teacher took place shortly before the classroom observations. Typically, this might be in the week prior to the lesson. Immediately after the lesson a small representative group of pupils, four or five, would be interviewed. After the observation a second interview with the teacher would also take place. The early focus of both interviews was the observed 'key' interactions that took place during the lesson. The interviews would then explore issues raised by the informants. Then the data was transcribed, and relevant research data was analysed using dilemma analysis.

A dilemma is characterised by 'hesitancy, puzzlement, uncertainty, a sense of difficulty of stress' (Somekh, 1995), 'complexity, tension and contradiction' (Winter, 1982). Dilemmas in the data often emerged through the identification of different perspectives on a key interaction, or key issue explored at interview. The importance of this approach is that it analyses the data in a way that uncovers the tensions within and between values, rather than attempting to map the values that teachers hold. This approach does not attempt generalisation about the frequency of values in the data, but highlights factors that can preserve or undermine a value position. This approach analyses the transcripts, not in terms of the particular values that teachers hold, but in terms of the issues surrounding various values. A dilemma may identify a minority concern, but this concern can reveal the potential for change in a value position. It is particularly useful in looking at an individual's response to structures, such as the National Curriculum, GCSE and the attended assessment procedures. It allows for the exploration of underlying assumptions and can offer insight into Tate's concern for the development of shared values.

Transcripts of the interviews were sent to the teachers and early findings were discussed with a number of them, but opportunities for this were constrained by the demands on their time and energy that are familiar to all of us who have been, or are, secondary school teachers. The analysis and presentation of findings begins with the English teachers and then turns to the teachers of Science.

English is Valued for its Practical Application, and the Promise of More Profound Insight into the Human Condition

Two English teachers, Mary and Sandy, taught at the same all boys comprehensive school, *Boyscomp*, which served an inner city area with a large ethnic minority population. The children's family origins were in Pakistan or Bangladesh.

A striking feature of the *Boyscomp* interviews was the instrumental way in which the pupils viewed the subject. The majority of the teachers of English in the other schools also shared this perception, although in *Boyscomp* there was a significant difference in practice between Mary and Sandy.

> **Mary**: English is totally unique as a subject ... it lends itself more than any other subject to my philosophy ... particularly through literature ... where else is there an opportunity to explore all the kinds of issues that concern us as human beings? Where else can you find yourself? Where else can you discover the inner person?

Mary emphasised a continuum, where instrumental concerns were used as a basis from which to explore the intrinsic. For her, English was a subject where pupils could explore issues relating to the 'inner person'; issues which concerned pupils as 'human beings'. This was a practical approach to the study of English, but it did not shut the door on the intrinsic. It recognised that for many pupils the satisfaction of intrinsic values (such as the 'inner person') would follow as a consequence of pursuing practical concerns. For example, when exploring the issue of propaganda in Orwell's '1984' she examined the techniques of propaganda (the use of rhetorical questions, repetition and assertion) and invited pupils to comment upon the validity of such techniques.

> **Mary's Pupils**: *What was the purpose of the lesson that you have just had?* Partly to prepare us for homework. It's all building up to an essay that we are going to write sooner or later on George Orwell. A task that could be useful for life; to pick up information and compare things.

The pupils' response to this was to consider the underlying values to be important because they were practical, or instrumental. The study of English helped them with the business of life, and helped them to analyse events, not just for the purposes of the exam (although we should not underestimate the significance of this). The lesson suggested a future use and development of the values offered by the teacher. The values could be developed in themselves, but also the pupils valued the examination success that this study could bring. The pupils were a top band set, and were expected to do well.

Sandy taught a lower ability group that was in the early stages of studying Macbeth. From the attitudes of the pupils, the researcher's observations and Sandy's comments, the pupils appeared to have an over optimistic view of the GCSE grade that they were going to achieve. This lack of 'realism' was also reflected by a disengaged approach to the classroom. The pupils did not show an understanding of the amount and quality of work required. The reasons for this can only be speculative, but it may be that they well understood their situation, and were determined to maintain their self esteem through other means. In terms of values, there was a similar dissonance.

> **Sandy**: language is power ... It helps you to express your feelings, which is going to help you be a more successful, happy human being ... and then there is obviously the huge literary tradition ... you can introduce people to something that is going to give them pleasure all of their lives, because they can go back to Shakespeare, Jane Austin and back to Dickens and back to poetry all their lives.

Sandy talked in the interview of the power of language, and its ability to improve the quality of life. Sandy was keen to emphasise the literary tradition in her lesson. She approached the work from the intrinsic perspective, that works of literature could offer pleasure and value in themselves. This was an approach that was not observed amongst the other English teachers, where a more instrumental approach was used as a starting point. Her emphasis upon the pleasure to be gained from the literary tradition found little resonance amongst her pupils.

> **Sandy's Pupils**: *What did you think of Macbeth?* It's all right. *Is it something that you should be studying?* Yeah. *Why?* To learn about what are good things about life, and what are bad things ... To get used to the language as well. So you know what things they used to do in them days ... To see where we were from, or ancestors and stuff. *Were your ancestors from Shakespeare's time in England?* P1 I think mine wor. P2 I don't know about mine.

Whilst the pupils did recognise the value of coming to terms with the language and morality of Shakespeare's characters, they were also sending out confusing messages about the relevance of Shakespeare to their own lives. They referred to 'getting used to the language', but also curiously they said that they valued the subject to 'see where we were from'. As was stated earlier, the majority of these pupils' families had a background deriving from Pakistan and Bangladesh. During the whole class viewing of the Macbeth video a number of pupils found difficulty in maintaining concentration. There was little to suggest that the class derived pleasure from the literature itself. The pupils did not appear to recognise their origins in an 11th century Scottish king.

The pupils maintained greater concentration when they considered the work to be directly relevant to their GCSE, eg. completing assignments. Even then it was not clear if these students really engaged with the values of the subject in a meaningful way.

It is, again, speculation to consider the reasons why the pupils appeared more motivated in the top ability group of Mary's than in the lower ability group of Sandy. It was clear, however, that Mary's group had an understanding of some of the instrumental values associated with the study of English, whilst being open to the possibilities of intrinsic values. At the same time, Sandy's class, described as a lower group, appeared strangely disengaged from the values of her classroom.

Jenny and June taught at *Engirlcomp*, a school where the origins of the majority of the pupils' families also lay in Pakistan or Bangladesh. Jenny, like Sandy, was also teaching through Macbeth. Jenny, like Mary at *Boyscomp* used a similar, instrumental approach to values, and her pupils were fully engaged in the instrumental values of the subject, and recognised the potential for exploring the intrinsic values of English.

> **Jenny's Pupils**: *Macbeth, it's a long time ago. Is it useful to you as a young woman growing up in Bradford?* It can be in some ways because it can tell you what is right and wrong. It can give you a better understanding of different situations you could get into. *Does the teacher ever tell what is right and wrong?* P1 No, she lets us make that choice. It is up to us what we think of it. P2 She gives us advice on what she thinks. P3 She gives us a guideline on what she thinks, but it is basically up to us really ... P2 to study poems in detail ... She will ask you 'what does this mean?' What does this word or sentence mean? Then you think about it and really get into it, and it is really nice.

The English classes at *Engirlcomp* were unusual in the sample, in that they were both mixed ability. The inclusion of pupils of different abilities and achievement in the same class was used by the teachers to encourage pupils to listen to each other and to contribute to debates, no matter what their status in terms of 'academic ability'. This encouraged pupils to communicate ideas, and to explore values from different perspectives. There was not a perceived 'common sense' view of the literature, even in terms of what Jenny called 'community values', everything appeared to be available for interrogation by class discussion.

The Values of English can be Explored through Different Pedagogies

There was a greater degree of certainty about values in *Engirlcomp* than in many of the other classrooms. This was particularly interesting, as the teachers and pupils' overlapping perspectives were largely expressed in terms of agreed classroom pedagogies and a commitment to 'community values'. These community values were not articulated, but were arrived at through the discussion of 'different texts' and 'different moralities'.

> **Jenny**: There is the value of allowing everyone to reach their potential and developing confidence and language skills ... the more control you have over our language ... and know when to use it then the better able you are to be equipped for a lot of situations ... when you are engaging with different texts you come across a whole series of different moralities, and I think that can be discussion points around that. I don't think that you can seek to impose a particular morality at all. But I think if you understand how texts have been written, and how they work then I think it is like developing independence really is what I am getting at.

Whilst teaching Macbeth Jenny aimed to bring her pupils into contact with different moralities, so that they could explore them, but not to impose any particular one. Her class presented scenes they had selected from the play in a style of their own choosing. She did not wish to impose her own values, although she felt that the 'community values' of the school were also 'common values' of tolerance and learning to live with other people who may not share the pupils' own cultural perspective. The purpose of this framework was to allow the pupils to develop skills associated with independence of thought. Jenny's pupils reflected this approach, recognising the complexities of different situations, and the difficulties of making decisions in the 'real world'.

June was using an anthology of poems published by the exam board and, like Jenny, her values were expressed largely in terms of pedagogical procedures.

> **June**: It is particularly positive in a school like this for broadening students horizons ... I think that there is room for them to gain experience of different cultures, especially the particular types of text that we are required to teach: different poems from different cultures and traditions and so on ... they get a chance to read about other cultures, about other experiences ... it gives room for discussion about quite important issues and you can incorporate that within the text that you are doing instead of teaching it. I'm sure that personal and social education is important as a separate subject, but in English you, a lot of the issues are raised naturally.

The observed lesson involved the study of a poem by Simon Armitage, which dealt with, among other things, domestic violence. June's approach was similar to Jenny's, encouraging co-operation, and the consideration of many issues that arose from the reading of the poem. June felt that it was important that English should broaden horizons and enable youngsters to explore personal and moral issues: a view shared by her pupils.

Significantly, the teachers considered that many of the issues relating to personal and social education would arise 'naturally' through the study of English if taught in this way.

> **Jenny's Pupils**: *What sort of a person would Ms XXXX like you to be?* To stand up for ourselves. Like all our teachers ... they talk positive. They make you think that you can achieve what they want you to achieve.

> **June's Pupils**: *Do you get the chance to say what you really think in these lessons?* Yes. That is what it is all about in English. It is good in groups. And she goes round and asks our opinion and everything. That is what I like about it. Everybody takes part in it. *Do you ever discuss what is right and wrong in English?* We do, but then again, when every person has said this is right and another person this is wrong, when we have discussed as a class, it is not right or wrong. *Is life like that?* P1 Yes. P2 Yes. *What was the point of the lesson?* To do poetry. *In your town?* To look, using the skills, to look for patterns. To use them later in life. It depends what you want to do. But it is in every job.

The classes at *Engirlcomp* were organised and strongly structured by the teachers to encourage discussion, and the sharing of ideas amongst the pupils. Seating arrangements were based on the premise that pupils needed to interact, not just with the teacher but with each other and, although the teacher had important expertise that the pupils did not possess, it was important that pupils should see each other where at all possible. Jenny's class was arranged in a circle the day they performed their scenes from Macbeth, and June's class was grouped around tables where discussion amongst the pupils could be encouraged. Through the expression of views about the subject matter, a respect for each other's contribution, no matter what the pupils' perceived abilities, and the underlying principle of adhering to community values, these classrooms displayed aspects of what could be termed democratic behaviour.

At *Coedcomp*, a larger comprehensive with a profile of pupils not untypical of an urban industrial town, the approach of the two English teachers, Roger and Gerry was more teacher centred in their classroom style.

> **Roger's Pupils**: *Does he ever give his opinion about things? P1* Yeah. All the time. It is like, he stands at the front and teaches, and he gives over his opinion and takes in other peoples, and gets debates going so that you think about the work that you are doing. *P3* It makes it more interesting. *P1* You are thinking about the work without realising. *How would you describe him? P3* A very good teacher. *P2* My favourite teacher. *Why? P2* Because he is funny and he kind of communicates with like what you are saying. *P1* We'll have little chats and that. *P2* He's just got an imagination ... he is more straight forward with you, he is getting a message over ...

> **Gerry's Pupil**: *Do you get to hear about XXXX's opinions?* Yeah. That is a good thing. Because you get to hear other people's opinions, not just your own. So you know more about what other people think. *Do you ever disagree with teachers' opinions?* Sometimes, yeah. *Would you prefer not to hear their opinions?* No, you don't get a good grasp of it, because you don't know what you are supposed to think, or if something is right or wrong.

Roger and Gerry shared a philosophy of the value of English. They were more overt about specific ethical values that could be promoted through the subject than were June and Jenny.

> **Gerry**: ... respect for individuals, the worth of the individuals, tolerance of individuals, equality of opportunity. Violently, almost violently anti-racist, with the kind of books that we read ...

Roger: Tolerance, understanding, sympathy ... If English is taught well that should come out of it. *Tolerance and understanding are there at the back of your mind when you are teaching?* Without a doubt. I think that it should be at the top of the teacher's list and what they are trying to do, tolerance and understanding. If a kid goes out of Yr 11 with a 'U' or a 'G' but has some understanding of tolerance of other people, then I think that I have achieved a lot.

Gerry taught a top set, where he emphasised specific ethical values. The pupils took responsibility for their own learning, and negotiated and monitored their own progress in consultation with the teacher. The class was seated in groups where communication between them was made easier. This was an approach that was not dissimilar to that of *Engirlcomp*. Where this approach differed to that of *Engirlcomp* was in the overt expression of values. The pupils felt that it was important for the teacher to express an opinion. They wanted to know what his opinions were on the text (they were studying 'Educating Rita'), because it helped them to 'sort out' their thinking, and helped them to get a 'good grasp' of the material.

Roger's class was studying 'Of Mice and Men'. He taught largely from the front, and the seating was arranged in rows facing towards him. In promoting tolerance, understanding and sympathy Roger communicated directly with his 'lower ability' pupils through exposition, for the purpose of getting the pupils to think about their work and the attendant values of intolerance, misunderstanding and antipathy. His pupils recognised that he was promoting a message, but they acknowledged the relevance of this to the work that they were studying. His didactic approach built the pupils' confidence. He talked to the pupils, not at them. He talked to the pupils from the front of the class as individuals, and he would respond to them, often from the front of the class, as individuals. He used allegory and anecdote to link the text with the pupils' lives and the issues that they faced. One pupil, who claimed not to like any kind of reading, was drawn into the work precisely because he saw relevance in the values that were explored. The intrinsic values of the subject were opened up by Roger's classroom work.

Most English teachers encouraged pupils to explore their own values. Gerry, and the teachers at *Engirlcomp* did this in relation to the text, and the views of the rest of the class, whilst Roger and Mary's focus were more in relation to the text and their views. The important factor was that there was meaningful communication. Communication was bounded by the conventions of schooling, which recognised the authority of the teacher and the parameters of debate determined by them. The National Curriculum did not prevent the teachers of English from using teaching methods which allowed pupils to clarify values. Within the subject there was a meaningful exploration of the values both in the text and in the context of their own lives.

Pupil Engagement with Values is Sometimes Beyond the Teacher's Control

At *Churchcomp*, an urban coeducational Catholic school, Barry's 'middle ability' set was reading 'Kes' as a whole class activity. In teaching from the front, clearly advocating certain values, and encouraging individual responses to them Barry used a similar teaching style to Roger.

> **Barry:** *What values does your subject offer?* The classic humanist values ... I think that we have lost our way with the National Curriculum. It's knocked us sideways. Instead of it being a Catholic school we're now an Ofsted school. *(It should be)* an extension of mother's knee. The choice of reading is made according to your values and your interests and what you're enthusiastic about. Well, the choice is now limited to what the consensus is about ... I think that there is a lot of affection in that class ... there's a lot of growing up going on. They are cheerfully indifferent to speak to ... What I wanted was a continuity of the book. Either that works or you have nothing.

He recognised the pupils' 'indifference' and suggested that the 'consensus' values of the National Curriculum had more than a little to do with it. He wanted the school to be free to explore Catholic values, and the restraints of the National Curriculum, and the inspection system, made this difficult.

Some pupils were seen to be 'going through the motions' or 'even playing the system'. When this happened the pupils were often doing the minimum required. In some cases this can mean examination success, but also a resistance to engage in the exploration of their values in relation to those of the subject. In these circumstances a classroom teacher's best efforts to engage pupils can face an uphill struggle. Barry faced such a situation.

Barry's Pupils: *Do you ever discuss right and wrong in English? P2* Yeah, lots of things. *P1* That thing, that party. *P2* Oh, yeah. *Can you say what that was about? P1* We had to organise a party, with all different things in it. What were allowed to do, what were right for a party. *So, what was the message from that? P5* There weren't no messages. *P2* It was just an exercise. *Do you learn about right and wrong in school? P2* In EPR we do. *P3* We don't learn about right, really. We learn about what we are not supposed to do. *P2* We don't do it in English we do it in EPR.

The pupils were asked to identify the main character, and to consider the bullying, by his brother, and by his teachers. The pupils would respond to the questioning, but would not make the link between the values encountered in English and their own lives. They were not prepared to transfer the experiences, attitudes and values of the book to their own experience, attitudes and values. The pupils were in some ways disengaged from the processes of the classroom, despite the efforts of the teacher. The pupils welcomed the efforts of the teacher to communicate with them, but their attitudes to the school, and to schooling were somewhat negative. They would participate in Barry's lesson, and spoke of it with some fondness, but they had already sectioned off their schooling from their own 'real' lives.

The analysis of the English data has led us to common ground with Science. Hans taught at *Scigirlcomp* a girl's school that served the local urban community. The girls who attended here were similar in one way to those of *Engirlcomp*, in that their families' origins lay largely in Pakistan and Bangladesh, but in terms of engagement with values they were very different. He too, was faced with a situation where attitudes to his subject, attitudes formed and influenced outside the school, were having a negative effect on the pupils' perceptions of the value of Science.

Hans's Pupils: *Why do you think you study Physics? P1* No idea. *P2* In case we become Physics teachers ... For us it is just boring because we are into other stuff ... *P4* I mean you don't hear your mum say 'well forget the cooking, well here's a magnet' ... *P2* Physics isn't really a woman's thing is it? Well, it's not mine ... I'm not into weighing copper bits and blowing things up and that ... *P4* Yeah, but you don't blow things up. That's what is so boring about it. Sometimes when you do experiments you think 'why bother'? People have done this so many times before. You don't learn anything new. It's like a right and a wrong, and I can't do things that are right and wrong.

There was, amongst Hans's pupils, the perception that Physics was not a girls subject. Physics faced another difficulty. Hans felt that his subject was not well understood in wider society and so its importance was unrecognised. The affected pupil perceptions of his subject before they came to the Physics classes. It was seen as difficult and not particularly relevant. This reminds us that schools are part of a wider community, and that this wider community, and that this wider community can have negative, as well as positive effects upon the work of the teacher.

Hans's pupils also revealed a common difficulty. The behaviour of some of the pupils discouraged the teacher from taking risks. There were two types of risk. The first was the sense of the physical dangers inherent in the study of physics in a lab, and the second was the potential for classroom disruption if more open ended, practical and exciting approaches to the subject were taken. This had an affect upon the potential for the exploration of instrumental values. The limited and controlled opportunities presented in the classroom did not lead on from the instrumental to the intrinsic. Hans's pupils found little relevance and meaning in the demonstration approach to Science. Hans's pupils were not alone in finding this to be the case.

The Exploration of Values in Science is Often Inhibited by Pedagogy

Hans's 'middle ability' class at *Scigirlcomp* was, by the teachers' own admission very mixed in terms of ability and motivation. It was a class of 26 pupils, which was large for a practical session, and these factors made classroom management difficult. The topic of the lesson was electromagnetism, and required experimentation as part of scientific investigation. The lesson was conducted as a demonstration with the girls seated around the teacher's desk. They then had to return to their seats to write up what they had witnessed. This approach was justified in terms of lack of equipment and the volatile and sometimes uncooperative nature of the girls. However, the girls had little interest in watching somebody else's experiment, and learning somebody else's interpretation of the world. This appeared to be compounded by the belief that to do this was unlikely to offer them the same academic success as that of the 'top' group. The girls wished to experience the true excitement of experimentation, not the repetition of previous experiments. They wanted to find the 'truth' for themselves. But the teacher's hands were in some senses tied by the class size, the disruptive nature of some of the pupils, the demands of the curriculum, and cultural influences.

> **Susan's Pupils**: *Do you get chance to explore and say, 'Oh look, I've got a different answer'? P1* No. *P4* Not really, no. But then you hardly ever do anything different to how she demonstrated it. *Why?* Because she shows you step by step how to do it, so it is basically you are doing the same experiment and so it is usually the same results. *Do you find experiments exciting, things to do? P3* They are exciting when you do the things yourself, but when the teacher does it, it is not exciting. You are just sat there watching, real bored. But when you do it yourself you enjoy it more.

Susan's Science pupils at *Churchcomp* echoed the frustration of Hans's pupils with the demonstration approach, however, when the pupils moved on to replicate the experiment there were other difficulties. These were related to class size, and a lack of equipment. Colin's pupils, also at *Churchcomp*, understood his predicament.

> **Colin's Pupils**: *P1* This school's skint. *Do you think that affects teachers? P3* Yeah, because if they haven't got what they need to teach they get agitated and have to use rubbish stuff, like balloons in science instead of proper apparatus. So if they had money to buy proper apparatus which could explain it easier, we would learn better. *Do you think it affects XXXX? P3* Yeah. *P2* Yeah, he gets frustrated sometimes. Like not enough water baths. *P3* Not enough starch. *P1* That experiment. There were too many people in the classroom, and every one was too close on the tables, and I couldn't learn at all.

Science faced practical difficulties that English did not. Time and again pupils and teachers talked of the lack of appropriate equipment, and class size.

Instrumental Values Without Intrinsic Aims

Teachers of Science were sometimes frustrated by the nature of what they had to teach, and the resources they had to teach it. They felt that Science should offer such intrinsic value as curiosity, understanding of the world, interest and challenge.

> **Colin**: *What values does Science offer?* It gives reason and explanation to the world. It helps pupils understand what is going on ... It gives reason, explanation; it helps them enquire.
>
> **Susan**: I'd like to think that every lesson fosters some sort of curiosity. I think that if you are not curious then you can't possibly be a good scientist, because that is what it is all about.
>
> **Hans**: It if is related to everyday life it will take them more conscious of other things that they take for granted. Ok, I don't know about this so I can understand what is going on in the world. Of course it is part of the syllabus, they have to pass exams. In the future there will be issues about making electricity, making energy, making there will be a crisis and there will be no electricity in the future, so they would be able, culturally and socially, to make a decision about those issues in the future. It is interesting, it is a challenging.

The difficulty for Science teachers is that the constraints that they face do not enable them to allow the pupils to genuinely explore, and pursue these values. Hans made an appeal to the relevance of his subject in the same way that Sandy praised the virtues of Shakespeare. Both were unable to develop pupil understanding in an instrumental way: They can't offer pupils the means by which they will make sense of their world through a study of electromagnetism, or Shakespeare.

> **Betty**: If you are talking about a practical lesson where you are doing an experiment, ... and something happens which is not quite what they expect, and they will say to you, 'why is this happening' and sometimes you may have time to go off and do a bit of an aside, as it were, but other times you don't, you have time constraints. Not only that but you are constrained by the fact that if you are spending time with that one group with the sort of class sizes that we have got then you are not supervising what is going on in the rest of the class ... You don't have the time to devote to the pupils on an individual basis that is necessitated if you are going to follow curiosity when it crops up.

Betty, who taught a middle band group at *Coedcomp*, also explained that the pursuit of curiosity and exploration was not a reality given the class sizes that she had. Dennis, who taught a 'top band' Chemistry put it another way.

> **Dennis**: *Is curiosity and exploration a reality in science?* We have got to teach them a certain area of the subject. Now if a kid came to me and said, 'how can we find out about this?' then ideally, we would do, but in reality you can't because of your class size and so on. But, we might say 'we are going to investigate how this affects this', and they will do an experiment, and at the end of it I will say 'right, what have you found out from your results? How does this affect this?' It is not their curiosity as such. I suppose it is me telling them how to find something out.

Curiosity, given the constraints, is often a matter of 'me telling them how to find something out'. This leads in some cases to a preoccupation with measurement, and recording, and the following of procedures. The examination system does not allow for too much risk taking, and so the basics of measurement, recording and the following of procedure have to be mastered to ensure that the pupils have a basis for addressing the GCSE. This is particularly true perhaps for the less well motivated. The lack of access to the intrinsic values of curiosity, or exploration in the attempt to make sense of the world leads to frustration amongst pupils and teachers. Science becomes dry for some pupils, and loses its connection to the instrumental, so that even the use of scientific method as a means of investigation, as a means to an end, loses its relevance for pupils.

Values Should Not Be Taken Out of Science

Class size and lack of equipment leading to 'unsurprising' experiments, are not the only problems. The nature of legitimate knowledge is also a problem. Teachers have to teach what is in the Programmes of Study, and this does not appear to lend itself to the exploration of values in the way that English does. The curriculum is crowded, but the pupils also feel that it lacks an immediate connection with their interests.

> **Dennis's Pupils**: *How could lessons be improved?* *P1* He can't unless he changed the syllabus ... More trips ... *P3* and different kinds of experiments so that it isn't always heating up a substance over a Bunsen burner or something. *P2* Something that has got the element of surprise.

The central determination of the curriculum does not allow teachers to tailor subject matter to the needs of children in quite the way that they would like.

Dennis explained how a study of salts, and the opportunities afforded by the salt mines of Cheshire, would be a far more useful starting point than 'limestone' or 'blast furnaces'. These had become increasingly irrelevant to most pupils with the huge reduction in employment in the steel industry, and the lack of opportunities to visit a blast furnace or steel works. His pupils also had their own ideas about the type of Science that they would like to study.

> **Dennis's Pupils**: *P1* 'I want to do about genetics'; *P2* 'Psychology'; *P3* 'Physiotherapy'.

Pupils wanted to explore issues and areas of knowledge that they were curious about. They wanted to explore those things that gave meaning and explanation, as they saw it. Dennis felt that the syllabus had not changed substantially for forty years. The pupils were excited by the prospect of what Science could offer, but they weren't sure that National curriculum Science could offer it.

Teachers of Science were unsure as to the place of values in their subject. Dennis had covered the development and uses of ammonia earlier in the year. He had explained how ammonia was developed for agricultural purposes but was in fact used in the First World War as a weapon, which had helped to cause injury and prolonged the war. His pupils remembered that he said that in his opinion ammonia should never have been used in the First World War. This 'top ability' set saw nothing wrong in this:

> **Dennis's Pupils**: *P1* ... we understand that it is only his opinion, and it is not a fact ... He doesn't like to say 'that is what it should have been; this is what my opinion is'. We are hearing it about other things, but not about Chemistry.

> **Betty's Pupils**: ... she doesn't give us a proper opinion. You don't do it much in Biology. We don't talk about it. We hardly ever talk about it. *Do you think she should give their opinion? P1* Definitely. Because we want to know more about the environment that we live in ... It should go in depth, we should learn about the things around us, the environment.

Betty's pupils, like Dennis's, also welcomed the idea of more discussion of opinions *about Science* with the teacher, about controversial issues. They understood that it would give them a real grasp of the subject. It could help them pass exams, but it would also help them to understand, and to address their concerns about their world.

> **Betty's Pupils**: *P2* They could involve you more in what they do. Have more discussion. *P1* Upto date video's! *P3* Like '70s! *Do you have discussions in science? P3* Sometimes. *P4* Yeah, sometimes. *Are they planned or just happen? P4* No, just happen really. *Do you want to hear more about the teacher's personal opinions? P1* Yeah, and then we could have a discussion about it. ... she talks about steel and why we need it. *Is Chemistry useful to you? P4* I don't know really. Because we are doing like tests on making iron and stuff, but we are not exactly going to be making iron in that industry.

Teachers did not feel comfortable with the idea of exploring the values of their subject. Indeed, one department declined to take part in the research because they felt that their subject did not leave room for values, as they simply taught the National Curriculum.

Betty was wary of values if they were largely concerned with morality, and she felt that teachers of Science had no business involving themselves in this. But she welcomed the opportunity to discuss the values in Science in general, but more specifically in Biology, her speciality.

> **Betty**: I don't think that there is anything wrong with giving an opinion, as long as you make it clear that that is what it is.

Her pupils welcomed the opportunity to discuss her opinions *on her specialism*. But they felt that she did not often have the opportunity to do this, and they recognised that there might be difficulties with it.

> **Betty's Pupils**: I don't think she brings her own opinions into what she is teaching because she might think that if she has that effect on what we think then we will all think the same. *Do you want to hear more about her personal opinions?* ... It depends what it is about. If it is on like animal testing.

They wanted to discuss the values associated with Biology with their Biology teacher. Although this did happen to a limited extent they thought that she was inhibited by a concern for indoctrination.

Derek taught a 'lower ability' class in *Boyscomp*, and although he didn't feel any great optimism about the exploration of values in Science, he did feel that it was a vehicle for exploring broader social values.

Derek: For some, probably they will never appreciate any value. They will never really appreciate that Science is impinging on their everyday life ... I suppose that most people value things that they feel could be useful to them ... Indirectly you can have co-operation ... In that lesson it might have been done in an argumentative way, but that is not a problem, in science argument is a very essential part. I have told them that they have not just come here to learn about Science, they are also here to learn about life, the way things work or don't work, and how to deal with different situations ... We are dealing with behaviour modification of individuals or groups.

Derek was teaching about electromagnetism, as Hans was in *Scigirlcomp*. However, Derek's approach was very different.

Derek's Pupils: *P2* We always do (experiments) in two's. *P1* So we can help each other. ... And if you do it singly it takes a long time and it is easier if you are co-operating together. *P1* The practical work, sir. It was fun, sir. You could see all the sparks and how the electromagnet was working. *P1* And you learn something. *P3* But like doing it ourselves, we learn more. We can't get much in our head by telling us by saying it, or telling us by saying it, or telling us on a piece of paper. *(The teacher)* was fair.

His pupils conducted their own experiments in pairs, an experience that they enjoyed. These were potentially disruptive pupils, as they were at *Scigirlcomp*. It is worth noting that at *Scigirlcomp* there were 26 in the class and at *Boyscomp* there were nine. Derek used this opportunity to explore values, but these were not values concerned with the unique contribution that Science makes to our understanding of the world.

Conclusions

Meaningful exploration of values took place where instrumental values were used as a starting point, and where pupils were aware that this could help them to explore values of a more intrinsic nature. A practical, relevant starting point for the exploration of issues that were of genuine concern and interest to pupils was a good starting point, but it was not sufficient for instrumental values to be ends in themselves. Instrumentality has by its nature to serve a purpose. It was important that this purpose was not lost in the pursuit of task completion. It was also important not to simply exhort pupils to engage in the intrinsic, but to make the link explicit in the immediate practicality of the instrumental. Encouraging pupils to use cooperation and accurate and careful experimentation, as instrumental values, in order to discover the role of electromagnetism in making a bell work, and using the power of language, as an instrumental value, to understand the nature of human relationships in Macbeth were two examples.

Examination success was believed to be an important value of schooling. Pupils derived satisfaction from this in itself, or saw it as instrumental in achieving those things that they valued. When pupils considered there was little value in the examination results that they were likely to achieve then they saw little purpose in the activities of the classroom, or in the subject itself. The consequent loss in motivation amongst pupils led teachers, on occasions, to an overemphasis on instrumental tasks, such as an accurate description of an experiment in Science, or a comprehension in English. This risked turning a means to an end into an end in itself.

The research observed the value of a subject being explored in two ways. The first was through 'democratic pedagogy'. This approach relied upon the establishment and operation of clear procedures that would allow the class, under the direction of the teacher to establish commonly held values, and to explore them in a way that encouraged full participation by all class members. The second approach was that of 'pupil-teacher value exchange'. In this case the teacher expressed value positions and engaged individual pupils in a discussion of these values.

Pupils wanted to engage with the values of the subject and the teacher's values as a *subject specialist*. The pupils thought that this would give purpose, meaning and sense to the subject. Teachers of National Curriculum English felt more at ease with the curriculum, and the opportunities it offered for values exploration than did the teachers of Science.

Teachers of English and Science were uncomfortable with the promotion of moral values outside the context and aims of their own subjects. The teachers' main purpose was the teaching of their subject, which involved knowledge, skills and attitudes. Attitudes, as responses to stimuli, are underpinned by values. In this context some teachers were prepared to explore these values, but not to impose them.

Subject teachers were not in a position to ensure that all pupils would consider their subject's values. This was particularly the case in Science, where the curriculum was sometimes inappropriate, and class size and lack of appropriate materials made it difficult for teachers to use appropriate pedagogical approaches. Pupil attitudes to the subject were sometimes negatively shaped by their attitudes to school, and, on occasions, attitudes within society also had a negative effect upon pupil attitudes to the subject. These negative attitudes influenced pupils' engagement or disengagement with the subject values.

Pupils were not indoctrinated through schooling. They were active evaluators, not passive receivers of values. Pupils viewed teacher motives with a certain amount of healthy scepticism. Pupils explored values if they perceived this to be in their interests, but they did not respond well to exhortation. Rather than indoctrination there was a danger that pupils would be denied the opportunity to see in their teachers that people are different, and can do things differently. A number of teachers considered themselves to be at odds with the concept of 'the teacher' as they felt that they did not conform to the 'successful' model. A common perspective of the 'model teacher' was of a person who was beyond reproach, efficient, powerful and career minded. This was not how many teachers saw themselves, nor how they wanted to be. Pupils should see different styles of teaching, different personalities, different values and be encouraged to challenge them.

Values should not be taken out of subject study. Indoctrination should not be feared. It was not a matter of 'instilling' values, but of linking instrumental values to the worthwhile intrinsic values of life. Pupils evaluated the worth of a subject, its teacher, and its values. Teachers have a passion for their subject. They should be allowed to express it. We should not be so wary of curriculum constraints that we are afraid of using subject study to explore the values in the world around us and to use those values to make sense of our world.

References

Dewey (1944) *Democracy and Education*, London, Free Press.
Pearsall, J. (1998) (ed) *The New Oxford Dictionary of English*, Oxford, Clarendon Press.
QCA (1997) The promotion of pupils' spiritual, moral, social and cultural development: pilot project, QCA.
QCA (1999) *The National Curriculum*, London, DfEE, QCA.

Somekh, S. (1995) "Analytical Methods" in *Academic Development*, Vol.1, No.1, pp.65-67.

Tate (1996) in Carvel, J. "Curriculum Chief Condemns 'Politically Correct' Teachers", *The Guardian*, 15th January, p.6.

Winter, R. (1982) '"Dilemma Analysis": A contribution to methodology for action research', in *Cambridge Journal of Education*, Vol.12, No.3, pp.161-174.

7 Excluded or Empowered: The National Curriculum and Exclusions

ROBERT BERKELEY

Introduction

Exclusion from school in England rose markedly during the nineties. The debate about why rages on and a great deal of government time and effort has recently been expended on considering the issue and producing targets for its reduction. A theme that regularly arises out of the literature on exclusions is that of the role of the National Curriculum as a catalyst for the increase in exclusions from school. In this chapter, I will argue that the role of the National Curriculum is not clearly a direct cause for increased exclusion and that instead of a means for exclusion, the National Curriculum could be interpreted as a powerful tool for increasing social justice in English schools and society.

The return of a New Labour government in 1997 has been followed by an emphasis on education. Tony Blair's now famous 1996 statement that his priorities for government were 'education, education, and education' have not been superseded in his rhetoric. Education was immediately more closely linked with employment policies as the departments were merged. Since 1997 there has been ongoing consultation and a flurry of policy which schools have had to deal with - a considerable part of which has been to do with exclusions from school.

The newly formed cross-departmental Social Exclusion Unit was immediately asked to consider exclusions from school, reporting in 1998 (SEU, 1998). The Education and Employment committee of the House of Commons commissioned a report into disaffection in schools. There have been five DfEE circulars and publications specifically concerned with exclusions from school and their administration (DfEE, 1997, 1998a, 1998b, 1999a, 1999b). OFSTED (1996) and the House of Commons

Education and Employment Select Committee (1998) have published reports concerned with exclusions.

The outcome of this concern has been the adoption by government of a range of recommendations. The most significant of which is the reduction by a third of permanent exclusions by 2002. This was announced by the Secretary for Education and Employment in these terms:

> We are working towards a simple but challenging goal: to raise educational standards for all our young people, who deserve the best possible chances in life. Regular attendance and high standards of pupil behaviour are vital to this goal. To help achieve it, we have set out to reduce the level of unauthorised absence and exclusions by one third by 2002. (DfEE Circular 10/99, 199b)

In 1996/7 0.04% of primary school pupils were permanently excluded, 0.34% of secondary pupils and 0.54% of special school pupils (Parsons, 1999) (13,453 children in total). In 1997/8 the figures had changed only slightly, but may have marked the beginning of a downward trend. The DfEE (1999c) found the reported figures to be lower (due to differences in data collection protocol, the DfEE collect permanent exclusions data as part of the Schools Census in January, while Parsons et al. collected data from LEAs). The number of permanent exclusions in the DfEE survey was 12,668 in 1996/7, falling to 12,298 in 1997/8. This confusion in data recording has become more significant in the light of the government's attempts to introduce punitive measures for high-excluding schools and LEAs.

The increasing interest in exclusions from school is in part a result of the (until recent) growth in the number of children which this effects. The number of children permanently excluded from school has increased over 400% since 1991.

The great majority of exclusions (85%) were from secondary schools. The most common years for exclusion were years 10 and 11 (Parsons, 1999). In 1997/8 over 47% of exclusions occurred when the children were aged 14 or 15. The fact that the excluded are generally older has implications for their re-integration to mainstream school (see below). The schools in Greater London appeared more likely to exclude pupils on average than those in County or other Metropolitan boroughs (DfEE, 1999). This average however hides a large differential between authorities and schools, in some LEAs exclusion rates are ten times higher than in others.

In 1997/8 1,513 secondary schools did not make a permanent exclusion, 192 schools made 7-8 exclusions and five schools made over 20 permanent exclusions. In Inner London exclusion rates varied from 0.12% of the school population in Newham to 0.36% in Westminster.

Exclusions from school have been the source of a great deal of recent research attention. There is little consensus on the reasons for the marked increase in their number. Proposed explanations range from the socio-psychological to the socio-economic. The National Curriculum has been the source of some interest in the debate as its introduction coincides with the beginning of the rise in exclusions.

The National Curriculum as an Exclusionary Pressure

> If educational dysfunctions ... are to be addressed, then the curriculum for 14- to 16-year olds needs to be changed radically. The National Curriculum ... will ... have to go. It is too coercive, too centralised, too prescriptive, and too inflexible.
> (O'Keefe and Stoll, 1995)

> The [National Curriculum] fails to address the question of how to provide a coherent learning experience for each student that will recognise, support and utilise the diversity of experiences linguistic, cultural, economic, religious, gender and ethnic which provides a basis for each student to question and evaluate the worlds of knowledge and lived experience.
> (Hardy and Veiler-Porter, 1990)

O'Keefe and Stoll, and Hardy and Veiler-Porter highlight here the main arguments surrounding the issue of the National Curriculum and exclusions from school. The National Curriculum is blamed for an increase in disaffection among young people in schools. This disaffection, it is argued, is played out in truancy, disruptive behaviour and ultimately exclusion from school. It is held that changing the existing curriculum, increasing its flexibility and relevance, could reduce the levels of disaffection and subsequently, levels of exclusion from school.

It is argued that the curriculum needs to be more flexible in order to cater for the needs of different children. This is based on the premises that different curricula and that some level of curriculum delivery is better than receiving nothing at all. Curricula need to be sensitive to the particular contexts which children find themselves in.

> The curriculum, apparently, will be relevant to everyone, even though it will have no regard to where they live, what sex they are and what their racial background is: it will be the same for all, and yet relevant to all! (Jones, 1989)

A major way in which the National Curriculum fails to live up to the ideal of relevance, it is argued, is that from its very basis it is a middle class curriculum, imposed on the working class. Parsons (1999) refers to Bernstein in highlighting the role of the National Curriculum in reinforcing the class system:

> How a society selects, classifies, distributes, transmits and evaluates the educational knowledge it considers to be public reflects both the distribution of power and the principles of social control. (Bernstein, 1975)

If the curriculum is biased in terms of class, and at base designed to reproduce the existing class structures, it is no wonder that it is educationally irrelevant to young people from outside the favoured groups. Instead, following Bernstein, the National Curriculum can be viewed as a tool for social control. It is argued that this also translates to children from minority ethnic groups (McNeil, 1990).

The middle class emphasis of the National Curriculum leads to increased attention being paid to the (narrowly defined) academic at the expense of other benefits of schooling. As Inman and Buck note:

> The preoccupation with subject assessment and the National Curriculum over the past 10 years has meant that serious consideration of where provision of pupils' personal and social development should stand in relation to the overall purpose of education has been low on the national education agenda.
> (Inman and Buck, 1998)

It is argued that while the agenda has been about setting targets and achieving assessment levels in the academic curricula, concern with the 'whole-child' has been squeezed in order to concentrate on the purely academic. This argument can be taken further to suggest that pressures to achieve academic targets lead to teachers removing children who begin to get in the way of these targets being met:

> ... this could be seen as encouragement to remove elements which hinder the academic or cognitive development of pupils in a class; so-called difficult pupils may constitute such elements. (Parsons, 1999)

The National Curriculum has also been blamed for increasing the workload and reducing the patience of teachers (Blyth and Milner, 1993). This, coupled with measurement of only narrow academic indicators, has meant that teachers have less time to spend on educating the whole-child and indeed may be less ready to do so in any case. Requirements of the National Curriculum have made the teachers' role more specific and the oft heard 'I'm a teacher, not a social worker' more easily defensible.

The link between the National Curriculum and exclusion thus characterised is persuasive but not convincing. The effects of the National Curriculum when considering exclusions from school are, in my view, much harder to identify and in some cases 'National Curriculum' is used as shorthand for the entire 1988 Education Reform Act.

Separating Out the Effects

> It is important to note a methodological problem, that within the context of recent cumulative policy changes it was difficult for teachers to single out the specific effects of the National Curriculum on current curricular and pedagogical practice. (Mac an Ghaill, 1993)

Mac an Ghaill notes a major problem in considering the main effects of the National Curriculum for the researcher. The curriculum was not an isolated innovation and forms part of wider reforms. The outcomes of the curriculum may have been very different if it did not arrive at the same time as league tables. The outcomes could have been different if Local Management of Schools reforms had not been introduced at the same time. The Education Reform Act (1988) introduced the quasi-market in the education system in England and Wales. There is a range of arguments used to link the quasi-market with the increase in exclusions from schools. These arguments tend to take the reforms as a whole in order to judge their impact. This would appear to be the only sensible way in which to proceed. The arguments above should not, therefore, be seen as an attack on **a** national curriculum per se, more on **The** National Curriculum as its effects have been felt during and after the development of a new educational settlement.

The National Curriculum came in the midst of a long battle between government and the teaching profession which left the profession disillusioned and marginalised. The profession was much weakened by the 1986 payment disputes. So much so that the National Curriculum, which had undoubtedly far-reaching implications for all schools, was rushed through in 1988 after less than a year's consultation.

> Teachers were handed down a curriculum that was planned in great haste, with no clear aims and values, and without a coherent design, and were expected to teach and assess it after minimal opportunities to prepare for it.
> (Lawton, 1996)

It was not until five years later that the teacher unions were in any position to take a unified approach to resisting the excesses of the curriculum. The political context in which the education reforms were introduced has a great bearing on the effects that can be attributed to a National Curriculum.

The National Curriculum has not been a constant given. It was negotiated even in 1988 and the story of its development has been well-documented (Pring, 1989; Fowler, 1998; Graham and Tytler, 1993). Co-ordination of the curriculum was poor and there was little consensus even about basic aims and values. The Dearing Review (1994) reduced the content of the National Curriculum, gave more discretion to teachers, improved the administration of assessments and asserted that the national curriculum could not be a substitute for the whole school curriculum. This began the potential empowerment of teachers regarding the curriculum, but was an attempt at a quick-fix as problems still remained with the amount of time given to develop cross-curricular themes such as PSHE. Given the changing nature of the National Curriculum, it would be expected that an increase in flexibility after 1994 would be reflected in the levels of exclusion, (in any case a crude measure of disaffection). This is not the case. The first recorded downturn in the number of permanent exclusions throughout the nineties came in 1997/8 (DfEE, 1999).

Despite a five-year moratorium on the development of a new National Curriculum, suggested by Dearing, there have been significant innovations and changes in guidance from government. Guidance from OFSTED and the government has made it clearer that the National Curriculum is only part of the whole-school curriculum, the Standards and Effectiveness Unit of the DfEE has been instrumental in sharing 'best practice' on curriculum measures and programmes such as 'Excellence in Cities' have encouraged innovation.

In seeking explanations for the increase in the number of exclusions from school based on the introduction of the National Curriculum, the continuities in approach to curriculum delivery are easily overlooked. Many of the arguments against the National Curriculum are actually arguments against all formal curricula imposed by the middle classes. Bernstein's analysis of the class relations typified and extended through curricula, apply not only to the National Curriculum but also to a curriculum decided on a local or even school-specific basis, in that they are curricula set by middle class teachers for working class children.

It is doubtful that the required flexibility of different curricula for different children existed in very many places before 1988. There was an increasing move towards a common curriculum (HMI, 1977; DES, 1981). There was also increasing concern that lack of a common curriculum was not always producing beneficial outcomes:

> ... some children in both primary and secondary schools were certainly given curricula which were inferior. Diversity did not always produce excellence.
> (Lawton, 1996)

Mac an Ghaill (1993) points to a changing attitude to the National Curriculum on behalf of teaching staff over the years, from regarding it as intrusive and overly prescriptive to a useful tool to be implemented flexibly.

> What emerged in discussions with the headteachers was the current policy fluidity and complexity in which modern curricula are developed as hybrid cultural forms.

If this is the case then flexibility can be offered through the National Curriculum. It may be possible to go further and to consider some of the opportunities for developing inclusive and anti-racist practices that the National Curriculum has provided. Gillborn (1990) notes that:

> 'Reforms' of the educational system, introduced in the late 1980s and early 1990s, place curricular issues at the forefront of teachers' minds and herald a

new phase in the continuing struggle for a curriculum which is of relevance to all pupils.

Hardy and Veiler Porter (1990) assert:

> Anti racist teachers within the constraints of the National Curriculum can imaginatively subvert the nationalistic tendencies which we have highlighted ... it may be easier to direct [anti racist] curriculum development through LEA policy within the National Curriculum than is currently the case.

The National Curriculum has changed a great deal since its inception in 1988 (the period that these researchers refer to). Further, the political and social background against which it exists has also changed. Given the negotiated nature of educational policy, the imminent review of the National Curriculum, and public concern about the number of exclusions from school, not only the content but also the very existence of a national curriculum should be argued for. If Hardy et al. and Gillborn are correct in their support for a national curriculum on the basis of equality of opportunity, then the National Curriculum can and indeed should be adapted to provide this. My research, which is reported below, has tended to agree with some of the positive adaptations of a national curriculum, as a tool for inclusion and opportunity, rather than purely an exclusionary pressure. It has also suggested ways in which teachers, to deliver more equitable outcomes for their pupils have already adapted the National Curriculum.

Research Background

The data reported below, was collected as part of an ongoing research project entitled 'Exclusions from school; disciplinary structures or market forces'. The project aims to find out the causes of the increase in exclusions from school throughout the 1990s by examining the attitudes and practice of some of the participants within one educational quasi-market. The research was carried out within one metropolitan LEA and some bordering schools and colleges. Headteachers, deputy heads, LEA officers, special educators and pupils were interviewed and periods of observation spent in a small number of institutions. By concentrating on the relationships between institutions and actors in one area it was hoped that some insight into the micro-level of processes of exclusion could be provided adding some flesh to the statistical studies which highlighted an alarming increase in numbers.

The London Borough of Northdown, the venue for the research project lies on the edge of the Greater London conurbation, bordering the Home Counties. It is in many ways a unique place, and a place like many other. Geographically, the borough covers 9,065 hectares, of which over a quarter is Green Belt land. It has a population of around 330,000. It is not a homogeneous borough in terms of wealth, culture or ethnicity. The North of the borough has the largest concentration of 'inner city' or urban issues, while the concerns for the South of the borough are more suburban. The borough revolves around the major town and administrative centre of Northdown.

Northdown has over 80 primary schools (all but three under LEA control) and 23 secondary schools of which 12 were until recently grant maintained. There are seven Church secondary schools, and seven single sex secondary schools. No schools (apart from the CTCs) operate a formal selection process. Like most areas in London, there is a great deal of overlapping educational provision with the neighbouring boroughs. In the 1997 national examination league tables one secondary school was numbered in the top ten whilst another was 'named-and-shamed' and placed on special measures.

The National Curriculum in Schools

The teachers that participated in this research project were circumspect about the role of the National Curriculum in exclusions from school. When asked to point out the major changes in the past ten years that could have caused an increase in exclusions from school, none of them suggested the National Curriculum. Many pointed instead to competition between schools and the quasi-market. One headteacher pointed to different pressures to exclude which had been brought on by increased information-sharing about schools, another answered a question about the curriculum, directly linking it to inter-school competition:

> **Mr Parfitt:** Parents are understanding of the education system more. Schools are no longer these bastions of closed doors, they're more open. A school lives

and falls I would suggest more on its disciplinary reputation than its academic reputation.

Mr Williams: I do believe that the increased competition with producing exam results and the inspection - it's very interesting, does the school become more attractive with a high exclusion rate? I think you could argue that different groups of people probably see it in different ways.

The difficulty in isolating the effects of the National Curriculum from the more general educational settlement presaged by the 1988 ERA exist for teachers as well as researchers.

In each school there was a clear conviction that what they were offering their students was different and distinctive. The differences were talked about in terms of a whole school curriculum. Nearly all the secondary schools included in the study were proud of some innovation that they had taken or adapted in curricular terms and took these differences to show what was special about the school. This would suggest that in the view of these teachers, the National Curriculum, even at its most rigid, did not stifle teacher creativity. Indeed, teachers talked about curriculum development with some relish. Programmes, which concentrated on the personal and social development of children, were described to me.

Mr Anderson: Our aim very much is to complement what the children are doing in class and to complement their achievement in PSHE and I suppose we are successful on that.

Mrs James: We try to make sure by careful follow-up that [each girl's] talents are being used and that she is happy within the school. We think that success comes from being happy and again the more opportunities for that at school the better.

Other schools had gone further in making the curricula more flexible for those who were at risk of exclusion from school. The programmes that were being run in the area included two in-school units for children with preventative intervention to reduce exclusions, the use of three separate mentoring projects targeted at different ethnic groups, and increasing use of LEA Behavioural Support Services to keep children within school.

Mr Anderson: One of the [mentoring] groups works a great deal here. What they are doing, and this is a visionary thing I think, when we identify a child who is in danger of going irrevocably down the slippery slope, that's the time they will come in and talk with the child at home in the presence of parents. They do not do that as a one-off but over a period of time.

Mr Gray: We offer a programme which makes them look at their behaviour, their conduct and attitudes I'm sure that that's something which any school would be very interested in having.

Mrs Werburn [LEA Behavioural Support Teacher]: Schools have brought in extra support after going GM. Their school populations have often changed - they've got a lot of London over-spill and there's a big council estate that has grown and the headteacher has responded to that ... for example there was one particular school that prior to GM status had an allocation from me for five hours a week, they are currently buying 13.

These approaches to curriculum planning after the introduction of a national curriculum suggest that there is still some flexibility in the school system. This is evident not only between schools who are looking to offer distinctive choices, but also within schools for children with different needs. The ability to offer a diverse choice to parents and children should not be overstated. Gewirtz et al. (1995) suggests that schools are more likely to become uniform than diverse. Diversity in curriculum delivery, however, has not disappeared completely.

None of this is to say that the National Curriculum has been welcomed unequivocally in the schools in this research project. The pressures on teacher time were noted. Some teachers spoke of exhaustion with the flurry of often-contradictory government guidance. Others presented a range of extra-curricular events that had recently disappeared due to the amount of time teachers had to spend on paperwork.

The National Curriculum was seen as part of a wider whole school curriculum in this sample. As noted above it is not a static entity. The curriculum has developed over the period of the research project. Extra money and resources have been made available for curricular innovation through an EAZ in the South of the district, schools have returned to LEA control, support services have developed an enhanced role and exclusion levels in the area have become a source of much public debate.

When singling out the exclusionary pressures, teachers involved in this research project did not mention the National Curriculum itself, although they did find fault with some of the quasi-market reforms. When discussing the role of the curriculum in keeping young people in school they noted its importance. It was seen to be important enough, that within the area there were a number of curricular initiatives being carried out. The fact that many of these initiatives were offered only to certain members of schools, ie. those at risk of exclusion, also suggests that the curricula are designed to be flexible enough to be responsive to need.

The National Curriculum and Re-integration

> 6.7 ... Pupils should be admitted to a PRU based on clear criteria and each pupil should have targets for re-integration into mainstream or special schooling, further education or employment. (DfEE Circular, 11/99)

The National Curriculum is expected to be followed in all schools maintained by the government. This includes special schools and Pupil Referral Units. Many children who are excluded from mainstream schools receive their educational provision in these schools (around 30% in Autumn 1994 (Parsons, 1999)). The National Curriculum is followed so that, if desirable, children can be re-integrated into mainstream schools. As would be expected, however, the curriculum is adapted to suit the special needs of the students in these schools.

The head of a special school for students with EBD noted that re-integration remained important for the children attending his school. This remained true despite the fact that very few of them were actually successful in gaining entry to mainstream schooling. The National Curriculum, interpreted in the right way, gave his students an opportunity and hope of a move back into the mainstream system:

> **Mr Morris**: [we follow the] National Curriculum for key stage 2 and 3. We are looking now at new modules that are coming in for disaffected pupils, children with emotional and behavioural difficulties, they've actually started to recognise that they can actually narrow down the curriculum at key stage 4 ... science is another one that is starting to become marginal but we've found that the kids quite enjoy science so we're keeping that in but it really does sometimes come down to the specialisms of the staff that we have available ... we might even be looking for GCSEs for them in a couple of years time if we carry on with the present staff we've got at the moment ... we just try to be as

imaginative as possible for [basic skills training] you know with the older ones it's a slower process.

The methods of reintegration into the mainstream are complicated and dependent on developing relationships with mainstream schools. These relationships are based on providing the best outcome for the child. In many cases at the special school and the PRUs in the area, dual registration was used as a means of leverage. Headteachers at mainstream schools were willing to accept pupils from the special schools and units but one of their main concerns was the extra support that the children would need to re-integrate. Schools, even those that are undersubscribed are loath to take on children that have been excluded from elsewhere. One headteacher noted the rigorous re-integration programme that he and his staff follow:

> **Mr Govan**: We never ever take in a student on the casual intake without interviewing them, we need to talk to them, we need to talk to their parents and guardians, we need to have a real picture about what has happened, what they've been excluded for, the standard that they've reached academically, basically what has gone on prior to coming here.

Without the shared experience of following the National Curriculum, however modified, these young people would be even more unlikely to get back into mainstream school. In the area that the research was carried out in, it was fairly typical for an excluded child to spend two to three terms out of mainstream school, one of those terms on home tuition.

Re-integration was also important to the children who had been excluded. They saw it as the route back from being sidelined.

> **Fitzroy**: I know that I had to learn the hard way even my parents did tell me don't mess about and I still did mess about so now I have to work doubly hard to get back into school and it's a challenge.

> **Darren**: I want to go back to school and get on because I have to concentrate on my future now. I want to get a job when I'm older and the only way to do that is to get back into school and pass my exams.

Given the importance of re-integration for the children, the staff at the units and special schools were keen to stick with the National Curriculum, even though it posed a range of specific problems for them. Some of the lessons observed were unsuccessful and even in the small classes of six it was often difficult to match the teaching to the different standards the children were at. However, the staff persevered and one of the most effective classroom tactics would be to ask, 'What do you think they'd be doing back in mainstream now?'

The National Curriculum has an effect on children who are excluded from school. If they are to be re-integrated, they need to be able to move between schools with some ease. Following a shared core curriculum makes this a possibility. Re-integration after exclusion is a difficult task, even when the academic work is not taken into account; the existence of a National Curriculum is an aid to this process.

A Tool for Empowerment?

> According to ideas about distributive justice ... it would seem to follow that pupils should have access to the same kind of curriculum unless good reasons can be shown for providing different curricula ... the basic provision - the common curriculum - should be organised so that it is open to everyone. Anything less than this for normal pupils will not be socially just.
>
> (Lawton, 1975)

It has been suggested that the National Curriculum has been a contributory factor in the rise in exclusions from school. Here I have argued that this need not have been the case and indeed that a national curriculum, can be a tool for empowerment.

The diversity of curricula before the National Curriculum did not always mean that more responsive or flexible curricula were in place. The National Curriculum has increased transparency in schools but as a by-product could also have provided a forum through which to consider curricular development. The distinctiveness of schools and their provision would appear to remain, although the boundaries of their individuality have been circumscribed.

The reforms of 1988 may well have forced increasing pressures to exclude on teachers. The manner in which the National Curriculum was initially overloaded (Dearing, 1994) may also have squeezed the time available in schools for the personal and social development of young people, leading to increased disaffection. The effects of the National Curriculum could however, be interpreted as a step forward in ensuring that at a basic level education is delivered in a more egalitarian manner.

As David Halpin notes:

> Once we admit the principle of universal schooling, it seems impossible to resist the suggestion that there should be a common core curriculum.
> (Halpin, 1990)

It is not important merely that everyone goes to school, as the current concern with exclusions and truancy would suggest (SEU, 1998); what everyone learns there must also be of importance. The National Curriculum in its original form was a hastily put together, a confused and confusing piece of legislation. The possibilities it delivers for marginalised groups in mainstream and special provision schools, however, are manifold. While it may be convenient to consider the pre-National Curriculum days as halcyon, it may be that a national curriculum could be the tool through which to empower children at risk of exclusion from school and society.

References

Bernstein, B. (1975) *Class, Codes and Control*, London, Routledge and Kegan Paul quoted in Parsons, C. (1999) *Education, Exclusion and Citizenship*, London, Routledge.

Blyth, E. and Milner, J. (1993) *Exclusion from school: the first step in exclusion from society?* Children and Society 13(1).

Dearing, R (1994) *The National Curriculum and its Assessment: Final Report*, London, School Curriculum and Assessment Authority.

Department of Education and Science (1981) *A Framework for the School Curriculum*, London, HMSO.

DfEE (1997) *Excellence for all Children*, London, HMSO.

DfEE (1998a) *The LEA (Behaviour Support Plans) Regulations*, London, DfEE.

DfEE (1998b) *Behaviour support plans*, Circular 1/98, London, DfEE.

DfEE (1999a) *Social Inclusion: the LEA role in Pupil support*, Circular 11/99, London, DfEE.

DfEE (1999b) *Social Inclusion: Pupil Support*, Circular 10/99, London, DfEE.

DfEE (1999c) *Statistical First Release*, 11/1999, London, HMSO.

Fowler, W. (1998) *Towards the National Curriculum*, London, Kogan Page.

Gewirtz, S., Ball, S.J. and Bowe, R. (1995) *Markets, Choice and Equity in Education*, Buckingham, Open University Press.

Gillborn (1990) *'Race', Ethnicity and Education: Teaching and Learning in Multi-ethnic Schools*, London, Unwin Hyman.

Graham, D. and Tytler, D. (1993) *A lesson for us all: The making of the National Curriculum*, London, Routledge.

Halpin, D. (1990) *Making Sense of the National Curriculum* Forum 32(2) quoted in Mac an Ghaill (1996) *The National curriculum and equal opportunities* in *The National Curriculum - is it working?* Ed. Clyde Chitty, Longman.

Hardy, J. and Veiler-Porter, C. (1990) *Race, Schooling and the Education Reform Act in The ERA: 1988, its origins and implications*, eds., Flude, M. and Hammer, M. Basingstoke, Falmer Press.

Her Majesty's Inspectorate (1977) *Curriculum 11-16*, London, HMSO.

House of Commons (1998) *Disaffected children - 5th report of the Education and Employment Committee, Volume 1. Report and proceedings of the Committee*, London, HMSO.

Inman, S. and Buck, M. (1998) *The personal and social development of young people* in *Take Care, Mr Blunkett*, London, Association of Teachers and Lecturers ATL.

Jones, K. (1989) *Right turn: The Conservative Revolution in Education*, London, Hutchinson.

Lawton, D. (1975) *Class, Culture and the Curriculum*, London, Routledge and Kegan Paul.

Lawton, D. (1996) *Beyond the National Curriculum*, London, Hodder and Stoughton.

Mac an Ghaill (1996) *The National Curriculum and equal opportunities* in *The National Curriculum - is it working?* Ed. Clyde Chitty Longman.

McNeil, C. (1990) *The National Curriculum: A Black Perspective* in *New Curriculum - National Curriculum*, Moon, B. (ed.), London, Hodder and Stoughton.

O'Keefe, D. and Stoll, P. (1995) *Understanding the problem: truancy and curriculum* in O'Keefe, D. and Stoll, P. (eds.), *Issues in School Attendance and Truancy*, London, Pitman.

OFSTED (1996) *Exclusions from Secondary Schools*, London, HMSO.

Parsons, C. (1999) *Education, Exclusion and Citizenship*, London, Routledge.
Pring, R. (1989) *The New Curriculum*, London, Cassell.
Social Exclusion Unit (1998) *Truancy and School*.

8 Exploring the Policy Influence of England's National Curriculum on School Exclusion: A Dilemma of Intended Entitlement and Unintended Exclusion?

E. RUSTIQUE-FORRESTER

Introduction

This chapter begins with the observation that establishing a National Curriculum policy for pupils with a wide range of abilities and needs is, has been, and will always be, a highly contested terrain within education. An educational policy might set out in theory to ensure that pupils receive an 'equal provision' and a 'broad and balanced' curriculum. However, in truth and in practice, the quality and access of what is learned by pupils cannot occur through policy alone, but depends more upon the practices of schools and teachers. Put simply, access to the curriculum does not occur through the rhetoric and will of policymakers, but results from the willingness of schools and efforts of teachers to deliver knowledge in ways that enable each and every individual pupil to engage in a process of meaningful learning. In other words, the extent to which teachers are both able and willing to be inclusive in their methods and expectations of pupils depends critically on their capacity to do so. And teachers' capacities depend, in turn, on the conditions in which they teach and interact with pupils. Whilst these conditions of teaching and learning can be influenced by the school, here in Britain, such conditions are also profoundly determined and shaped by the current system's national policies.

The National Curriculum provides a case in point and the focus of this chapter. Under Britain's current educational system, national law requires all state-run schools and teachers to follow a system of nationalised curriculum, known also as the National Curriculum. But it appears that whilst the National Curriculum may have intended in theory to provide all pupils with an 'equal access' to a 'broad and balanced' curriculum, the effects from other educational policy changes have actually constrained the full achievement of this goal. Indeed, the influence of the system's policy dynamics on teachers' and schools' practices, particularly those emanating from present national policies on accountability, choice and assessment, have worked in confluence to create a set of pressures that are actually quite hostile to the needs of low- and under-achieving pupils. Closer scrutiny of the system suggests that rather than creating supports and incentives for teachers to be inclusive in their expectations and practices, there are more pressures and incentives for schools to be 'exclusive', rather than 'inclusive', in establishing expectations for pupil achievement. Evidence for this can be seen in the shifts in teachers' beliefs and schools' practices over the past decade.

In discussing the challenges surrounding school exclusion and the dilemmas experienced by schools, teachers and pupils, this chapter attempts to explain how the National Curriculum, in confluence with other national policies, appears to have created a set of conditions and dynamics in schools, which, may have unintentionally encouraged the recent growth in school exclusions. What this chapter aims to explore is the possible relationship between school exclusion and the underlying pedagogical dynamics that have arisen from the current system of National Curriculum and assessments. First, in following a prescribed National Curriculum along a nationally-defined time schedule, teachers have been limited and restricted in the ways that they can apply and adapt the content and pace of the curriculum to make its content more accessible to pupils who experience difficulties. Second, as a result of the wider policy pressures to perform well on the exams and assessments that are linked to the National Curriculum, schools and teachers have found it increasingly difficult to spend additional valuable time, resources and attention on their most challenging and difficult pupils. The effect of these two dynamics over the past decade, I contend, has been a greater likelihood for exclusion: a rigid learning environment characterised by a lack of time and tolerance, in which pupils, in experiencing difficulties, are less likely to be taught in ways that are more relevant and suited to their particular needs. The result for pupils is a greater likelihood for frustration and disaffection with school, disruptive behaviour and, above all, exclusion from school.

This chapter, which is based in part on an ongoing research study on school exclusions in secondary schools (Rustique-Forrester, in progress), attempts to develop a theory about the complex policy dynamics between the National Curriculum and school exclusions. The possibility that such a relationship might exist between curriculum and exclusion arises from the findings of several areas of research: first, studies that have documented shifts in teachers' beliefs and practices over the past decade in relation to the curriculum; and secondly, studies that suggest that pupils with special educational needs, bilingual pupils, and pupils with behavioural and learning difficulties have experienced difficulties in accessing the curriculum. Drawing upon interviews conducted with teachers in secondary schools, this chapter seeks to explain why school practitioners, in discussing their perceptions of the causes and dynamics of school exclusion, appear to attribute their particular dilemmas and difficulties to the pace, pressures and prescriptive nature of the current national educational policy climate.

The intent of this chapter, however, is not to provide a full report of research findings. Rather the discussion seeks to raise important questions about how and why in Britain, a National Curriculum which has the potential to provide an equal entitlement to all students, appears for some pupils, to have resulted instead in a complex and frustrating cycle of disengagement and unintended exclusion from learning. The chapter is organised into each of the following sections: first, an explanation of the policy dynamics related to the growth in school exclusions; second, an analysis of the impact of the National Curriculum on schools and teachers; third, an analysis of the conditions of teaching and learning; fourth, a discussion of policy implications; and a final section of concluding thoughts.

Part I

Background

The Policy Dynamics of School Exclusion

Much of the recent attention and concern surrounding school exclusions has centred on the rapid rise and unprecedented number of school expulsions (also known as 'permanent exclusions') and suspensions (referred to as 'fixed-term exclusions'). In England alone, permanent school exclusions have risen nearly 500% over the past decade (Social Exclusion Unit, 1998; Parsons, 1999), increasing from 2,500 secondary school pupils in 1992 to 12,500 in 1998. Although the current number of exclusions represents a small minority of the overall student population, the increased costs of providing alternative provision for excluded pupils continues to raise widespread concern amongst researchers, educators, and policymakers alike (Donovan, 1998; Commission for Racial Equality, 1998; House of Commons, 1998).

Expulsions are not only costly in terms of providing alternative provision, but because very few students who are excluded from schools successfully return to mainstream school (Parsons, 1999; Gillborn, 1996), school exclusions represent an ever increasing financial burden on the services and resources of local school authorities. Even more critical are the long-term consequences of school expulsion, which have been linked to crime, unemployment, and other forms of social exclusion such as lack of housing and poor health, and which increase without schooling, formal education, or training (Commission for Racial Equality, 1998; House of Commons, 1998; Social Exclusion Unit, 1998). Finally, evidence of disproportionate numbers of Afro-Caribbean boys and pupils from poor backgrounds who have been excluded from schools raises additional moral and ethical concerns over the social and gender dynamics of exclusion, and further questions about the extent to which schools have actually provided all pupils, regardless of race and class, equal access to the curriculum (ibid),

In examining the rationale and justification amongst school practitioners for decisions to exclude, Kinder et al.'s (1999) national study of school exclusions found that although many teachers believed that the act of removing a pupil was 'an undesirable and potentially damaging response' (p.19), most teachers and school managers still saw exclusion as a necessary policy for managing school discipline, an action justified in terms of protecting school staff and pupils from physically threatening and violent behaviour and preventing the disruption of others from learning. The perception suggests two possible interpretations. One is that the growth in expulsions and suspensions in schools might reflect a greater increase in behavioural problems in classrooms. A second interpretation, however, may be that schools and teachers have become either less tolerant of what is perceived to be disruptive behaviour, less able in managing such behaviour, or perhaps a combination of both. In other words, schools and teachers may be using a wider definition of what constitutes disruptive behaviour and perceive fewer possibilities for pupils who cannot adapt and adjust in their behavioural and learning styles within the mainstream curriculum. This second view may explain further why schools may have resorted more increasingly to exclusion.

The possibility that schools and teachers have become less tolerant of disruptive behaviour has been supported by the findings of OFSTED's report (1996) on secondary school exclusions, as well as other studies which have examined the national figures on school exclusion (Social Exclusion Unit; 1998; Gillborn, 1996; Parsons, 1996; 1999). Indeed, analysis of schools' exclusion figures indicate that most decisions to permanently exclude pupils arise from incidents of disobedience and disruption, and *not* from physically threatening behaviour, which accounted for only one in four permanent exclusions:

> The Education Department's figures indicate that: Disobedience in various forms - constantly refusing to comply with school rules, verbal abuse or insolence to teachers - was the major reason for exclusion.
> (DfE, 1992, p.3, cited in Gillborn, 1996)

According to Gillborn (1996), the figures indicate that 'offences leading to exclusion are more varied and poorly defined than is usually assumed' (p.2). In practice, therefore, the uses of school exclusion appear to range far more widely than what is frequently believed. The reasons for such wider uses of exclusion thus raises further questions about what might be happening in schools and classrooms that may have encouraged greater numbers of expulsions and suspensions in response to disruptive behaviour.

Indeed, in recent years, a line of research studies and national reports has suggested that the effects of the system and the accompanying pressures of increased competition between schools and diminished resources might provide possible explanations for the general rise in exclusion (Charlton and David, 1993; Cooper, 1993; Blyth and Milner, 1994; Hayden, 1997; Osler et al., 1999). According to the Social Exclusion Unit (1998):

> Schools have been under such pressure to meet demanding academic standards and to compete with each other that excluding borderline cases could seem more attractive ... Performance tables have often blamed for this ... and some feel that many behavioural problems are the response of those [pupils] who have fallen behind and are not being helped to catch up, for whom an academic curriculum seems increasingly difficult, uninteresting and irrelevant.
> (p.11)

Whether or not teachers may be experiencing difficulties in managing behavioural problems, however, remains a relatively unexplored area. This gap in knowledge suggests that further examination of the policy pressures operating in schools and their influence on teachers' beliefs and classroom practices might illuminate the underlying forces for growing incidents of school exclusion. Yet, few studies have pursued this line of policy enquiry and explored whether the causes and dynamics of school exclusions may be linked to particular aspects of national policy.

This lack of awareness might be due to the traditional focus of previous studies, which looked first and foremost, at pupil behaviour as both the cause of and solution for school discipline problems; and secondly, at pedagogy and schools' practices (Rustique-Forrester, 1999). This view of school exclusions appears to be further reinforced by the powerful tradition of educational psychology, that has long dominated school-based research and continues to provide the current basis for educational assessment (Davis, 1999).

Greater understanding of the causes and dynamics of exclusion, however, will not come from looking simply at the pupil behaviour and linking the causes of exclusion to pupils' social and family background. As a number of academics have argued, the causes of behaviour that lead to exclusion should not be assumed to originate within the child or assigned to family pathology (Parsons, 1996; Cooper, 1993; Lloyd-Smith, 1984). Rather, the problem of exclusion might be viewed more widely, which includes a recognition of excluded pupils' difficulties as well as other factors, such as that of pedagogy and policy (Watkins and Wagner, 2000;

Parsons, 1999; Castle and Parsons, 1997; Lovey and Cooper, 1997; Rayner, 1998).

Re-Conceptualising Exclusion: Exploring Policy Dynamics of School Exclusion

Rather than conceptualising school exclusion from a single perspective associated with an individual pupil's background and behaviour, exclusion might be further explored as a complex interaction between policy and pedagogy. The causes and dynamics of exclusion might be better understood if viewed as a phenomenon with four interrelated dimensions and levels: first, as a manifestation of an individual pupil's behaviour; second, as a process and decision of schools, reflecting different professionals' perceptions of what constitutes 'appropriate' and 'acceptable' behaviour; third, as a reflection of the demands and pressures of the current educational system; and fourth, as a manifestation of larger social trends and patterns, such as race, gender, cultural dynamics, poverty and ill health. In other words, school exclusion might be better examined as a consequence of an interrelationship of pupil, school, social and policy factors.

Exclusion should thus be examined not simply as a manifestation of pupil behaviour, but as a possible consequence of the competing tensions inherent in teaching, learning, pedagogy and policy. Such further study of school exclusions would involve first, a wider lens to examine the broad educational policy context in which school exclusions have grown; and second, a scrutiny of the relationship between specific national policy changes and teachers' beliefs and practices. The justification for this perspective stems from studies such as Osler and Hill (1999), which revealed that teachers, in explaining their attitudes toward school exclusion, located their beliefs and practices within the context of the current educational system:

> Teachers and headteachers ... were not asked about the impact of recent educational reforms ... but as they reflected on pupil behaviour and their own attitudes to excluding pupils, they made regular reference to the changing social policy context in which they are working. They referred frequently to the impact which market forces in education have made on school discipline, increased teacher workloads, changed parental expectations, and to how the

National Curriculum had limited the scope for schools to meet individual needs and address pupils' personal and social behaviour.

(Osler and Hill, 1999, p.46)

The views expressed by teachers and the observations of educational researchers seem to suggest that whilst school exclusion may be related to behaviour, it is also part of wide policy dynamics which emanate from the wider system. As Parsons and Howlett (1995) argue, school exclusion results from the 'difficult dilemmas' faced by schools and a perceived set of pressures to exclude: "If schools are to be judged on standards, and particularly on performance in national examinations, there is pressure to exclude those pupils who exhibit disruptive behaviour" (p.14).

The Relationship Between Curriculum, Behaviour and Exclusions

Research suggests that within schools, the curriculum is a critical factor that can often predict and explain the difficulties that pupils experience in schools and classrooms. According to Ainscow (1991) the curriculum plays an important role in determining whether teachers are able to create opportunities for engaging pupils who have a wide range of different skills and interests:

> When children experience significant difficulties in schools - they arise as a result of the interaction of a complex set of factors. In practice, the problem is a curriculum one. What we are witnessing is the inability of a teacher or group of teachers to provide classroom experiences that are meaningful and relevant given the interests, experiences and existing skills and knowledge of particular children. (Ainscow, 1991)

However, in the years following the implementation of the National Curriculum, concerns emerged over the ability of teachers to provide such individual experiences. Cooper (1993) observed that with the impact of the National Curriculum and the accompanied changes brought about by national assessments, school choice, and league tables, "some schools may put less effort than before into catering for the needs of pupils who are unlikely to contribute to their performance profile, and may actively seek to exclude pupils who might have a negative impact on their ratings" (p.187). Cooper (1993) further warned that access to a 'broad and balanced' curriculum in a mainstream school, pupils with emotional and behavioural difficulties could be limited, rather than enhanced. Indeed, in the years immediately following the implementation of the National Curriculum, suspicions that increases in exclusion rates were influenced by greater competition between schools were confirmed by reports of 'dramatic increases' in the exclusion of pupils in inner-city areas such as Birmingham, Sheffield and London (Pyke, 1991; Merrick and Manuel, 1991).

Although research studies have described a link between school exclusion and the influence of school and pupils' social background factors in school exclusion and disaffection (Parsons, 1999; McManus, 1987; McLean, 1987; Galloway, 1982; Galloway et al., 1985; Rutter, 1983; Rutter et al., 1979; Reynolds, 1984; Reynolds and Sullivan, 1981), the role and interaction of such school-based variables in shaping teachers' particular beliefs and practices in relation to exclusion remain complex and unclear. Indeed, when asked why school exclusions had risen over the past decade, teachers and school managers revealed in Rustique-Forrester (2000), a number of interrelated beliefs and theories that linked: a) pupil behaviour to learning conditions; b) learning conditions to teaching conditions; c) teaching conditions to school conditions; and d) school conditions to the impact of the present educational system, which includes the National Curriculum. According to views expressed by teachers, the causes and dynamics of school exclusion do not stem from one single factor, but rather are a consequence of the interaction of several factors. In describing those pupils who were excluded or at risk of exclusion, teachers perceived these students as individuals who were 'failed by the system' and who exhibited great frustration and behavioural problems in the classroom because of difficulties accessing and engaging with the National Curriculum.

The policy relationship between the National Curriculum and school exclusions, thus, cannot be simply explained in a few simple sentences. As the next sections will attempt to explain, the difficulties experienced by teachers as a result of the National Curriculum stem not just from the nature and content of the curriculum itself; but from the conditions and effects of the system on the capacity of schools to provide meaningful learning opportunities to pupils with a diverse range of needs and abilities. The capacity of teachers, in particular, depends crucially on the conditions under which teachers and school managers view and implement other policies, such as student assessment and school accountability. In other words, it may not simply be the impact of the National Curriculum that is a critical factor in explaining pupil's disaffection and disengagement from learning, but the confluence of the present policies of national assessments, exams and school choice. A closer examination of the policy effects and dynamics of the National Curriculum and their impact on teacher's beliefs and practices might explain how and why incidents of school exclusion have increased over the past decade.

Part II

Review of Research Findings

The Impact of the National Curriculum on Teachers' Beliefs and Practices

The impact of the National Curriculum on schools and teachers might be understood in terms of several documented shifts in teachers' beliefs and classroom practices. One is a shift in the pedagogical focus of teachers from a previously pupil-centred focus to a subject-specific orientation. A second is a shift in assessment from qualitative forms of pupil assessment to quantitative measures, which has been also accompanied by a system-wide pressure to raise national test results. A third area of change can be seen in the pace, style and methods of how teachers teach. Related to this is a fourth shift in how teachers formulate expectations for pupils' achievement and measure academic performance.

The impact of these shifts in beliefs and practices, I argue, is a climate in schools and classrooms that is relevant in understanding the context in which schools exclusions have grown. The impact of this climate can be linked to exclusion in three ways: firstly, through a decreased likelihood that teachers know how and are willing to adapt their teaching approaches to suit individual pupils' needs and abilities; secondly, through a lowered tolerance of schools for pupils with behavioural and learning difficulties; and thirdly, through a narrow definition of 'achievement' and fewer opportunities for pupils to experience success 'outside' the National Curriculum.

The Shift in Teachers' Pedagogical Focus: From Pupil-centred to Subject-specific Approaches

> Regrettably, during the last 20 years, little approbation has been directed towards curriculum approaches with focus on the child, rather than upon the subject. There has been a preoccupation, particularly since the 1988 Education Act, with subject knowledge and outcomes. The heritage of child-centeredness, from which a pastoral curriculum has grown, has been brutally dispensed with.
> (Garner, 1999, p.95)

Over the past decade, educational researchers and policy analysts have observed a shift in the pedagogical focus of teachers from the previous 'generalist' approach in pedagogy toward a more subject-specialist orientation, which has resulted in more content-driven methods of teaching (Hacker and Rowe, 1997; Parsons, 1999; Carpenter, 1997; Silvernail, 1996). The reasons for this shift, however, did not seem to arise from the belief that a subject-orientation was the best approach for pupils, but that in order to cover the wider range and number of subjects required by the National Curriculum, teachers had to move away from a pupil-centred focus to an academic subject-orientation.

> Still, the sheer magnitude and detail of the curriculum have forced teachers to narrow what they can teach ... at the primary school level, teachers are required to teach each of the ten foundation subjects. However, many primary teachers are not trained to teach all ten disciplines ... and over half indicated they lacked the full range of academic background necessary to teach the national curriculum, and some openly admitted that they were not teaching each discipline equally well.
> (Silvernail, 1996, p.24)

Silvernail (1996) concluded that despite the 'Herculean effort' of teachers to implement the National Curriculum, nearly 70% of teachers believed they had to narrow their curriculum in order to teach the National Curriculum and prepare their students for national assessments, also known as SATs (p.24). The unintended effect of this, however, was a decrease in professional morale and confidence, particularly amongst those teachers who found it distressing to teach subjects for which they felt unprepared and did not believe they could be effective (ibid).

Carpenter's (1997) analysis of the impact of the National Curriculum on pupils with special educational needs also revealed the concerns of teachers of pupils with SEN who believed that the shift away from pupil-centred approaches decreased the likelihood that pupils would be taught in ways that were appropriately suited to their specific individual needs (p.6):

> Many teachers were convinced that the advent of the National Curriculum would divert attention away from the paramount needs of the pupils, especially [with regard to] their personal and social development ... they did not like the subject emphasis ... and found it hard to see the relationship between the National Curriculum and the school curricula painstakingly developed prior to 1988. (Carpenter, 1997, p.6)

Despite the policy assurances that the National Curriculum would provide an equal entitlement, fears of exclusion from the curriculum were still raised by SEN teachers, who sought clarity over the exact meaning of 'entitlement' amidst 'real fears of probable exclusion from the National Curriculum', and 'the belief that such exclusion from curriculum might lead to eventual exclusion from the education service' (ibid). Worries were also expressed by teachers about the reduced amount of teaching time available to address the additional needs of pupils with particular behavioural or learning needs. Delivering the full National Curriculum required teachers to cut out major elements of the pupil-centred approaches offered traditionally by schools, such as personal and social development and the use of community leisure activities (Silvernail, 1996; Carpenter, 1997).

The Impact of Assessments and Tests: The Pressure to Perform and to be Accountable

The pressure on teachers to ensure that pupils perform well on national assessments can also be linked to the National Curriculum. In both primary and secondary schools, the content of what teachers teach and the pace of what is taught directly reflects the concepts and material that teachers must cover so that pupils meet specific attainment targets are prepared for national assessment and exams. The pressures felt and experienced by teachers, however, are not simply the result of reduced professional autonomy and flexibility, but further compounded by a national system of school accountability and school choice. Schools' and teachers' delivery of the National Curriculum is enforced through a process of national inspection, better known as OFSTED, and measured by national rankings, also known as 'league tables'. Through OFSTED inspection and league tables, schools and teachers are monitored and judged on their 'effectiveness' at delivering the curriculum, which is measured by pupil's performance on assessments and exams.

The impact of these policies on teachers' beliefs and practices translates profoundly, however, into a pressure in schools where teachers must ensure, first and foremost, that their pupils perform well on exams. In such a system, expectations for pupils' performance are defined by their results on a standardised test, and few opportunities exist for pupils who cannot keep up with the pace of the curriculum. Furthermore, given the pressure of inspection and league tables, there is a lowered tolerance amongst teachers for behavioural difficulties in the classroom, irrespective it seems, if such disruptive behaviour stems from a pupil's frustration with learning. As one teacher explained:

> In the past, you could accommodate [the pupil], but now with the constraints of the curriculum ... it affects the learning of other pupils in the class. As a head of year, I feel you have to balance the needs of the individual child and [those of] the wider group. So if you have a child in Year 10 where children are starting to get involved in exam courses, you have got to balance that with the needs of a child who has a problem and is causing a fuss with the wider audience in the classroom. I feel it as a pressure ... something I am trying to tackle. I have pupils with behavioural problems, which need addressing, but I see the wider needs of the group.
>
> (Interview with Mr. Jones, Head of Year 10, Secondary School in Northwest England)

For Mr. Jones, the pressure of preparing his pupils for exams poses a difficult dilemma. Either he finds ways to address the needs of his pupils with behavioural difficulties, or he uses his time and energy to ensure that the rest of his class are prepared for exams. In having to choose between the needs of the class and the more challenging needs of pupils with learning and behavioural difficulties, exclusion might provide a quicker and easier solution. Although teachers like Mr. Jones might feel an obligation to address pupils' behavioural difficulties, such efforts require time and energy that few teachers can afford, given the competing pressures of covering a specified number of topics and ensuring that pupils are prepared for exams.

The Impact of Curriculum Pace and Prescription: Constraints on Teachers' Time

In having to focus upon the delivery of the curriculum, the assessment of a uniform set of standards, and the preparation for exams, tremendous pressures are placed on schools to 'cover' the curriculum along a tightly regimented schedule. For teachers, this translates into reduced time available to communicate with other teachers or individual pupils, either to discuss problems in depth or to help those pupils who may be struggling with particular aspects of the curriculum. As Mr. Jones explained:

> With the children following an exam course, things are more constrained. You follow a syllabus, which is tested ... and so therefore the teacher is trying to get on with those commitments under that sort of pressure. Because you have only two years to get through, it is critical to get through the work. In a school where we have a high proportion of children who are weaker academically, [these pupils] find it difficult to follow these sort of courses, and it shows with the way they react in classes and their attendance. (Ibid)

In the current system, teachers must gallop at a rapid pace to get through the curriculum and to ensure that pupils are 'ready' for national assessments and exams. The demands of a relentless schedule of assessments, tests and exams, together with the additional pressure to achieve certain results and targets, further compounds the pressures on teachers. Not only are there enormous pressures felt by pupils to perform well on exams, but such pressures can directly affect the classroom climate under which pupils are taught. Such conditions, in creating anxieties for teachers and pupils can have an adverse impact on teaching and learning, and can thus aggravate some pupils' frustration and difficulties.

As one secondary teacher in London explained, the enormous pressure of national exams, combined with the highly regimented schedule of prescribed coursework, did not create a positive or optimal learning environment, and actually lowered the patience and tolerance levels of both teachers and pupils:

> In Year 11, you see that tolerance diminished rapidly. Pupils are stressed. Teachers feel the pressure. No one likes it. At our school, we even call it 'exam confusion' because students get confused with all the deadlines, the coursework, and the schedule for preparing for exams. Everyone gets

aggressive, panicked, and upset ... and it comes out in pupils' behaviour and attendance. Pupils, who can't cope, they act out, they bunk off, they don't come to school. We try hard not to exclude, we really do, and we try to sympathise with what the pupils must go through.

(Interview with Mr. O'Reilly, Head of Year 11,
Secondary School in London)

Clearly, the process and pace of preparing pupils for exams reveals that under such conditions, some pupils will inevitably experience greater levels of pressure and frustration. The likelihood for behavioural problems are thus further exacerbated by the lack of time and flexibility available to teachers for ensuring that all pupils can individually access the material taught. Such pressures and constraints can thus limit the capacity and effectiveness of teachers, and therefore reduce the quality and access of the curriculum.

The implications of the shift from pupil-centred to academic-oriented approaches; the pace and pressure of following a prescribed curriculum; and the lack of time available for addressing the needs of pupils with behavioural problems - might explain how and why schools' and teachers' abilities to respond to such challenging pupils may be limited and constrained. Although the views and experiences expressed by Mr. Jones and Mr. O'Reilly are not necessarily the same for all teachers, their experiences and dilemmas raise important questions about the common pressures of the current national system. First is a pressure on teachers to focus their attention on those pupils who are more likely to achieve and second is a pressure on schools to minimise the disruptions that threaten other pupils' learning. Such system-wide pressures, in diminishing teachers' time and tolerance, would suggest a lowered capacity amongst schools to manage disruption and respond to certain pupils' needs - and thus might explain why schools across Britain have resorted more quickly to exclusion.

Low Expectations for Pupil Performance: The Impact of Quantitative Assessment

A final example of changes in teachers' beliefs and practices are those which can be linked to the pressures of national testing and assessment, and the current emphasis on quantitative measures to measure pupils' academic attainment. Under the National Curriculum, what pupils are expected to achieve derives not from teachers' qualitative assessment of students' individual strengths and weaknesses, but is specified by nationally-set attainment levels, which are defined according to age. Pupil performance and progress are measured through a series of national tests and assessments, which are used in turn by policy makers who monitor and indicate a school 'effectiveness' in delivering the curriculum and meeting nationally set targets.

Translated into practice, a teacher's view of their pupils' potential for academic success is therefore likely to be influenced by the perceived likelihood that the pupil will perform well on National Curriculum assessments and exams. However, for some teachers, helping pupils to achieve specified exam results did not always equate to what they believed were better ways of motivating and helping certain pupils find 'success' in school. Indeed, Silvernail's (1996) study revealed that the national curriculum and assessments sometimes led teachers to teach in ways that went against their own notions of 'good' educational practice. In describing the dilemma and pressures of staying within the prescribed content and topic of the National Curriculum, one teacher revealed a conflict with what she believed to be in the best interests of her pupils:

> I have done things I am philosophically and morally opposed to. Last year I knew that three of my boys knew Level 3 skills in one area, but they wouldn't get the Level 3 content until next year. So I gave them the content so they could do the Level 3 SAT. They did it and I reported them at Level 3. (Ibid)

According to Silvernail (1996), irrespective of whether or not their particular students fully understood the National Curriculum material, schools and teachers perceived little choice and flexibility in departing from the pace and content prescribed by the National Curriculum. Adapting the curriculum to make learning more optimal for pupils with learning and behavioural problems might provide a more successful chance at engaging in learning; however, the presence and demands of national tests and assessments leave teachers with little room for such flexibility and negotiation.

Indeed, adapting the National Curriculum was shown to be particularly difficult for schools with a high proportion of pupils from bilingual backgrounds. Hacker and Rowe's (1997) study of the effects of the National Curriculum on bilingual pupils revealed that teachers delivered minimal expectations with minimal standards of teaching in order to deliver the National Curriculum, concluding that 'in terms of any additive definition of 'equal opportunity' to our bilingual pupils, [the National Curriculum] is a blunt instrument, which fails to recognise and respond to their distinctive needs and interests, as with so many groups:

> We believe, then, that present National Curriculum provision is far from offering 'quality'. In rendering invisible [bilingual pupils] language repertoire, it renders invisible a key part of their lives and identities; this cannot in the longer term promote effective training and identification with the goals of education for such pupils. (Mitchell and Brumfit, 1997, p.117-8)

De Pear's (1999) study of the perceptions of exclusion by pupils with special educational needs similarly revealed that the National Curriculum discouraged teachers from adapting their teaching in order to develop alternative ways for pupils to achieve academic success:

> Pupils seem to be labelled early on and the school procedures act upon them in such a way that exclusion seems inevitable. Some youngsters appear to feel so powerless in academic terms that they turn to disruptive behaviour as the most feasible form of defense in the uncomfortable situations in which they find themselves ... The data show that it might not be the fact that pupils had no wish to take responsibility in the learning situation, but that some teachers in dealing with them, prior to exclusion, gave them little opportunity to succeed.
> (p.50, 62)

According to De Pear (1997), under the current system, teachers received little support for such attempts and thus perceived little value for curriculum innovation: 'Teachers described a sub-optimal system, rooted in control and within which any attempt at advocacy would be fought off by the prevailing culture' (p.50). De Pear further reported that 'a large number of professionals involved with the care and the education of children have experienced frustration and anger at the exclusion of 'problem' pupils who have had little chance for advocacy and who have been denied appropriate resources and provision' (ibid).

Other curriculum-related factors that may have lowered pupils' self- and teachers' expectations could well be the increased use of streaming, setting and ability-grouping of pupils (for a review of studies, see Hallam and Toutounji, 1996; Sukhnandan and Lee, 1998). Whilst grouping students by ability might allow schools to more quickly identify those pupils who are likely to perform well on assessments and exams, such practices have been shown to result in the reinforcement of teachers' low expectations of certain pupils, translating powerfully to pupils' perceptions of their own failure and achievement (Oakes and Lipton, 1990; Holt, 1966). Moreover, over the past decade, in the shift from pupil-centred to academic-oriented pedagogy, teachers have reverted to teaching methods that may be less effective for pupils with learning difficulties. This includes rote memorisation and the use of traditional models of stand-and-deliver in which teachers are the deliverers of information and pupils are the receivers (Hacker and Rowe, 1997).

In this climate of teaching and learning, pupils' opportunities for achieving success are narrowly defined and limited by what teachers believe they can achieve on national assessments and tests. Such an environment in schools translates powerfully and profoundly to those pupils who become marked and labelled by their poor performance on exams and sorted by ability through their tests results. For pupils with special educational needs, emotional or behavioural difficulties, and other learning challenges, the current system offers little time and flexibility for schools and teachers to help such pupils succeed in the current curriculum. The lack of opportunities for low- and under-achieving pupils to demonstrate their learning, except through test-based means, translates into fewer chances to succeed in school. This is further reinforced by the narrowly-defined quantitative indicators through which teachers are asked to view, value and interpret their pupils' learning. Evidence of schools' and teachers' decreased capacity to meet the needs of pupils with behavioural and learning difficulties might be seen in the growing use of GNVQs, a vocational-based curriculum alternative to GCSEs (Mansell, 1999) and the increased reliance by schools on Pupil Referral Units (PRUs) where teachers and schools can place 'unmanageable' pupils and where they are exempt from the National Curriculum (Parsons, 1999).

Part III

Analysis

The Impact on the Conditions of Teaching and Learning

Although a number of surveys have suggested that as a profession, teachers as a whole, are supportive of the National Curriculum (Cox, Evans, Sanders, 1992; Graham and Tyther, 1993; and Davies and Landman, 1991; Silcock, 1990; 1992; Watts and Grosvernor, 1993), the dilemmas and conflicts experienced by teachers cast a different light on the unintended consequences of the National Curriculum in creating a climate that has aggravated the growth in school exclusion. Indeed, Silvernail (1996) explained that whilst teachers supported the theory behind the National Curriculum, 'however, when one begins to probe teachers, a very different view surfaces'. Silvernail (1996) concluded that although teachers believed in providing a 'broad and balanced' and 'equal entitlement' to pupils, 'teachers feel that the *specific* national curriculum and assessment program, as it has been implemented, is detrimental to British children' (Silvernail, 1996, p.23).

The pressure on teachers to ensure the uniform delivery of topics rather than to focus on the suitability of the content and style of what many teachers believe should be taught might help to explain why some schools may have experienced greater difficulties in responding to pupils with behavioural and learning difficulties. Moreover, the prevailing culture of the system and school's reliance upon narrowly defined indicators of pupils' ability and test results do not recognise the diversity of pupils' strengths, weaknesses, interests and styles. In relying upon test results as a main indicator of learning, teachers are discouraged from developing approaches that might allow greater recognition of the diversity of pupils' needs. The lack of opportunity for pupils to achieve success and the narrow indicators upon which their learning is labelled and measured might further explain how and why increasing numbers of pupils might be less motivated by exams, and exhibit greater frustration and disruptive behaviour in classrooms.

Among the most deeply felt effects of the National Curriculum on schools and teachers is a climate of teaching and learning in which teachers have little time, are discouraged from using individualised methods and styles of teaching, and have few incentives and opportunities for attempting innovative, school-based solutions. In such a climate, employing thoughtful and meaningful ways of addressing the needs of pupils with learning and behavioural difficulties is far less likely, and exclusion from the curriculum and school more likely. Such findings such as those reported in De Pear's (1999) study, which found that excluded pupils perceived little opportunity to succeed, should not be crudely concluded to mean that teachers and schools would prefer to exclude. Rather, this should raise further questions about whether and why, as a consequence of the system and its policies, schools have resorted increasingly to exclusion to cope with the difficult learning challenges presented by those pupils.

In sum, the pedagogical shift from generalist, pupil-centred approaches to the subject-specialisation of teaching, the constraints on teachers' time; the frenzied pace of superficially covering the myriad number of topics of national curriculum; the pressure of league tables and assessments; the reduced flexibility of adapting content and methods to suit individual pupils' needs; and a climate of expectations in which quantifying pupils' abilities and raising test results are national policy priorities - have all worked effectively first, to reduce and erode teachers' time to address the needs of challenging pupils; and second, to diminish the tolerance and capacity of schools of adapting pedagogy and curriculum to fit the needs of individual students.

Part IV

Policy Implications

The Need to Improve the Knowledge and Capacity of Teachers

In considering the implications for future policy, it is important here to recognise two profound areas of societal change, which present enormous challenges to schools and teachers. One is a rapidly changing global and the technological society. A second is a growing and increasingly diverse student population whose economic success depends on their participation in and access to education. These changes constitute the need for unprecedented levels of knowledge and skills from teachers. The recognition of these global forces of social transformation and the need for better teaching and learning have also increased the demands and expectations of schools and teachers in other countries such as the US, where policymakers have responded by investing more heavily in increasing the level of support, training, recruitment and salary levels of teachers in order to build and sustain the capacity for major educational change (Consortium for Renewing Education, 1998; National Commission on Teaching and America's Future, 1996; 1998):

> Schools can have little positive impact on students without teachers who know their subjects and who know how to teach important content to all students ... The importance of having expert teachers in classrooms cannot be overstated. Research has documented what most parents and students know intuitively: that the quality of teaching forms the single-most important school-related factor in school achievement. (Consortium for Renewing Education, 1998)

That teachers are what will matter most in ensuring the inclusion and success of all pupils may be an obvious statement of fact. Yet, in Britain, the growing complexities of teaching and the needs of teachers for greater levels of training, support, and trust have failed to garner the necessary public resources or understanding from policymakers. Despite recent calls and proposals for improving the quality of teachers and teaching, policies have resulted in placing greater burdens on school whilst simultaneously calling upon teachers to prove their competence and improve their performance.

In the decade that has followed the implementation of the NC, studies and reports have found that teachers' administrative duties have increased rather than decreased (Barnard, 1997); teachers' stress levels and morale have also been found to reach 'disturbing' levels (McEwen and Thompson, 1997):

> The stress imposed on teachers by the wider educational system is demonstrated by the finding that almost 60% of teachers report that they have too much to do. That such a high proportion of teachers are under time pressure suggests that the causes are structural rather than due to poor time management alone ... it is clear that a disturbing proportion are experiencing levels of stress that go beyond the threshold of the normal grievances and tensions found in almost any occupation.

Higher levels of stress among the teaching profession, which traditionally and historically, does not exhibit 'unnaturally high levels of physiological or psychological stress ... due to their high level of job discretion' (McEwen and Thompson, 1997) might be explained by the reduced autonomy and conflicts experienced by teachers in their practice. Indeed, further studies conclude that teachers have become less innovative not due to lack of will, but because they have been encouraged by the system to revert to more traditional ways of delivering information (Hacker and Rowe, 1997; Mitchell and Brumfit, 1997), as well as to organise pupils by ability:

> Given the current climate of British education, with its emphasis on attainment and competition and the National Curriculum with its tiered system of examination entry, the incentive for schools to organise pupils by ability is understandable. However, what is clear from the findings of the research is that a particular system of grouping pupils, on its own, is not necessarily going to enable all schools to:
>
> - Enable all schools to raise their attainment levels and thus their position in the league tables;
> - Be an appropriate method of organising pupils across all subjects; and
> - Fulfil the needs of *all pupils* given the variation in their individual learning styles and personal/social attributes (level of ability, social class, gender, race, and age). (Sukhanandan, 1999, p.4)

What is clearly needed is a greater sophistication amongst policymakers to understand the complexity of teaching an increasingly diverse range of pupils. The reality of schools and their diversity means that one-size-fits-all mandates are likely to fail in providing pupils with an equal access and a high-quality environment for learning. If solutions for pupils who have difficulties in accessing the National Curriculum are to be developed, greater incentives must be introduced into the system so that schools and teachers are encouraged to develop innovative, school-based strategies. Greater flexibility must also be encouraged amongst teachers to develop curricular approaches in place of traditional exams and assessments, which emphasises conformity to a clear set of school rules and behaviours rather than a diverse set of approaches to pupils' needs. Proposals to improve the performance of teachers through performance-based pay incentives are less likely to promote inclusive styles and methods of teaching, and more likely to result in classroom dynamics that encourage teachers to focus attention and efforts on pupils who can produce measurable results. Ensuring inclusion and access to curriculum requires equipping and enabling teachers with more time, professional development and flexible working conditions. This might be a far more effective policy strategy for reducing exclusions, and would most certainly help schools and teachers to respond more effectively and thoughtfully to the complex demands of pupils with behavioural and learning difficulties.

Part V

Concluding Thoughts

Ensuring Access to Curriculum: Removing the Pressures to Exclude

Exclusions have grown and risen to record levels over the past decade, it would appear, not because there is a National Curriculum, but because of the pressures emanating from the wider educational system to which the present National Curriculum is structured, linked and assessed. It is not simply that the National Curriculum which has reduced teachers' flexibility and autonomy, but more importantly the effects of the system that has eroded the time and tolerance needed by teachers to be more thoughtful and patient in trying to find ways for pupils with particular difficulties to access the curriculum. It is not the curriculum alone, but the combined impact of policy pressures that have 1) shifted schools' pedagogical goals from an individual, whole-pupil focus to a narrowly-defined, academic subject-focus; and 2) discouraged teachers and schools away from teaching subjects in-depth and according to individual needs to teaching superficially and conforming to nationally-defined targets and directives.

Although recent statistics indicate that school exclusions appear to be declining (Godfrey and Parsons, 1998) the decrease is still small relative to the overall growth over the past decade, and thousands of children remain out of school and excluded from learning. The problem of school exclusions still raises important questions about the pressures in schools that may be continuing to encourage, rather than discourage the use of exclusions (Parsons, 1999). Therefore, in fully understanding the dynamics and causes of school exclusion, the answer will not be found by looking solely at the individual pupil's behaviour and the micro-incidents and decisions that occur in classrooms and schools. A more complex explanation for the rise in school exclusions lies in understanding the wider dynamics of the national policy context and educational system, in which certain pressures to exclude students appear to emanate from the influence and interaction of the national policies. In this interaction of policies and pressures, the current national curriculum has clearly played a crucial role and major factor.

Over the course of the last decade, the cumulative impact of the National Curriculum and subsequent educational reforms have made time, patience, tolerance and knowledge essential elements for combating disaffection and preventing disruptive behaviour increasingly necessary. Yet, these four basic needs of teaching and learning - time, patience, tolerance and knowledge - are what ironically, have been most eroded by the pressure and demands of the current system. Time, training and knowledge are what teachers say they need to cope more effectively with pupils whose behaviour and needs present difficult challenges in the classroom. Yet, tolerance and patience are what the system, over the course of the past decade, have failed to provide.

At the time of writing this chapter in January 2000, the policy constraints of the National Curriculum on schools' and teachers' capacities was acknowledged by a recent review conducted by the Qualifications and Curriculum Authority, the policymaking body which presently oversees the National Curriculum (QCA, 1999). The report released at the end of 1999 calls for 'a less prescriptive and more flexible national curriculum' - a step that has been applauded by schools and would be a move in the right direction. Yet, it is naïve to think that such diversity in teaching and learning approaches will simply emerge in schools and result from the calls of policymakers to emphasise higher-order thinking over the low-order skills of rote learning and regurgitation. It is also naïve to think that providing teachers with pay-based incentives, based on pupils' results, will also improve expectations and practices towards those pupils whose behaviour and ability, when such pupils actually present greater barriers to teachers achieving the results needed to 'earn' a pay rise.

The changes in teachers' practices and beliefs, and perhaps those related to school exclusion, resulted from system-wide changes that were brought about by national policy. Therefore, improvements in teaching and the reduction of exclusion are not likely to occur in schools without recognising first and foremost, the need for policy changes that provide teachers with greater support, training and more flexible conditions for teaching. Recognising the needs of the teaching profession must start with the difficult recognition of the inherent contradictions in the design of the overall educational system and the elimination of those pressures that work against the inclusion of all pupils, regardless of their perceived ability. Without a fundamental re-examination of the curriculum and the policies to which the National Curriculum is presently linked, the process of school exclusions provides schools with a far more efficient, swifter and easier solution for responding to behavioural problems rather than changing the ways that schools are structured and teachers teach.

The fundamental question with which this author has been concerned is not whether a National Curriculum is right or wrong, good or bad, effective or ineffective, but rather, whether the basic goals of the current curriculum in Britain, which are aimed at providing a 'broad and balanced' access to learning are best achieved by offering a fail-proof package to standardised and prescribed subjects that teachers uniformly deliver to every pupil, or whether such entitlement might be better realised by ensuring that schools and teachers have the needed time, knowledge, tolerance and patience for endeavouring to meet every individual student's needs. Emphasis on the latter shifts the challenge of ensuring access to the curriculum away from top-down directives issued by policy makers towards improving the capacity of schools and teachers. Such efforts, I think, might perhaps present profoundly different possibilities for ensuring that no child can be excluded from learning, and that every child who is entitled to access to national curriculum, actually receives it.

References

Ainscow, M. (1991) Effective Schools for all: An Alternative Approach to Special Educational Needs in Education, *Cambridge Journal of Education*, Vol.21, No.3.

Barnard, N. (1997) Exclusion linked to paperwork, *The Times Educational Supplement*, 7 November 1997, p.15.

Blyth, E. and Milner, J. (1996) *Exclusion from School: Inter-professional issues for policy and practice*, London, Routledge.

Carpenter, B. (1997, Spring) Curriculum Perspectives: An Overview of Recent Developments In Special Education, *Curriculum*, Vol.18, No.1, pp.3-14.

Castle, Frances and Parsons, C. (1997) Disruptive Behaviour and Exclusions from Schools: Redefining and Responding to the Problem, *Emotional and Behavioural Difficulties*, Vol.2, No.3, Winter 1977, pp.4-11.

Charlton, T. and David K. (1993) *Managing Misbehaviour in Schools*, London, Routledge.

Commission for Racial Equality (1988) *Exclusions: The Public Cost*, London, CRE.

Consortium on Renewing Education, The (1998) *20/20 Vision: A Strategy for Doubling America's Academic Achievement by the Year 2020*, Vanderbilt University, Peabody Center for Educational Policy.

Cooper, P. (1993) *Effective Schools for Disaffected Students: Integration and Segregation*, London, Routledge.

Cox, T., Evans, J. and Sanders, S. (1992) How Primary School Teachers View the National Curriculum 1 Year on, *Educational Review*, Vol.44, pp.19-29.

Davies, J. and Landman, M. (1991) The National Curriculum in Special Schools for Pupils with Emotional and Behavioural Difficulties: A National Survey, *Maladjustment and Therapeutic Education*, Vol.9, No.3, pp.130-135.

De Pear, S. (1999) Perceptions of Exclusion by Pupils With Special Needs, in *On the Margins: The Educational Experience of 'Problem' Pupils* edited by Lloyd-Smith, M. and Dwfor Davies, J., Staffordshire, England, Trentham Books, pp.49-65.

Donovan, N. (1998) *Los Olivados - UK 1998*, The Stakeholder, pp.15-16.

Galloway, D. (1982) A Study of Pupils Suspended from Schools, *British Journal of Educational Psychology*, 52, pp.205-212.

Galloway, D., Martin, R. and Wilcox, B. (1985) Persistent Absence from School and Exclusion from School: The Predictive Power of School and Community Variables, *British Educational Research Journal*, Vol.1, No.1, pp.51-61.

Garner, Philip (1999) *Pupils With Problems: Rational Fears ... Radical Solutions?* Staffordshire, England, Trentham Books.

Gillborn, D. (1996) Exclusions from School, *Viewpoint*, No.5, September 1996, London, Institute of Education.

Godfrey, R. and Parsons, C. (1998) Exclusion: The Facts and Figures, *Parliamentary Briefing May 1998*, p.64.

Graham, D. and Tyther, D. (1993) *A Lesson for Us All: The Making of the National Curriculum*, London, Routledge.

Hacker, R.G. and Rowe, J.M. (1997, November) The impact of a national curriculum development on teaching and learning behaviours, *International Journal of Science Education*, Vol. 19, pp.997-1004.

Hallam, S. and Toutounji, T. (1996) *What Do We Know About the Grouping of Pupils by Ability? A Research Review*, London, University of London, Institute of Education.

Hayden, C. (1997) *Children Excluded from Primary School: Debates, Evidence and Responses*, Buckingham, Open University Press.

Hayden, C. (1997) Exclusion from primary school: children "in need" and children with "special educational need", *Emotional and Behavioural Difficulties*, Vol. 2, No. 3, Winter 1997.

Holt, J. (1966) *How Children Fail*, London, Pitman.

House of Commons (1998) *Disaffected Children: Education and Employment Committee, Fifth Report, Vol. 1, Report and Proceedings of the Committee*, London, The Stationery Office.

Kinder, K., Kendall, S., Downing, D., Atkinson, M. and Hogarth, S. (1999) *Raising Behaviour 2: Nil Exclusion: Policy and Practice*, Slough, NFER.

Lloyd-Smith, M. (1984) (ed) *Disrupted Schooling*, London, John Murray.

Lovey, J. and Cooper, P. (1997) Positive alternatives to school exclusion: an empirical investigation, *Emotional and Behavioural Difficulties*, Vol.2, No.3, Winter 1997, pp.12-22.

Mansell, W. (1999) Vocational results hit record high, *The Times Educational Supplement*, 5 November 1999.

McEwen, A. and Thompson, W. (1997, May) After the National Curriculum: Teacher Stress and Morale, *Research in Education*, No.57, pp.57-66.

McLean, Alan (1987) After the Belt: School Processes in Low-Exclusion Schools, *School Organisation*, 7, 3, pp.303-310.

McManus, M. (1987) Suspension and Exclusion From High Schools: The Association With Catchment and School Variables, *School Organisation*, 7, 3, pp.261-271.

Mitchell, R. and Brumfit, C. (1997) The National Curriculum Experience of Bilingual Students, *Educational Review*, Vol.49, (June 1997), p.159-80.

National Commission on Teaching & America's Future (1996a) *What Matters Most: Teaching for America's Future*, New York, National Commission on Teaching & America's Future.

National Commission on Teaching & America's Future (1996b) *Doing What Matters Most: Investing in Quality Teaching*, New York, National Commission on Teaching & America's Future.

Oakes, J. and Lipton, M. (1990) Tracking and Ability Grouping: A Structural Barrier to Access and Achievement in *Access to Knowledge: An Agenda for Our Nations' Schools*, edited by Goodlad, J. and Keating, P., New York, The College Entrance Examination Board.

OFSTED (1996) *Exclusions from Secondary Schools: 1995-96. A Report from the Office of Her Majesty's Chief Inspector of Schools*, London, The Stationery Office.

Osler, Audrey and Hill, J. (1998) Exclusion from school and racial equality: an examination of government proposal in the light of recent research evidence, *Cambridge Journal of Education*, Vol.28, No.1, pp.33-59.

Parsons, C. (1996) Permanent Exclusions from Schools in England in the 1990s: Trends, Causes and Responses, *Children & Society*, Vol.10, pp.177-86.

Parsons, C. (1999) *Education, Exclusion and Citizenship*, London, Routledge.

Parsons, C. and Howlett, K. (1995) Difficult Dilemmas, *Education*, 22-29 December 1995, pp.14-15.

Pyke, N. (1991a) Rise in exclusions linked to ERA, *Times Educational Supplement*, 3 May 1991, p.3.

Pyke, N. (1991b) Alarm at sharp rise in exclusions, *Times Educational Supplement*, 4 October 1991, p.1.

Qualifications and Curriculum Authority (1999, August) *National Curriculum Consultation: Developing the School Curriculum. QCA's Report and Recommendations Following the Statutory Consultation on the Secretary of State's Proposals for the Review of the National Curriculum in England*, Suffolk, England, QCA Publications.

Rayner, S. (1998) Education Pupils With Emotional and Behaviour Difficulties: Pedagogy is the Key! *Emotional and Behavioural Difficulties*, Vol.3, No.2, Summer 1998, pp.39-47.

Reynolds, D. (1984) *The school for vandals: a sociological portrait of a disaffection-prone school*, in Frude, N. and Gault, H. (eds) Disruptive Behaviour in Schools, Chichester, Wiley.

Reynolds, D. and Sullivan, M. (1981) The Effects of School: A Radical Faith Re-Stated in Gillham, B. (ed) *Problem Behaviour in the Secondary School*, Beckengam, Croom Helm.

Rustique-Forrester, E. (in progress) *The Dynamics and Dilemmas of School Exclusion: A Study of Teachers' Perceptions of the Policy Pressures to Exclude*, London, Institute of Education.

Rustique-Forrester, E. (1999) The Dynamics and Dilemmas of Growing School Exclusion in the UK: A Review of the Research and Policy Literature, Paper presented at the 1999 Annual Meeting of the British Educational Research Association, University of Sussex, England, September 1-4.

Rustique-Forrester, E. (2000) Uncovering the Policy Dynamics and Dilemmas of School Exclusion: School Practitioners' Perceptions of the Policy Pressures to Exclude, Paper presented at the 2000 Annual Meeting of the British Educational Research Association, Cardiff University, Wales, September 6-9.

Rutter, M. (1983) School Effects on Pupil Progress: Research Findings and Policy Implications, *Child Development*, 54, pp.1-29.

Rutter, M., Maughn, B., Mortimore, P. and Ouston, J. (1979) *Fifteen Thousand Hours: Secondary Schools and Their Effects on Children*, London, Open Books.

Silcock, P. (1990) Implementing the National Curriculum: Some Teacher's Dilemmas, *Education 3-13*, Vol.18, No.3, 3-10.

Silcock, P. (1992) Primary School Teacher-Time and the National Curriculum: Managing the Impossible? British Journal of Educational studies, Vol.40, No.2, 163-173.

Silvernail, D. (1996) *The Impact of England's National Curriculum and Assessments on Classroom Practice: Lessons from Across the Atlantic*, New York, National Center for Restructuring Education, Schools and Teaching.

Social Exclusion Unit (1998) *Truancy and Social Exclusion*, London, The Stationery Office.

Sukhanandan, L. (1999) Sorting, Sifting and Setting: Does Grouping Pupils According to Ability Affect Attainment? *NFER News*, Spring 1999, Great Britain, National Foundation for Educational Research.

Sukhnandan, L. and Lee, B. (1998) *Streaming, Setting and Grouping by Ability: A Review of the Literature*, Great Britain, National Foundation for Educational Research.

Walford, G. (1990) 1988 Education Reform Act for England and Wales: Paths to Privatisation, *Educational Policy*, Vol.4, No.2, pp.127-144.

Watkins, C. and Wagner, P. (2000) *Improving School Behaviour*, London, Paul Chapman.

Watts, R. and Grosvenor, I. (1993) The Implementation of the National Curriculum in History, *Forum*, Vol.35, No.2, 48-50.

9 Horse Before the Cart: Developing an Evidence-Based Approach to Educational Policy

FAY SMITH AND FRANK HARDMAN

Introduction

In a lecture given on 2nd February 2000 to academics at an Economic and Social Research Council (ESRC) seminar at Church House, London, David Blunkett, Education and Employment Secretary, called upon social science researchers to join with policymakers in breaking down the 'seam of anti-intellectualism running through society'. He went on to state 'we need social scientists to help to determine what works and why, and what types of policy initiatives are likely to be most effective'.

Since the Labour government's election in May 1997, there have been numerous major policy initiatives in the field of education. One such large-scale initiative has been the National Literacy Strategy (NLS) designed to address standards of literacy in English primary schools. This major policy initiative followed from recommendations made by a Literacy Task Force established on 31st May 1996 by David Blunkett, then Shadow Secretary of State for Education. It was charged with developing, in time for an incoming Labour government, a strategy for substantially raising standards of literacy in primary schools over a five to ten year period. In a bid to achieve this end, the National Literacy Project (NLP) was piloted in approximately 250 schools in 18 local education authorities serving largely urban, disadvantaged areas and was due to run for five years. This in turn led on to the National Literacy Strategy (NLS), launched in August 1997 (DfEE, 1997), and the recently issued Framework for Teaching (DfEE, 1998). The framework has been operating under a quasi-statutory status in all state primary schools since September 1998. It sets out the teaching objectives for pupils from reception to Year 6 and gives guidance on the 'literacy hour' in which the teaching should take place. The prescription consists of an introduction of 30 minutes, 20 minutes independent work and a ten minute plenary, where pupils are expected to spend approximately 60% of their time being directly taught and 40% working independently.

It is claimed that the strategy has had a major impact on many aspects of primary education, including teaching styles and the organisation of the school day. At the current time, over £71 million has been set aside for the implementation and development of the NLS making it the largest and most costly attempt to improve literacy standards in primary schools to date. Such a 'top-down' initiative also represents a major shift away from approaches to curriculum development which characterised previous government literacy initiatives.

In this chapter we will argue that before centralised curricula changes, such as the NLS, are imposed on state schools there needs to be rigorous, systematic and independent research of such policy initiatives. We will illustrate our arguments by critically reviewing the research evidence that has been made available to support the introduction of the NLS and, building on our own research, suggest ways in which educational researchers can join with policymakers to provide sound, relevant and intelligible research.

Putting the Cart Before the Horse?

Following widespread criticism that there was little research-based evidence to support the launch of NLS, particularly concerning the progression prescribed, the teaching methods advocated and the detailed format of the literacy hour, Roger Beard of Leeds University was commissioned to write a report to review the literature (Beard, 1999). In the report it is claimed that the strategy draws upon programmes supported by research from different parts of the world (eg. Clay, 1993; Slavin, 1996; Crevola and Hill, 1998) which are designed to raise standards of literacy, particularly in relation to the needs of disadvantaged pupils. The programmes share common features by specifying teaching methods (eg. a fast-paced, structured curriculum; direct, interactive teaching; systematic phonics in the context of interesting texts; a combination of shared and paired reading and writing; early intervention for pupils who have not made expected progress after one year at school) which are supported by teacher effectiveness research so as to ensure that primary teachers and schools are well-informed about best practice and have the knowledge and skills to act upon it. However, in the report, it is acknowledged that none of the programmes have fully run their course and in each case there is a need for further empirical research to evaluate the impact of such programmes on learning outcomes, classroom practices and teachers' thinking.

Beard's review of the evidence on the NLS contains little empirical research that is directly related to the effectiveness of the strategy. Only two sources of evidence are cited: an evaluation of the NLP carried out by the National Foundation for Educational Research (NFER) (Sainsbury, 1998) and by Her Majesty's Inspectorate (HMI) (OFSTED, 1998). In the NFER research, children's progress in reading between October 1996 and March 1998 using two standardised reading tests was measured. According to Beard, the test results revealed a 'significant and substantial' improvement over the 18 month period. Pupils in participating schools had scores below the national average at the outset. Final test scores improved by approximately six standardised score points, so that they were still below, but significantly closer to, the national average. Children eligible for free school meals, those with special educational needs and those learning English as an additional language had lower scores, although all these groups nonetheless made significant progress. Attitudinal data showed that children gained in reading confidence in the course of the project, saying they needed less help with their reading at the end than they had initially. Questionnaires to Headteachers also showed a positive response to the introduction of the literacy hour.

In addition to the NFER data, the HMI evaluation refers to National Curriculum test results which at ages 7 and 11 showed overall progress made in three-quarters of the NLP schools in line with, or better than, the national average and by more than the national average in approximately half of the schools. The report does acknowledge, however, the limitations of year on year comparisons when different cohorts of pupils are involved. Comparison is also made difficult because the National Curriculum tests had not been standardised as in the reading tests used in the NFER evaluation.

Given the paucity of evidence, we carried out our own research into the effectiveness of the NLS on learning outcomes (Smith and Hardman, 2000). We concentrated on one local, urban education authority in the

North East of England which had been involved in the piloting of the NLP. By using a quantitative and qualitative approach we identified predictors of success (success being defined by exam performance). Predictors of success included such variables as: percentage of pupils on free school meals, age of pupils, time of NLS implementation, teaching and learning style and management of the literacy project within the school. We had several types of data available including a standardised reading test, value added data and national examination results. We also carried out a case study of a representative sample of three schools. By interviewing key members of staff within each school we were able to investigate the effects of teachers' thinking, teaching and learning styles and class management skills upon the success of the project.

The first cohort (Cohort 1) of primary schools in the authority began implementation of the NLS in January 1997. It included 19 schools who had been involved in the NLP because of their low National Curriculum test scores. Cohort 2 began full implementation in 20 schools in September 1997. A further cohort (Cohort 3) of 21 schools began in September 1998. Finally, all 93 schools in the LEA became involved in the NLS. Our study focused on the 39 schools in the first two cohorts. Cohort 1 was not randomly selected. The schools in Cohort 1 were identified as priority schools due to their lower National Curriculum exam scores compared to other schools. This is important because any comparison between Cohorts 1 and 2 should focus upon the progress made rather than exam results *per se*.

For the quantitative study, three different types of test results were available: value added data (Performance Indicators in Primary Schools), National Curriculum English test results at Key Stages 1 and 2 (SATs) and Suffolk Reading Scale. For the case study, three schools were chosen because of their varying socio-economic status, different size and different points of entry into the NLS. One of the schools was part of Cohort 1 and therefore been part of the NLS for longer. This school also took part in the NLP. The other two schools are part of Cohort 2. The headteacher, a Key Stage 1 teacher, a Key Stage 2 teacher and the NLS coordinator from each school were interviewed (some teachers took on more than one of these roles).

The analysis of the quantitative data suggests there was a significant improvement in 1997/8 test scores compared to 1996/7 for both cohorts when looking at the Suffolk scores. There is also an improvement in the value-added and SATs scores but not significantly. Overall, the findings of the analysis supported the belief that the NLS is having an impact upon the schools but that this impact has been slight and only significant for the Suffolk results. In addition, the findings show that there are variations across years within schools and that schools' results vary from year to year. This suggests that while schools in the short-term are improving, maintaining progress can be difficult. Cohort 1 schools also made less progress than Cohort 2 schools despite their longer involvement in the NLP/NLS. This could be explained by the socio-economic profile of the Cohort 1 schools as success as defined by exam scores in National Curriculum tests, value added tests and the Suffolk reading test is related to free school meals: schools with higher numbers on free school meals obtained lower exam results. The percentage of pupils with English as an additional language (EAL) also played a role in some cases.

Special Educational Needs in the Literacy Hour

Evidence from the interviews with teachers suggests that there is a gap opening up between their more able and less able children. The 'average' and above average pupils are seen as benefiting from the NLS, but those with special educational needs are being left behind: this means that a polarisation effect could be developing. However, the scores presented from these surveys represent aggregated information and thus give no detailed insights into the progress of groups of pupils nor *individual* pupils with special educational needs. There is, therefore, the need for more evidence on how the NLS is addressing the needs of pupils with special educational needs in mainstream primary schools.

Currently, as has been suggested, there is little empirical evidence on the suitability and effectiveness of the literacy hour, particularly for those pupils who have been identified as having problems with literacy. Although Beard (1999) suggests the NLS draws on programmes from Australasia and the USA, the framework (DfEE, 1998) differs from these programmes in two highly important aspects: firstly, it makes no specific reference to the early identification of pupils at risk for literacy learning; secondly, there are no in-built approaches aimed at reducing the gap between the least able and the most able pupils. Indeed, any reference to pupils with special educational needs was not made available until after the initial document was produced. In contrast to the NLS, the New Zealand programme (Clay,

1993) has a well-defined strategy for pupils who fail to achieve literacy early on. This consists of identifying pupils at the end of their first year of schooling, implementing individual tuition in their second year and then, if necessary, providing additional focused support in the third year of education. The 'equivalent' response in England and Wales is to identify pupils in years 3 and 4 and to offer them 'Additional Literacy Support' through auxiliaries and nursery nurses in school.

The absence of any clearly defined approach to identifying and meeting the needs of pupils at risk for literacy learning raises questions about how effective the NLS can be for these individuals and is in need of further investigation. Recent international studies into the performance of primary pupils in reading (Brooks, Pugh and Schagen, 1996) suggest that England and Wales perform in the mid-range of countries, below countries like New Zealand, Finland and France. An unusual feature of the performance in England and Wales is the distinctive trailing edge of pupils for whom literacy learning is very limited. This raises issues about the need to improve the performance of this poorly performing group of pupils and to explore ways of developing their literacy skills. Future studies will need to track the individual progress of these pupils to determine the impact of the NLS and to inform developments in the teaching of literacy to raise standards for all pupils.

In examining the claims of an overall improvement in learning outcomes resulting from the NLS, it should be remembered that the findings of the evaluations are correlational; therefore, any improvements in literacy scores cannot be directly attributed to the NLS. For example, the learning gains could be explained, as Galton et al. (1999) suggest, by the greater emphasis on the teaching of literacy in terms of time that is being allocated to it in the school day, or by the 'Hawthorne effect' or novelty factor that usually follows the introduction of any educational innovation. The findings of all three evaluations discussed above suggest there is a need for longitudinal studies to measure the effectiveness of the NLS and to evaluate its impact on classroom practices and teachers' thinking. There is also the need for reliable evidence data to measure individual attainment alongside aggregations at school and LEA level. Such analysis as an individual level would provide information on how effective the NLS is with children of different levels of ability, including those with special educational needs. This would also include the development of assessment measures with high curriculum validity and sensitivity to test what is actually taught in the literacy hour.

In addition to the learning gains resulting from the NLS, the NFER and HMI evaluations claim that there has been an improvement in the quality of literacy teaching. They suggest that effective teaching within the literacy hour is characterised by consistency, clear structure, high quality interaction and good pace. This is as a result of the prescribed emphasis on direct teaching in the first half of the literacy hour and maintenance of this approach with groups and then with the class again, in the second half. The NFER study based its evidence on descriptive reports from project LEAs and LEAs ratings of how well the project was implemented in their schools. The HMI evaluation of the quality of the teaching was based upon observations of over 300 literacy hour lessons. However, the reliability and validity of OFSTEDs methodology for collecting data has been called into question (Fitz-Gibbon, 1996). As will be discussed in the next section, the assumption that the literacy hour is resulting in high quality interactive teaching is challenged by research into classroom discourse.

Interactive Whole Class Teaching

The concept of 'interactive whole class teaching' is seen as a major feature of the NLS. In his report reviewing the research evidence for the NLS, Beard (1999) acknowledged that the emphasis on this more directive form of teaching draws mainly upon the school effectiveness and school improvement literature. Citing the work of Reynolds and Farrell (1996) it suggests that 'interactive whole class teaching' will play a vital role in raising literacy standards. However, as Galton et al. (1999) argue, the concept of interactive whole class teaching is not well defined and little evidence has been presented to show it differs from traditional whole class teaching. Nor does it explicitly appear in the framework document (DfEE, 1998). According to Reynolds (1998) it encompasses rapid question and answer sessions when teachers are finding out what pupils know, followed by 'teacher-led discussion' involving slower paced, 'higher order' questioning designed to promote higher levels of pupil thinking.

Studies of classroom discourse from North America and the United Kingdom (eg. Mehan, 1979; Dillon, 1994; Edwards and Westgate, 1998; Hardman and Williamson, 1998), however, show that whole class teaching across all stages of schooling is dominated by what Tharp and Gallimore (1988) call the 'recitation script'. In its prototypical form teacher-led recitation consists of three moves: an *initiation*, usually in the form of a teacher question, and a *follow-up* move, in which the teacher provides some form of feedback (very often in the form of an evaluation) to the pupil's response. This three-part exchange structure, as revealed by Sinclair and Coulthard (1992), is therefore seen as a 'teaching technology' which is particularly prevalent in directive forms of teaching and consists of a series of unrelated teacher questions that require convergent factual answers and pupil display of (presumably) known information. Recitation questioning therefore seeks predictable correct answers and only rarely are teachers' questions used to assist pupils to more complete or elaborated ideas.

Nystrand et al. (1997), Wells (1993) and Wood (1993), however, suggest that in the hands of different teachers, teacher-led recitation can lead to very different levels of pupil participation and engagement by making different use of the *feedback* move. Through feedback which gets beyond evaluation of the pupil's answer, the teacher can extend the answer to draw out its significance, or to make connections with other parts of the pupils' total experience during lesson topics so as to create a greater equality of participation for the pupils as advocated by Reynolds (1998) in his characterisation of interactive whole class teaching.

In the absence of any empirical evidence showing that interactive whole class teaching is distinctive from the more traditional whole class, we investigated (Mroz, Smith and Harman, 2000) whether the literacy hour was promoting 'higher order questioning' and 'teacher-led discussion' as suggested by Reynolds, or as Galton et al. (1999) suggest, pressurising primary teachers into doing more of what they do already: teacher-led recitation. An opportunity sample of ten teachers across the 5-11 age range from seven primary schools serving a range of wards in one local authority in the North East of England was selected. This ensured the schools were representative of a range of catchment areas (eg. ranging from a school in an area of high unemployment with 84% of children on free school meals and 58% on the special needs register to a school with an above average socio-economic mix where 13% of children were on free school meals and 10% were on the special needs register). All ten teachers had been involved in the piloting phase of the NLP and had been identified by the local advisor as being effective teachers of the literacy hour. Each teacher was video recorded as they taught the literacy hour. The lessons were then transcribed and coded using a framework adapted from Sinclair and Coulthard's (1992) system of discourse analysis.

The descriptive apparatus for spoken discourse developed by Sinclair and Coulthard proposes that lessons can be analysed as having five *ranks*: lesson, transaction, exchange, move, act. A lesson consisting of one or more *transactions*, which consist of one or more *exchanges*, which consist of one or more *moves*, which consist of one or more *acts*. The study analysed the discourse at the rank of the teaching exchange as it is here that Sinclair and Coulthard are confident that the system is most reliable as it draws on linguistic considerations in describing what is going on. Sinclair and Coulthard identify 11 categories of teaching exchanges with specific functions and unique structures (the reinitiation exchanges were merged for the purposes of the current study). The four main functions of exchanges are: informing, directing, eliciting and checking. The *teacher inform* exchange is used for passing on facts, opinions, ideas and new information to the pupils and usually there is no verbal response to the initiation. The *teacher direct* is designed to get the pupils to do but not say something, whereas the *teacher elicit* is designed to get a verbal contribution from the pupil. The elicit exchange which occurs inside the classroom has a different function from most occurring outside it because the teacher usually knows the answer to the question which is being asked. This accounts for the *feedback* move being an essential element in an eliciting exchange inside the classroom because the pupils, having given their answer, want to know if it was correct.

Having transcribed and coded the lessons into the different categories of teaching exchanges, the results could be quantified and turned into percentage scores to compare the patterning of the teacher/pupil interactions across all ten lessons. The analysis of the patterning would therefore show whether teachers were using interactive whole class teaching strategies to actively involve pupils in the lesson or replicating more traditional patterns of teacher-led recitation. Figure 1 shows the patterning of the teaching exchanges based on the percentage scores for all ten teachers teaching the literacy hour. The graph shows there was little overall variation in the patterning of the teacher exchanges used by the ten teachers as they taught across the three year groups. Teacher-presentation (teacher informs) and teacher-directed question-and-answer (teacher elicits) dominated most of the classroom discourse in all ten lessons, accounting for 82% of the total teaching exchanges.

Figure 9.1   Patterning of Teaching Exchanges for All Ten Lessons

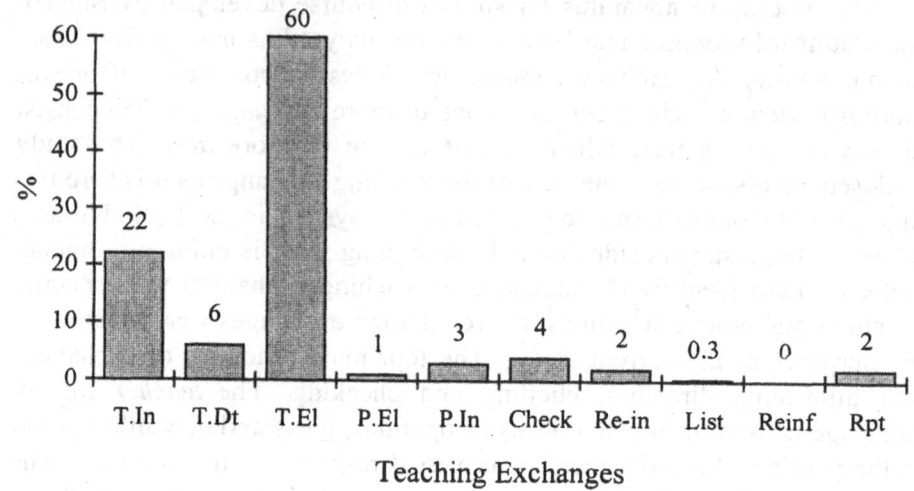

Key: T.In   = teacher inform
       T.Dt   = teacher direct
       T.El   = teacher elicit
       P.El   = pupil elicit
       P.Inf = pupil inform
       Re-in = re-initiate
       List   = listing
       Reinf = reinforce
       Rpt   = repeat

The ubiquity of the three-part exchange structure in all ten lessons meant that they were predominantly conducted within the teacher's frame of reference. Because of the teacher's claim to prior knowledge of the subject content, and right to control the pacing and sequencing of its transmission, pupils rarely managed to impose their own relevance outside the teacher's frame of reference. This is reflected in the type of moves they were usually restricted to within the classroom discourse, often being denied access to initiation and evaluation moves, resulting in the very low level of pupil questions (pupil elicits) and statements (pupil informs). It also minimised the amount of responsibility which the pupils were able to take for their own learning as they were usually dependent on the teacher's sense of relevance.

In all ten lessons, the teacher was predominantly seen to be retaining control over the direction and pace of the lesson and the lines of knowledge which were to be pursued. All ten lessons were conducted through teacher recitation where interrogations of the pupils' knowledge and understanding was the most common form of classroom interaction. The following extract, taken from a whole year 5 class in an urban primary school, is typical of the discourse style used by all ten teachers when interacting with pupils in whole class and group-based work. Here the teacher is exploring various grammatical features in a newspaper report (the *moves*, Initiation, Response, Feedback, make up the three-part teaching exchange which in turn are made up of *acts*: cl = clue, com = e = evaluation; el = elicitation; i = inform; rep = reply; s = starter):

Exchanges			Moves	Acts
Teaching	T	looking at the text now I want you please to tell me what tense the first paragraph is in	I	s
				el
2	P	the past tense	R	rep
3	T	yes it's in the past tense	F	e
4	T	how do you know it's in the past tense	I	el
5	P	because it says August 1990	R	rep
6	T	you know by the date it's in the past tense	F	e
7	T	but you know by something else you know you know by the doing words in the text that change	I	s
		what's a doing word		el
		what do we call a doing word David		n
8	P	a verb	R	rep
9	T	a verb good	F	e
10	T	will you give me one verb please out of this first paragraph	I	s
		find one verb in this paragraph		el
		Stephen		n
11	P	rescued	R	r
12	T	rescued excellent excellent	F	e

		and that's in the past tense		com
13	T	does the tense change when it comes to the next paragraph	I	s
		remember it's the verb that will tell you		cl
		skim find the verbs that was the past that happened before this is now it's happening now		I
		does the verb change Julie		n/el
14	P	it's the present	R	rep
15	T	it's the present tense of the verb	F	e
16	T	can anybody find me one verb in there in the present tense	I	s
		skim down see if you can find a verb in the tense		el
		Lucy		n
17	P	catch	R	rep
18	T	catch right	F	e

This section illustrates clearly the teacher's pervasive use of the three part exchange and the elaborate nature of many of her sequences of elicits which are chained together to form a lengthy transaction. The extract also illustrates how the teacher often uses *starter* acts (Turns 1, 7, 10, 13, 16) as a matter of routine in opening moves. These are similar in function to what Edwards and Mercer (1987) call 'cued elicitations' and French and MacLure (1979, 1981) term 'preformulations' where she provides advance warning that a question is imminent and provides some clues as to how to answer it.

We also see her 'reformulate' a question (Turn 7) in the sequence in an attempt to arrive at the answer she desires, by simplifying and building into its restatement some of the information needed for the acceptable answer and where the ingredients of an appropriate answer might lie. It shows the way in which teacher-directed talk of this kind creates the impression of knowledge and understanding being elicited from the pupils rather than being imposed by the teacher. The extract also reveals the rapid pace of the teacher's questioning and the predictable sequence of recitation. There is a large amount of teacher elaboration through the use of *starters* and the rephrasing of questions in contrast to the brief responses expected from the pupil which show a high incidence of simple recall. The pupils' responses are evaluated and commented on by the teacher who has the right to determine what is relevant within her pedagogic agenda.

Teacher-presentation and teacher-directed question and answer therefore dominated most of the classroom discourse during the whole class teaching sections of the literacy hour and when the teacher worked with groups. There was also a notable absence of the higher order questioning and teacher-led discussion which is said to characterise interactive whole class teaching so as to allow pupils to develop more complete or elaborated ideas. In other words, the findings suggest teacher-led recitation was the most frequently used form of interactive teaching where the third move was rigidly used to evaluate rather than extend pupils' contributions. The findings, therefore, reveal a strong tendency to preserve more traditional patterns of whole class teaching despite the appearance of organisational and curriculum change within the literacy hour.

Our findings are supported by other studies of educational innovations (see Edwards and Westgate, 1994 for a summary) which reveal that at a deeper pedagogic level there is a resilience to change and strong continuities in teacher-pupil discourse. For example in researching the impact of the National Curriculum on primary schools, Alexander et al. (1996) found that despite a scenario of change in curriculum planning, content, management, assessment, record keeping and collective culture of schools there was a continuity in teacher-pupil interaction in the privacy of classrooms. They argue that after seven years 'the 1988 Education Reform Act at the level of the curriculum as transacted in classrooms and experienced by children may not be so far-reaching as proponents claim or critics fear' (p.116). Alexander et al. conclude that pupil-teacher discourse is a central aspect of 'deeper' layers of teaching and that studies of educational change and pupil outcomes ought to be directed towards it. Extensive research in the United States of America by Hestenes (1998) also found that managing the quality of classroom discourse is the most important factor if there is to be genuine interactive teaching. He goes on to suggest that wide differences in learning outcomes among teachers using the same curriculum materials and purportedly the same teaching methods can be accounted for my differences in the quality of classroom interaction between teachers.

Similarly, Galton et al. (1999) found, building on an earlier study (Galton et al., 1998), that since the introduction of the National Curriculum there has been an increase of whole class teaching and that the majority of questions used by teachers were either closed or factual. The Observational Research and Classroom Learning Evaluation (ORACLE) project, devised by Galton et al. (1980), classified teachers' questions in terms of their reactions to pupils' answers rather than the teachers' apparent intentions. Only if the teacher accepted more than one answer to the question would it be judged as 'open' rather than 'closed'. Such incidents, as in our study of the discourse of the NLS, were rare. Galton et al. (1999: 67) therefore conclude that 'Today's teachers devote even more of their time to telling pupils facts and ideas or to giving directions than their counterparts of twenty years ago'. Given the even greater emphasis on directive forms of teaching in the literacy hour, opportunities for pupils to question or explore ideas may be even lower than those found in the ORACLE project. This hypothesis is in need of further investigation given the advocacy for whole class teaching during the literacy hour.

Such an emphasis on directive forms of teaching in the NLS goes against the widely accepted social constructivist theory of learning (eg. Driver, 1983; Bennett, 1992; Harlen, 1992; Barnes and Todd, 1995) and recent government initiatives to promote 'Thinking Skills' in schools (McGuinness, 1999). Research into the constructivist function of dialogue and learning suggests that classroom discourse is not effective unless pupils play an active part in their learning. This view of learning suggests that our most important learning does not take place through the addition of discrete facts to an existing store of knowledge, but that we relate new information, new experiences, new ways of understanding to our existing understanding of the matter in hand. One of the most important ways of working on this understanding is through talk, particularly where pupils are given the opportunity to assume greater control over their own learning by initiating ideas and responses which consequently promote articulate thinking. Research (eg. Barnes and Todd, 1995) suggests that if the pupil is allowed to contribute to the shaping of the verbal agenda in this way, the discourse is more effective in developing the pupil's own cognitive framework.

According to this widely accepted view of learning, such an approach should allow for alternative frames of reference which are open to negotiation and where the criteria of relevance are not imposed. It therefore questions the value of the linguistic and cognitive demands made on pupils within the traditional teacher-led recitation format, as demonstrated in the present study, where the pupils are mainly expected to be passive and to recall, when asked, what they have learned and to report other people's thinking. The social constructivist view of learning therefore suggests pupils' linguistic and cognitive development may benefit from wider communicative options. There is also strong research support (eg. Slaving, 1986; Johnson and Johnson, 1990; Bennett and Dunne, 1992; Galton and Williamson, 1992) for the view that such collaborative forms of discourse can produce significant gains in learning because pupils are led to talk about their understanding in their own ways which is an important aid to increasing knowledge and improving understanding.

Alternative Discourse Strategies

Research into classroom discourse and thinking skills (McGuinness, 1999) suggests the need for the exploration and evaluation of alternative teaching and learning strategies. These are designed to help to raise the quality of teachers' interactions with their pupils, and which will promote wider communicative (and hence more cognitively demanding) options to those in which pupils are often mere listeners or respondents. Considerable evaluation work needs to be completed linking the thinking skills approaches to learning outcomes for both individual and whole class learning. Much of the emphasis in the NLS training materials has been on subject knowledge and content in the curriculum rather than on pedagogy so that teaching styles have only been superficially addressed.

To improve the quality of teachers' interactions with their pupils, Nystrand et al. (1997) advocate that teachers pay more attention to the way in which they evaluate pupil responses so that there is more 'high-level evaluation' whereby teachers incorporate pupils' answers into subsequent questions. In this process, which they term *uptake*, they suggest that teachers' questions should be shaped by what immediately precedes them so that they are genuine questions. This is in contrast to recitation where there is usually a prepared list of *test* questions with prespecified answers from a list of 'essential' information against which a pupil's knowledge can be checked. Through this process teachers can engage pupils in a probing and extended discussion in which they signal to them their interest in what they think and not just whether they know and can report what someone else thinks or has said. Therefore when high level evaluation occurs, the teacher ratifies the importance of a pupil's response and allows it to modify or affect the course of the discussion in some way, weaving it into the fabric of an unfolding exchange. They therefore chain together teacher questions and pupil responses so that the discourse gradually takes on a conversation-like quality with teacher and pupils taking turns in speaking, thereby encouraging more pupil-initiated ideas, questions and responses and consequently promoting higher-order thinking.

Similarly Dillon (1994) and Wood (1992) suggest that the balance of control needs to be shifted in the pupils' direction, the achievement of which demands teachers paying attention to their use of questions and alternative conversational tactics to recitation. Their alternative discourse strategies involve 'low control' moves from teachers whereby instead of asking frequent questions they give their own thought and ideas in the form of statements in which they speculate, surmise, interpret, illustrate, or simply listen and acknowledge what pupils have to say. These alternatives to teacher questions which include telling, suggesting, negotiating and listening are designed to free pupils to give their own views, to reveal their knowledge and areas of uncertainty, and to seek information and explanation through questions of their own. Once the pupils have helped to shape the verbal agenda, teacher questions are more likely to involve a genuine attempt to explore their knowledge and to promote 'real' discussion. Here there would be an exploration of a topic, an interchange of ideas and questioning by pupils, with pupils and the teacher following up on each other's statements.

Teachers' Professional Development

The evidence of powerful continuities in teacher-pupil discourse discussed above supports Leat's (1999) view that curriculum innovations like the NLS are probably a weaker influence than factors specific to the teacher, the classroom, the institution and the professional culture. Leat goes on to argue that if curriculum innovations are to be successful much greater attention needs to be paid to the researching of teacher development. A new curriculum, as in the NLS, offered from 'above', even though its ideals may be applauded by teachers (Dadds, 1999), will not easily replace an existing curriculum. Research into teachers' professional development and teaching style (eg. Joyce and Showers, 1995; Tharp and Gallimore, 1988; Galton et al., 1999) suggests there is a process of adaptation which leaves old teaching styles and patterns of interaction largely untouched. Such studies suggest that teachers are slow to change their ways of teaching and new teaching methods or innovations are not readily taken on. What Joyce and Shower call the 'hybridisation' phenomenon could help to explain why many promising innovations have been judged to have failed, when it is probably nearer the truth to say that they were never effectively implemented.

Hargreaves (1992, p.ix) puts the need to consider teacher development into sharp focus:

> ... we have come to realise in recent years that the teacher is the ultimate key to educational change and school improvement. The restructuring of schools, the composition of national and provincial curricula, the development of bench-mark assessment - all these are of little value if they do not take the teacher into account. Teachers don't merely deliver the curriculum. They develop it, refine it and interpret it too.

In order to bring about changes in the way teachers interact with their pupils, Leat (1999) suggests the need for monitoring and self-evaluation to become a regular part of in-service training, thereby giving teachers a degree of ownership of the process of school improvement. Dillon (1994) suggests that coaching and talk-analysis feedback may be useful tools for professional development whereby sympathetic discussion by groups of teachers of data (recordings and transcriptions) derived from their own classrooms could be an effective starting point. Similarly, Tharp and Gallimore (1988: 191) suggest that because innovation and change always cost time, anxiety and uncertainty, it is essential that teachers have supportive interactions with peers through modelling and feedback if the 'recitation script' is to be changed to 'new repertoires of complex social behaviour necessary for responsive teaching'.

Next Step: Putting the Horse Before the Cart?

In his speech to the ESRC conference, David Blunkett concluded 'we need research of the highest quality ... which evaluates policy initiatives and systematically reviews existing evidence'. The question remains: what form should this research take and how should policy-makers make use of the research evidence to inform future curricula initiatives?

Fitz-Gibbon (1996) calls for more large-scale experimental and longitudinal research in education similar to controlled experiments in medical research. As a model of good practice, she discusses the example of a controlled research study in education which took place in the 1970s in the United States of America examining the effects of nursery education (Lazar, 1977). Randomly controlled field trials were set up to test the hypothesis that the provision of nursery education to severely deprived pre-schoolers would yield important benefits later in a child's life. The hypothesis was supported. The evidence from the study suggested that *deprived* pre-school children at least need to be given nursery education. However, this raised the question: would every child benefit? Given that there were limited resources, the policy issue became one of 'for what proportion of the population should nursery school be provided'. This led to a series of longitudinal experiments being carried out, premised on the policy that those most in need should receive the service. However, it was acknowledged that the cut-off point for 'most in need' was never going to be precise and could only be assessed with difficulty. There was inevitably going to be a borderline group about whom there would be debate because their level of need could not be precisely assessed. It was decided, therefore, that the only ethical way to assign children who were in the borderline group was by random assignment. Consequently, the borderline group was then randomly assigned to make a 'treatment' group and a control group so as to evaluate the nursery school policy and decide which kind of children would benefit the most. Fitz-Gibbon argues that the borderline control group design could be more extensively used to evaluate many educational policy initiatives such as: the placement of children in special needs classes; the development of classes for mentally gifted students; the provision of vocational courses as an alternative for some students. Had the NLS been evaluated in this way, for example, we would have much better information on how effective the NLS is with children of different levels of ability, including those with special educational needs.

If, as has been argued in this chapter, the character and quality of teacher-pupil interaction are pivotal to learning, then detailed exploration of classroom processes using qualitative methods alongside quantitative processes focusing on pupil outcomes is also needed. The focus on curriculum content, teaching objectives, lesson structure assessment in the NLS seems to have pushed pedagogy further into the background of teachers' professional concerns. The teaching of literacy in the NLS may not change substantially until pedagogy recovers its central position within teachers' professional thinking. Product-process research will play a crucial part in assessing the impact of educational policy initiatives. Without it, assertions about the impact of particular ways of teaching on what and how children learn will tend to be based on the kind of circumstantial evidence of the kind currently being used to support the NLS. We also need to know more about teacher development and how beliefs and attitudes impact on classroom practice. The evidence of powerful continuities in teacher-pupil discourse discussed above tends to support the view that initiatives like the NLS are probably a weaker influence than factors specific to the teacher, the classroom and the professional culture. Qualitative research will give us greater insights into these areas of concern, particularly in studying innovation and change at an individual and institutional level.

References

Alexander, R., Willcocks, J. and Nelson, N. (1995) Discourse, pedagogy and the National Curriculum: change and continuity in primary schools, *Research Papers in Education*, 11, 1, pp.81-120.
Barnes, D. and Todd, F. (1995) *Communication and Learning Revisited: Making Meaning Through Talk*, Portsmouth, NH, Heinemann.
Beard, R. (1999) *National Literacy Strategy: Review of Research and other Related Evidence*, London, DfEE.
Bennett, N. (1992) *Managing Learning in the Primary School*, Chester, Trentham Books.
Bennett, N. and Dunne, E. (1992) *Managing Classroom Groups*, Hemel Hempstead, Simon and Schuster.
Brooks, G., Pugh, A.K. and Schaghen, I. (1996) *Reading Performance at Nine*, Slough, National Foundation for Educational Research.
Clay, M.M. (1993) *Reading Recovery: A guidebook for teachers in training*, Auckland, New Zealand, Heinemann Education.
Crevola, C.A. and Hill, P.W. (1998) Evaluation of a Whole-School Approach to Prevention and Intervention, *Early Literacy Journal of Education for Students Placed At Risk*, 3, 2, pp.133-157.
Dadds, M. (1999) Teachers' Values and the Literacy Hour, *Cambridge Journal of Education*, 29, pp.7-18.

DfEE (1997) *The Implementation of the National Literacy Strategy*, London, Department for Education and Employment.
DfEE (1998) *The National Literacy Strategy: A Framework for Teaching*, London, Department for Education and Employment.
Dillon, J.T. (1994) *Using Discussion in Classrooms*, Milton Keynes, Open University Press.
Driver, R. (1983) *The Pupils as Scientist*, Milton Keynes, Open University Press.
Edwards, D. and Mercer, N. (1987) *Common Knowledge: The Development of Understanding in the Classroom*, London, Methuen.
Edwards, A.D. and Westgate, D.P.G. (1994) (2nd ed) *Investigating Classroom Talk*, London, The Falmer Press.
Fitz-Gibbon, C.T. (1996) Monitoring Education: Indicators, Quality and Effectiveness, London, Cassell.
French, P. and Maclure, M. (1979) Getting the right answer and getting the answer right, *Research in Education*, 22, pp.1-23.
French, P. and Maclure, M. (1981) (eds) *Adult-Child Conversation*, London, Croom Helm.
Galton, M., Hargreaves, L., Comber, C., Wall, D. and Pell, A. (1999) *Inside the Primary Classroom: 20 Years On*, London, Routledge.
Galton, M., Simon, B. and Croll, P. (1980) *Inside the Primary Classroom*, London, Routledge.
Galton, M. and Williamson, J. (1992) *Group Work in the Primary Classroom*, London, Routledge and Kegan Paul.
Hardman, F. and Williamson, J. (1988) The Discourse of Post-16 English Teaching, *Educational Review*, 50, 1, pp.5-14.
Hargreaves, A. (1992) Foreword, in Hargreaves, A. and Fullan, M. (eds) *Understanding Teacher Development*, London, Cassell.
Harlen, W. (1992) *The Teaching of Science*, London, David Fulton.
Hestenes, D. (1998) Who needs physics education research? *American Journal of Physics*, 66, 6, pp.465-467.
Johnson, D.W. and Johnson, R.T. (1990) Co-operative learning and achievement in Sharan, S. (ed) *Co-operative Learning: theory and research*, New York, Praeger.
Joyce, B. and Showers, B. (1995) *Student Achievement Through Staff Development*: Fundamentals of Schooling Renewal (2E), New York, Longman.

Lazar, I. (1977) The Consortium on Developmental, Education Commission of the States, *The Persistence of Pre-school Effects*, Washington, DC, US Department of Health, Education and Welfare.

Leat, D. (1999) Rolling the Stone Uphill: teacher development and the implementation of Thinking Skills programmes, *Oxford Review of Education*, 25, 3, pp.387-403.

McGuinness, C. (1999) *From Thinking Skills to Thinking Classrooms: a review and evaluation of approaches for developing pupils' thinking*, London, Department for Education and Employment.

Mehan, N. (1979) *Learning Lessons*, Cambridge, Mass., Harvard University Press.

Mercer, N. (1992) Talk for Teaching and learning in Norman, K. (ed) *Thinking Voices: The work of the National Oracy Project*, London, Hodder and Stoughton.

Mroz, M., Smith, F. and Hardman, F. (2000) The Discourse of the Literacy Hour, *Cambridge Journal of Education*, 30, 3 (forthcoming).

Nystrand, M., Gamoran, A., Kachur, R., and Prendergast, C. (1997) *Opening Dialogue: understanding the Dynamics of language and learning in the English classroom*, New York, Teachers College, Columbia University.

OFSTED (1998) *The National Literacy Project*, London, Office for Standards in Education.

Reynolds, D. (1998) Schooling for Literacy: a review of research on teacher effectiveness and school effectiveness and its implications for contemporary educational policies, *Educational Review*, 50, 2, pp.147-162.

Reynolds, D. and Farrell, S. (1996) *Worlds Apart? - a review of international studies of educational achievement involving England*, London, HMSO for OFSTED.

Sainsbury, M. (1998) *Evaluation of the National Literacy Project*, London, National Foundation for Educational Research.

Sinclair, J. and Coulthard, M. (1992) Towards an Analysis of Discourse, in Coulthard, M. (ed) *Advances in Spoken Discourse Analysis*, London, Routledge.

Slavin, R.E. (1986) Small Group Methods, in Dunkin, M. (ed) *The International Encyclopedia of Teaching and Teacher Education*, London, Pergamon.

Slavin, R.E. (1996) *Education for All*, Lisse, Swets and Zeitlinger.

Smith, F. and Hardman, F. (2000) Evaluating the effectiveness of the National Literacy Strategy: identifying indicators of success, *Educational Studies*, 26, **3** (forthcoming).

Tharp, R.G. and Gallimore, R. (1988) *Rousing minds to life: Teaching, learning, and schooling in social context*, Cambridge, Cambridge University Press.

Wells, G. (1993) Re-evaluating the IRF Sequence: A Proposal for the Articulation of Theories of Activity and Discourse for the Analysis of Teaching and Learning in the Classroom, *Linguistics and Education*, 5, pp.1-37.

Wood, D. (1992) Teaching Talk, in Norman, K. (ed) *Thinking Voices: The Work of the National Oracy Project*, London, Hodder and Stoughton.

10 National Curriculum Subjects are Repositories of Values that are Under-Explored
BOB BUTROYD

Introduction

The debate over values is a fashionable one. Hardly a week goes by without reference to values, normally in the context of morality and a perceived decline. For schools, this is a particularly difficult area. Schools are accountable now in a very public way. Schools are expected to respond to the concerns expressed by various individuals and organisations within society, and yet if they do they are aware that they are open to charges of moral relativism, political correctness and indoctrination in equal measure. What options do teachers have in terms of values? What opportunities are presented to them in their work? What do teachers themselves feel are values that are worth pursuing? This chapter looks at the values of a small number of teachers in secondary schools, and explores their values concerns in the light of recent curriculum developments.

It argues that a failure to recognise the values of the subject is not only a missed opportunity to engage pupils in the day to day experiences of the classroom, but it also fails to recognise the expertise and motivation of their teachers.

The Qualifications and Curriculum Authority (QCA, 1997), produced guidance for schools in the area of values development which considered the contribution of subject teaching in secondary schools and colleges. The QCA argued that:

> Spiritual development requires a supportive and challenging environment. This requires teachers to consider not only the types of experiences and activities which need to be provided for the pupils but also the underlying ethos of the learning situation. This includes the teacher's own values and attitudes.

The proposal for teachers to review their own role in teaching and learning was an encouraging pointer for those who consider that the subject teacher is a major influence on young people. However, since this publication there has been little reference to this important process in subsequent guidance or consultation material on PSHE and citizenship. This is an important oversight, as the subsequent research demonstrates.

The Context of Teachers' Work

1986 saw the DES (DES, 1986) publish criteria for a number of GCSEs. These publications defined the subjects' field of study, limited the number of legitimate fields, and in so doing reduced the teachers' control of the curriculum. Since this time schools have witnessed the introduction of a more centralised, state sponsored, educational environment.

In 1988, a National Curriculum for England and Wales, was introduced by the Education Reform Act (ERA). This Act introduced nine National Curriculum subjects for youngsters from five-14, with the addition of RE and, at 14, Modern Foreign Languages. This curriculum was subsequently updated in September 2000. ERAs intention was to determine subject matter and assessment for the school curriculum for all state educated pupils between the ages of five and 16.

In addition to standardising curriculum content, and testing in the state sector, ERA also introduced Local Management of Schools (LMS), which largely depended upon formula funding. This formula tied a minimum of 80% of school funding to pupil numbers; in many local authorities it was well over 90%.

LMS was an important innovation because the funding of schools was directly linked to the number of pupils on the school roll. An increase in the number of pupils led to an increase in funding, and a decline in pupil numbers to a decline in funding. However, changes in pupil numbers were to be agreed first by the Secretary of State. The Key Stage tests were to provide important information for the Secretary of State when making decisions about the expansion, contraction or closure of schools. To guide parents in their school choice, schools had to provide parents and local authorities with the performance indicators demanded by the 1988 Education Act. The school, and the teacher, were to be judged by outcomes. These outcomes determine the content of what is to be taught. Is this content likely to inspire and excite teachers in the same way that content largely determined by teachers would?

The use of performance indicators was one way to control teachers. Another major initiative was that of appraisal. The 1986 Education (No.2) Act, along with Statutory Instrument 1991/1511, introduced teacher appraisal in all maintained schools on a phased basis from 1992. Teacher associations welcomed the developmental aspects of appraisal and saw it as separate from procedures relating to pay and conditions. However, the law made reference to taking account of appraisal for purposes of promotion, dismissal and pay (DES, 1991). This difference of view between those responsible for the introduction of appraisal, and those responsible for its operation lead to a situation where appraisal had been 'ticked into touch' (Ward and Meikle, 1993). However, subsequent developments (DfEE, 1999) have seen the introduction of further 'performance related pay' schemes.

In addition to imposing an 'input-output' model of inspection, the inspection process attempted to address the question of teaching quality: Can this person teach? How well do they teach? At the same time contextual questions were asked about those factors which promoted 'good', 'satisfactory' or 'poor' teaching. The cumulative effect of these initiatives was to distance the curriculum, assessment and organisation of schooling from the influence of teachers.

Increased government control of the curriculum, pedagogy, monitoring procedures and school organisation, raised questions as to the nature of the school as an independent site, where ideological domination can be contested. The move from 'licensed autonomy', which Grace (1985), Lawn and Ozga (1986) and Ball (1988) argued started in the mid-1980s, with the removal of teachers negotiating rights, continued throughout the 1980s into a period of 'direct rule' in the 1990s.

In a period of reduced teacher autonomy what is it that sustains teachers in their work? Is 'success', as measured by the various performance indicators sufficient? Are they content to have decisions regarding the curriculum, assessment and pedagogy removed from them? How do they see that they can influence the school experience of youngsters in any significant way? Fieldwork, carried out during the 1996-7 academic year explored these issues.

The Focus of the Research

The research was designed to identify and explore the impact of motivational influences, values and practice on the secondary school teacher. Goodson's (1992) promotion of the 'teacher's voice' offered insight into the world of the teacher by assuming that the teacher was a complete human being, with emotions, friends, family and a life that wasn't completely bound and defined by school. Goodson (1992) also refers to the 'fundamental lie'.

> Curriculum as prescription supports the mystique that expertise and control reside within central governments, educational bureaucracies or the university community ... To continue to exist, teachers day to day power must remain unspoken and unrecorded. This is one price of complicity: day to day power and autonomy for schools and for teachers are dependent on continuing to accept the fundamental lie.

To unearth the 'unspoken and unrecorded' power of the autonomous teacher the research had to be grounded in the teachers accounts of their experiences and practices.

The Sample

The research in recognising the reduction in teacher autonomy looked for a sample that would reflect an experience and gender balance. If the mid to late 1980s was a period significant period of transition for teachers, then the time prior to this would represent a time of teacher autonomy. It was likely that teachers between the ages of 45 and 55 would have a number of years experience of teaching in this decade. This was sample 'A'.

Sample 'B', in the age range of 29-39 years would consist of teachers whose schooling would have taken place during this period of autonomy, but whose major years of experience would have been during the period of greater 'direct rule'.

Another reason for two age related samples was to accommodate Huberman (1992) who appeals for research to be completed on the influence of beliefs on the teacher's career cycle.

The intended balances were broadly maintained, although the practical release of teachers from cover, and their selection by the head, or deputy head teacher did influence the samples. Ten teachers were male, and nine female, whilst Figure 10.1 also illustrates the teachers main subject responsibility. Ten teachers were interviewed in Southside and nine in Northside Comprehensives. The names of the schools and the names of the teachers were changed to preserve anonymity that made this research possible.

Figure 10.1   The Sample

Southside	Northside
Sample A (44-55)	**Sample A (44-55)**
Louise - Language support	David - Science
Mark - Geography	Susan - Science
Eric - Art	Irene - Modern languages
Nancy - Maths	Terry - English
Anne - Modern languages	Jane - Modern languages
Sample B (29-39)	**Sample B (29-39)**
Pam - English	Nigel - PE
Frank - Science	Gerry - RE
Barbara - Modern languages	Ken - Technology
Colin - Maths	Helen - English
Ron - English	

The two schools were chosen on the basis that they were both fairly typical of any comprehensive school to be found in a northern industrial town. Southside was an 11-16 coeducational school with 173 pupils aged 15 in January 1995, with 32% of pupils achieving five or more grades A-C. Northside was an 11-16 coeducational school with 235 pupils aged 15 on January 1995, with 58% of pupils achieving five or more grades A-C.

The Interviews

The intention of the semi-structured interviews was to explore the complete person, not simply the teacher. The open nature of the questions meant that the interview would be able to pursue those influences, or motivations that the teacher considered to be important. The interviews lasted between 40 minutes and one hour, and took place on the school premises. In both schools cover was provided in order to allow uninterrupted interviewing. The holding of the interviews on the school premises may have influenced the findings. As we shall see later, the responses of the interviewees did not encompass the breadth of experience and influences that Goodson's 'teacher's voice' would suggest.

The Questions

There were seven questions that were asked of both samples in order to elicit information about formative influences, present attitudes and the nature of the lessons that they enjoyed. This word 'enjoyment' was used in order to ground any exploration of values in the practice of the teacher. Then, the samples were asked questions which focused on the loss of autonomy. For the more experienced group the questions focused upon their teaching, and for the younger group it focused upon their experiences as pupils. The use of words such as 'good', 'enjoyment', 'favourite' were deliberately used in order to encourage the interviewees to make decisions about those things that they 'cared about, or considered important' (Haydon, 1997).

The word 'values' was deliberately avoided in the Southside interviews, and until the last question in the Northside interviews for two reasons. Firstly, the research did not want to provoke Goodson's 'fundamental lie' by eliciting a response from the teacher that they would feel that a university researcher would wish to hear. Secondly, the word was being used at the time in a very specific context: moral values. The debate over the Bulger and Lawrence murders was still current in the press. I used values in Haydon's much broader sense because this definition addressed the difficulties associated with the idealisation of values, where 'they may have a higher dignity (morally and spiritually), but they are not real, and thus count less in the real business of life' (Marcuse, 1972).

Considering what people care about, or consider important, grounds the concept of values in the life, work and experiences of teachers. Marcuse suggests that if values are idealised then they may in fact have little impact upon the established way of life. This meant that the schedule (Figure 10.2) looked beneath what the teacher subscribed to in the interests of cohesion, or wishing to 'please' the researcher, to explore their intentions, pleasures, influences and practices.

The interview schedule for Southside was focused upon the teachers' practice and experiences. The purpose of this was to unearth values embedded here that could be further explored, particularly during the question beginning 'Earlier you said that ...'.

The interview schedule at Northside was modified in the light of the Southside interviews. The modifications to the interview schedule provided opportunities for greater articulation of values. The additional questions gave the opportunity for greater elaboration of whole school issues, and a direct question about the values 'that were important', which was asked towards the end of the interview at Northside, could be placed in the context of the teachers earlier comments about practice and the values that were embedded in them.

The result was richer data with regard to the values emerging from the Northside interviews. Although there were differences in the values held by the informants in the two schools the research was not designed to be a comparative study.

The Analysis

The research and analysis was both iterative, particularly with regard to the return to issues raised earlier in the interviews, and the inclusion of an overt question on values towards the end of the interviews at Northside; and discursive, in that premises and conclusions were revisited and modified in the light of further research analysis and reading. The research was exploring a complex and tangled and the mapping exercise was not, and could not exhaustively identify all the values held by the teachers. What it did was to identify a number of issues about values that were worthy of further exploration.

The reading of the transcripts identified a range of values that were difficult to form into patterns. This was partly due to the method of research. The semi-structured nature of the interviews, and the different schedules, with the different samples, made comparison difficult and possibly invalid. However, the researcher was attempting to dig beneath the surface appearances, to try to explore the deeper motivations of teachers.

This was, potentially, a very intrusive process, and had to be handled delicately. The interviews were designed to be explorative, not definitive.

Figure 10.2 The Interview Schedule

Interview Schedule for Southside
1. Have you always been a teacher? How long have you been teaching here?
2. Which subjects were you trained for? What are you teaching now? How do you feel about that?
3. Can you describe to me a lesson that you have recently enjoyed?
4. What do you enjoy about teaching?
5. What are the major influences on you?
6. Earlier you said that ...
7. Do other teachers share your views?

Sample 'A' only
8. When you first started teaching what was it like to teach then?
9. When you look back, are there any good things about the way things were done then that you miss?
10. Are there any things that you do now that you would rather not do?
11. Earlier you said that ...
12. Do other teachers share your views?

Sample 'B' only
8. Did you enjoy your time at school?
9. What were your favourite lessons at school?
10. Who were your favourite teachers?
11. Are other teachers different now to when you were at school?
12. Are you different now to how teachers were when you were at school?
13. Did other pupils share your views?
14. Earlier you said that ...

Additional Questions for Northside
Do other people take an interest in what you do? Do they really understand what you do?
How would you measure success as a teacher?
What should schools aim to teach pupils? Have your views changed at all?
What sort of interests do you have out of school? What do you find attractive about these?
What sort of people do you admire? Do any of these things affect the way that you work?
What values do you consider to be most important to you?

It was important that I did not 'see' in the data themes that were incapable of verification. Inductive coding (Altrichter, Posch and Somekh, 1993) was used as a method of allowing the values to emerge from the data. Inference was part of the analysis; inference based upon relatively unambiguous data, but also upon culturally shared meanings. Through reading and re-reading (Miles and Huberman, 1984) the reconsideration, verification or rejection of the developing values, took place. But it was still proving difficult to code the data, despite the eventual use of NUDIST (QSR Nudist, 1999), a software package for qualitative data analysis. A certain amount of categorisation of values did take place, but I was still left with a large number of apparently disparate values: how to make sense of them?

It was late in 1998 that I became aware of the QCA (1997) statements of values. Here was a conceptual structure that claimed to represent a consensus of the values that were important in society. How well did teachers reflect this consensus? I compared the values that I had identified with the criteria underlying the statements of values. The results, in large part verified the findings of the QCA (Figure 10.3), except for one important omission, the teacher's care for, or considered importance of, their subject. These were expressed specifically as 'a love of subject', or, more obliquely as 'academic achievement'. This raised the key question of whether the curriculum arrangements, particular those pertaining to the National Curriculum, and GCSE allowed the pursuit of this love of subject, or whether they constrained values exploration through the subject.

This overcame some of the problems of verification, because subject related values were expressed in samples 'A' and 'B' in both schools. There was sufficient 'triangulation' across sites, and samples to justify further analysis of the issues emerging from a consideration of subject values.

The Importance of Subject in the Development of Values

The data confirms that there was a good deal of general agreement about the types of values that schools should address, and David, a Science teacher, as well as a deputy head described some of them:

Figure 10.3 Research Values and the QCA Statement of Values

	T	Southside										Northside								
		Louise Lang S	Mark Geog	Eric Art	Nancy Maths	Anne Mod.L	Pam Eng	Frank Scie	Barb Mod.L	Colin Maths	Ron Eng	David Scie	Susan Scie	Irene Mod.L	Terry Eng	Jane Mod.L	Nigel PE	Gerry RE	Ken Tech	Helen Eng
Societal Values																				
Equal Opportunities/Fairness	8	*				*							*	*			*	*		
Pupil acceptance of events	2		*		*												*			
Deterrence	2									*						*				
Family values	1																*			
Self																				
Moral codes	6											*	*			*	*	*		*
Religion	5					*											*	*		*
Honesty/Truth	4								*			*		*				*	*	
Strong beliefs	4											*		*			*	*		*
Self discipline	3		*															*		*
Knowledge, skill, courage	1																	*		
Contemplation	1										*									
Relationships																				
Respect	9			*	*						*	*	*	*	*	*	*	*	*	
Co-operation with others	7							*			*	*	*	*	*			*		
Care and consideration	5						*					*			*		*	*		
Personal/social relationships	5			*								*				*	*		*	
Gratitude	2											*	*			*				
Trust	2													*				*		
Tolerance	2																	*		
Humanity	1					*														
Environment																				
Environmental Education	1		*																	
Educational Values																				
Love of subject	10			*	*		*	*					*	*			*	*	*	*
Academic achievement	6			*	*					*	*				*		*			

T = total number of teachers

Often there are a lot of things that you have to do that are just as important as the delivery of the subject, and they are not always as overt, they are just a slow steady process and just as effective ... Pupils have to see a point. It has to be developing the potential of the pupils, as fully as you can, and it has to be rounded off, by making them realise their place in the social world that they are going to live. That means that they have to realise the moral codes, and the other things that go along with taking a part in society when they leave us. You try to turn them out, as far as you can, as well balanced, well rounded individuals, with the best possible chance, so that they can take some control over their lives when they leave you, and they are not at the beck and call of things around them, but that they can make their own choices as to where they go. We have to give them as much as we can: the skills, the knowledge, the feeling for what society is all about.

David talks of the delivery of the subject in a way that suggests that it is separated from the central issues of 'finding their place in the social world'. There is the suggestion that 'moral codes' and 'taking part in society' are somehow estranged from subject study. The suggestion that the study of Science does not help pupils to have 'some control over their lives' raises questions as to the nature of a core subject that does not deal with these issues.

David described 'whole pupil' development as developing pupil potential, their place in the social world, and moral codes. Few teachers in the sample would have difficulty with these values as aims. However moving from a general statement like this to implementation does raise difficulties, as putting values into practice is dependent upon the context, and the context within secondary schools generally concerns a subject context. The potential danger of a context free identification of values is that a 'matrix' or managerial approach to values may result. This normally involves some form of audit that may fail to reveal the true nature of values exploration within the classroom.

To understand values exploration within subject matter would require an understanding of the subject matter and its preferred pedagogy. It is the link between subject matter, pedagogy and their attendant values that this paper investigates.

Love of subject came through strongly in ten of the interviews, and academic achievement in six of them. Taken together 14 of the 19 interviewees expressed a concern for subject related values. It could be argued that these values represent aspects of the search for truth, fairness, tolerance and other values to be found in the QCA value statements. However, this paper argues that as a focus for action subject values require greater recognition than the QCA presently gives them.

Subject Study and Pedagogy as a Source of Values

This section examines a small number of values that find a home within the QCA classification in order to illustrate the subject specific nature of their application. The first quote in the following extracts confirms the teachers' subject focus and the second quote raises some of the values which are present during, or a consequence of subject study.

Moral Codes, Self-Confidence, Co-operation and Respect

Susan, Biology

> I've always liked the subject that I was teaching and wanted other people to get the same sort of feel about it that I did ... I've always liked my subject and if I stopped teaching now I would still, wherever I went, collect things, build up certain collections.
> **What should schools aim to teach pupils?** Not only academic subjects, but also you are equipping them when they leave school at 16 to be safe out there, not to be worried about their own sexuality, to know the differences between right and wrong.

Frank, Physics

> I sometimes ask myself what would have happened if I had got myself a 2:1 and tried to do a PhD? But at the time when I was doing my Physics degree I had had enough Physics. Now it seems like a good idea, probably because I have had enough teaching.
> **Can you describe a lesson that you have recently enjoyed?** It was a Year 8 class, outside, to measure the speed of sound ... I'd only expected two people to do the timing, but we had five people with their own stop watches, and we ended up with seven times to write down. And I thought, 'they're taking an interest'. I felt good about that. I didn't enjoy certain aspects of it because there were a few lads who were messing about. That was a down side.

These two Science teachers, with different teaching experience and expertise, possess different pedagogical priorities. Susan was a Biology teacher of 25 years experience, and for her the development of pupils' self confidence in their own sexuality, and a sense of right and wrong were important parts of her teaching. However, for Frank, a Physics teacher of three years experience, co-operative behaviour from pupils, which led to their involvement in his lesson were more important.

Respect is considered to be a 'good' thing. However, different teachers have different interpretations of the word. This is, in part, shaped by the different aims of the subject and the different pedagogies. Within his subject of PE Nigel illustrates the link between co-operation and respect.

> Have I taken anything from the teachers that taught me? The answer is, yes I have: the idea that you can have an enthusiastic person and you like your subject, that comes across. So, no I'm not different, because I like my subject.
> **How would you measure success as a teacher?** Different in different situations. I would like to be able to walk into a changing room and ask kids to be quiet; that was a certain amount of success, because the kids have got enough respect to actually listen to what you have to say.

As a PE teacher Nigel makes a clear link between co-operation and respect, which in this case means the pupils doing what the teacher asks them to do. Irene, a modern languages teacher, also links co-operation with respect. Respect is considered here to be a matter of pupils going along with her plans of how the subject should be taught.

> **What is it that you enjoy about teaching?** If the situation is right I enjoy putting over my enthusiasm for my subjects and getting feedback on that.
> **How would you measure success as a teacher?** Pupils co-operating, and performing tasks that I put to them, and basically fitting in with my plans, how I see it. If that then comes through and they manage to have a go at what I ask them to do ... whether it is written, or speaking or listening ...

These different interpretations of respect rely upon pupil conformity. In an era of league tables linked to funding, the pressure to conform to the demands of published examination results leads teachers to require behaviour from pupils that will facilitate the success in the examinations. Whereas Barbara, also a modern languages teacher, is rather more concerned that pupils are able to express their point of view.

> Partly enjoyment and learning about different cultures. Having had a leaning that way. Also through having links through friends in different countries.

In this instance Barbara welcomes the National Curriculum because it does encourage discussion and the expression of opinions.

> I think it is better that we, in the case of languages, are getting children to give their opinions about things.

Whilst Barbara feels that her subject encourages pupils to express their own opinions, in practice this may well involve listening to other pupils' opinions as well, although the process of formulating opinions of their own, to express in another language, may be demanding enough.

Gerry is an RE teacher, and he also enjoys a situation where pupils put forward their own views, and 'see other people's opinions'.

> I never really enjoyed RE at school to be honest. Yet teaching is a fantastic subject. Why? It's so open ended for a start.
> ... I enjoy the arguments, 'cos I'm having lots of arguments at the moment (with the pupils) because of the nature of what I teach. Getting them to think in different points of view, and to see other people's opinions.

In this case the classroom process involves pupils empathising with other points of view, which involves respecting the circumstances and reactions of others.

In the context of Modern Languages the demands of the syllabus require pupils to communication, as expression of opinions are important activities for subject practice. This would also be true of RE, whilst the focus of PE is upon a more physical manifestation of respect.

General agreement upon the need for respect in schools may be easy to reach. However, the development of respect in different subjects may lead to very different practices and outcomes. Respect takes different forms for different teachers. These different interpretations, heavily influenced by pedagogy and subject matter, are constructed by teachers in the context of their classroom work. Although teachers are able to influence experiences of values within their classroom, teachers are themselves operating within circumstances not entirely of their own making.

Words of Caution

These are words of caution for those considering the place of values in education. Teachers do not develop in isolation from their environment. There are factors impinging upon the work of the school, which shape and constrain values development.

It is clear that teachers do not teach in circumstances of their own choosing. Their control over the curriculum is much reduced. There are time constraints placed upon them as a result of government imposed change. So, teachers have to teach subject matter that they would perhaps not choose to teach. As we will see, this does have an effect upon the motivation of teachers, and the resultant values. As we shall see, Gerry in RE has more freedom than most, and is able to explore issues that he enjoys. However, Eric in Art is not able to fully explore the subject matter that he thinks appropriate for pupils, particularly as he is 'pushing, pushing, pushing' his pupils to complete work. Another teacher claims that the importance attached to exam success through league tables is a dominant influence upon the work that they do.

Nancy, Maths:

> I just enjoy being with them, and see their enjoyment of the subject.
> **How do you measure success?** You want them to pass exams at the end of it. That is how they are measured. Education is a big selection process isn't it?
> **Would you want it to be any different?** In the ideal world, yes. But it won't will it? Cynical me.

Nancy says that examinations shape the whole educational process, equating education with selection. The selection process that Nancy refers to requires that pupils and teachers accept the importance and validity of selection. Pupils and teachers are urged by legislation, the media, ambitious parents, concerned governors and school managers to take the examinations system seriously. Indeed, Nancy suggests that this is taken so seriously that exams, and the selection that flows from the, subsume any other purposes, or values, of the school. Teachers and pupils who reject, or who are rejected by, this selection process will face difficulties in 'fitting in' to the school ethos.

So far I have argued that teachers are concerned with the values which are central to their experiences with pupils, and that many of these revolve around success in their subject. This success is dependent upon teachers having the time to develop appropriate relationships, particularly in practical subjects.

Ken, DT:

> **What were your favourite lessons?** I think the subjects that I teach now really: the design technology, graphics, games, those sorts of practical areas really ...
> The best teachers in my eyes encouraged me, they helped me. Maybe they put a little germ inside of me that has taken me to this stage in my career now.
> **How do you think that they did that?** I think with the enjoyment of the subject that they actually had, the humour that they put into the subject as well to make it enjoyable.

Eric, an Art teacher, described a similar process whereby a teacher gets 'through' to a pupil, but time is not on the teachers' side.

> The thing that has kept me going in teaching is my own love of art. Not of teaching, but of art.

The distinction between 'Art' and 'teaching' is an interesting one. His love of subject of separate to his work as a teacher. It is his love of his subject that has kept him going. It must surely be disappointing to pupils, parents and the teacher himself that his love of his subject is understood to be separate from his teaching. Love of subject must sustain, motivate and satisfy a subject teacher. The transference of these values would be at the centre of any genuine transmission of values. Does teaching his National Curriculum subject prevent him from sharing his passion with his pupils?

> (If) they were getting something out of it I thought it was quite legitimate to make a project last for months ... whereas now I seem to be working in six week bursts, pushing, pushing, pushing.

The development of relationships of the kind that foster learning requires time, and yet, the current curriculum arrangements make such demands upon teacher time that it inhibits the development of effective teacher-pupil relationships.

Nancy, who we have already met considered that the situation is such that children can become an irritant, as there are so many other demands made upon a limited amount of time and energy.

> We are just getting so worn down by it, so much paper work to do, almost I think that your teaching becomes low on your list of priorities. The children become almost a nuisance.

Helen, a teacher of English for 14 years, argued that teachers are in danger of failing to establish professional autonomy, as the profession does not have the opportunities to develop the related values.

> You don't have the opportunity to talk in any depth. It's 'put the world to rights in five minutes'. I do feel that I have a chance to speak to people, but not in terms of if you are going to do anything with it. No, you don't get the chance to talk as much as you should. People are very preoccupied in school. That is a major issue. With all these itsy bitsy things that you have to do. Then you get to your classroom and teach, and you come away and do this and that. Social chat is as far as it goes in the staffroom, but to actually pool ideas together, no.

Helen wanted more time to talk to other teachers about issues of real importance so that they could pool ideas. However, she felt preoccupied with inconsequential matters that filled her working day, and reduced her contact with other teachers to 'social chat' that was more to do with therapy and letting off steam (not unimportant matters themselves).

Helen, who expressed a deep concern for those values that the QCA classify as 'the self', painted a picture of professional dialogue amongst teachers that lacks attention to purpose. Exploration of purpose is important to a serious review of the values of subject and pedagogy. Helen argued that teachers were not in a position to engage in serious professional dialogue, a prerequisite of the development of professional autonomy. The suggestion that teachers should make time for professional development will of course be taken seriously by many teachers in present circumstances but many others will struggle to find the time, energy and support that they need.

Conclusions

Teachers address those values which help them in a practical sense. If attention to values helps subject success then teachers will consider their implications more seriously. If they do not consider that values have a part to play in the subject then teachers will view them as an imposition on a curriculum with more important priorities, and a distraction from the subject teachers' central purpose.

There is a danger that in such circumstances there will be a managerial, audit approach to values which attempts to track values across the curriculum, probably with some sort of matrix. This would be a mistake, a it will not encourage teachers and pupils to reflect upon their values. It would be disingenuous to suggest that teachers should simply be left alone to identify, interpret and focus upon values in education. This is a recipe for not acting upon the motivation offered by values in education.

Recognition, interpretation and implementation of values in education requires that teachers are able to communicate and develop ideas amongst other practitioners. Teachers need the time, space and encouragement in which to do this. Values development cannot be taken seriously if values like professional autonomy are lost to teachers.

The absence of a QCA category with an educational focus questions the purpose of the promotion of values. The QCA assumes that their values will underpin educational practice. But a failure to recognise the central purpose of the teachers' role, as seen by classroom practitioners, suggests a failure to understand the nature of the educational experience. Values need contexts, meaningful contexts. These meaningful contexts exist within the school subjects. They are an area of concern to teachers, and yet they receive little attention from the QCA.

Many values are entwined with pedagogy, and yet values in England and Wales are in danger of becoming extensions, or enhancements of the curriculum. The values in the data derive from specific contexts, and the teachers view them as integral to their operation as teachers. They are expressed in a subject specific way, and relate to the pedagogy and epistemology of their subject specialism.

The QCA recognised the importance of teachers exploring their values, but more emphasis needs to be placed upon the values that are transmitted in the classroom through daily pedagogy. If it is accepted that values are heavily dependent upon context, then a managerial, matrix approach would be largely meaningless, and might even be destructive if the reality of the classroom contradicts espoused values. An initiative that recognises and supports the consideration of subject and pedagogical values is more likely to lead to a meaningful pupil and teacher review of values within society.

References

Altrichter, H., Posch, P. and Somekh, B. (1993) *Teachers Investigate Their Work: An introduction to the methods of action research*, London, Routledge.

Ball, S.J. (1988) Staff Relations During the Teachers' Industrial Action: context, conflict and proletarianisation, *British Journal of Sociology of Education*, Vol.9, No.3, pp.289-306.

DES (1986) *GCSE: The National Criteria, Economics*, HMSO.

DES (1991) *Statutory Instrument 1991/1511*, London, HMSO, 1991, para. 14.1.

DfEE (1999) *Teachers meeting the challenge of change: technical consultation document on pay and performance management*, London, DfEE.

Goodson, I.F. (1992) Sponsoring the Teachers' voice: Teachers' lives and Teacher Development, in Hargreaves, A. and Fullan, M.G. (eds) *Teacher Development and Educational Change*, London, Falmer Press, pp.110-122.

Grace, G. (1985) Judging Teachers: the social and political contexts of evaluation, *British Journal of Sociology of Education*.

Hargreaves, A. (1994) *Changing Teachers, Changing Times*, London, Cassell.

Haydon, G. (1997) *Teaching About Values: A new approach*, London, Cassell.

Huberman, M. (1992) Teacher Development and Instructional Mastery, in Hargreaves, A. and Fullan, M.G. (eds) *Understanding Teacher Development*, London, Cassell, pp.122-142.

Lawn, M. and Ozga, J. (1986) Unequal Partners: Teachers under indirect rule, *British Journal of Sociology of Education*, 7.

Marcuse, H. (1972) *One Dimensional Man*, London, Abacus, p.121-122.

Miles, M.B. and Huberman, A.M. (1984) *Qualitative Data Analysis*, Beverley Hills, London, Sage.

Peshkin, A. (1988) *In Search of Subjectivity - One's Own Educational Researcher*, October, pp.17-21.

QCA (1977) *The promotion of pupils' spiritual, moral, social and cultural development: the contribution of subject teaching in secondary schools and colleges*, London, p.4.

QSR NUDIST (1991) *Qualitative Data Analysis Software for Research Professionals*, Melbourne, Qualitative Solutions and Research PTY.

Ward, D. and Meikle, J. (1993) "Teacher Unions to tick Appraisal into touch", *The Guardian*, 14th April, p.2.

11 ICT in the National Curriculum - Revised but not Resolved

MATTHEW PEARSON

Introduction

It is almost universally accepted that pupils should be taught Information and Communications Technology and should leave education as confident users of computers and associated technologies. Through the medium of the Internet, computers are making an impact on society in ever more powerful ways, and the public consciousness is now pervaded with the importance of mastering these tools. Policymakers and advisors seek to find the most dramatic way of expressing the importance of embracing the information revolution, and stress the need for formal schooling to take this revolution into account.

Given this background, it is no surprise that ICT appears within the National Curriculum, and the constant upgrading of its status is a clear sign of that politicians and policy makers see master of the subject as one of the key features of a competitive modern economy. Lord Stevenson is quoted in sound-bite mode on the title page of the latest National Curriculum Teachers' Handbook:

> The modern world requires new skills. Understanding ICT and, more importantly, being able to apply it to the problems we face is one of the most important. Increasingly ICT will be vital for our individual prospects and for our economic future. (DfEE, QCA, 1999, p.143)

At the beginning of the 21st century the National Curriculum for ICT should be entering its most important phase, offering mandatory guidance to schools so that they are able to equip pupils with the skills and knowledge needed to use this technology, ensuring the quality of this provision with a focused set of statements about knowledge, skills and understanding, and measuring progress within the subject through the application of attainment targets.

In this chapter I would like to do two things. The first is to interrogate ICT as defined within the National Curriculum and examine the crucial ways in which this subject differs from other subjects, or whether it can properly be called a subject at all. A close reading of the National Curriculum and associated policy documents will reveal the ways in which the subject has been constructed, formulated into a curriculum specification, and then shipped out to schools for implementation. The second is to compare the idealised world of the Curriculum orders with some of the real world challenges faced by pupils, teachers and schools as they attempt to perform the 'transformation skills' so wished for the by the statutory authorities.

ICT - Subject or Skill?

ICT is a new subject. Subjects such as Mathematics, English and History have been part of curriculum provision for a long time and have thus been the subject of longstanding debate. The social and cultural history of these mature subjects works to guarantee their place within the curriculum. One of the stated purposes of the National Curriculum is 'to promote public understanding', and 'provide a common basis for discussion of educational issues among lay and professional groups, including pupils, parents, teachers, governors and employers' (DfEE, 1999b). This common basis for discussion existed in traditional subjects before the National Curriculum. Almost all stakeholders in the formal schooling process have an idea of what a Mathematics or English curriculum should look like, no doubt based in part upon their own experiences of being taught these subjects at school. Although the National Curriculum has certainly not stabilised these subjects or prevented disputes about the definition of the subjects from breaking out, policy makers constructing the curriculum for these subjects had somewhere to start, and some rules of thumb with which to kick-start their formulations. Information and Communications Technology does not have this heritage, and the newness of the subject has prevented formulations which draw upon existing teaching and learning practices.

A pedagogical formulation of ICT which offers a model of the subject which is both robust from a philosophical point of view, and usable from a teacher's point of view has yet to be created. One of the barriers to achieving this is the rapid development of personal computing technologies. Compared with the speed which new hardware and software is developed and enters the market, the timescale of the National Curriculum is a document which works on a geological time scale. When the National Curriculum first introduced ICT into schools as a statutory subject, the personal computer industry was still in its infancy, but from the late 1980s onwards the speed of change in this field has been phenomenal. Most dramatic changes have been created by the growth of networked computing. The size and scope of the Internet has grown rapidly and broadened its base of users. Within organisations, implementations of internal networks (Intranets), has shifted the emphasis away from single machines and onto distributed computing. It is clear that the designers of the first National Curriculum for ICT were creating a curriculum to be used with stand-alone computers. The computer was viewed as a tool for processing information, and pupils were encouraged to identify tasks which computers could perform, and harness this power to help them complete work from within other curriculum areas. ICT is now a vastly more complex landscape than it was at the time of the Education Reform act.

Recent work carried out at the University of Huddersfield, has examined what primary pupils understand by the term *computer network* (Baron and others, 1999). The pupils were asked to draw computer systems, and over 80% of them drew networks extending beyond and individual desktop machine. The most sophisticated representations demonstrated that pupils understood the concept of the Internet as a global network of computers capable of sharing information. The pupils who took part in this study were able to articulate, through their drawings, how the computer used can connect with sources of information from all over the globe, and most importantly connect not just with other computes but also with other users of computers. Many pupils did draw a school on their depiction of a computer network, but a significant proportion did not draw links from the school to the larger network. In many cases the school was represented as an isolated node in the network. Pupils are aware of the ways in which the Internet is changing interaction with computers, but many of them see the school as located outside this revolution.

The designers of the ICT curriculum face the challenge of connecting the school to the Internet in order that the full educational potential of the medium can be harnessed. The current National Curriculum certainly makes many gestures towards the desirability of this end, and the use of e-mail by pupils is explicitly mentioned in the revised Programmes of Study, but its guidance is lacking about how schools should handle the complex technical and pedagogical questions which surround this transition. Most teachers believe in the educational potential of the Internet but converting this potential into educational practices which can be integrated with other curriculum areas is far from straightforward.

As this paradigm shift in the way personal computing is practised filters into the formal education system, the designers of the ICT curriculum are faced with the challenge of specifying content and approaches which are relevant in this new landscape. This change has been noticeable even within the acronyms used to describe the field, and the word *Communications* has gradually inserted itself between *Information* and *Technology* signalling the rising importance of the computer as a tool of communication, rather than merely as a processor of information. The latest review of the National Curriculum reporting in 1999 recommended the expansion of the acronym IT to include Communications, and the Qualifications and Curriculum Authority cited support for this change at 80%, with just 6% of respondents to the proposal opposed to replacing IT with ICT (QCA, 1999b).

The challenges emerging as a result of the light-speed development of personal computing are not restricted to formal schooling. Commercial organisations are struggling to keep pace with the developments, and there is a widespread belief that companies which do not develop coherent strategies to exploit the Internet are destined for failure.

The Language of the National Curriculum

It is worth remembering that the National Curriculum is only a set of words, and subjecting its rhetoric to a close reading can yield considerable insight into how the document goes about its stated task of specifying the curriculum of formal schooling in England and Wales. ICT is specified in the National Curriculum document as both a subject in its own right, and a subject area which can be used in other curriculum areas. Crawford (1997) outlines the three main ways in which the secondary school can deliver the statutory requirements for ICT. ICT can be taught only a subject in its own right, taught only within other subjects as a supporting discipline, or delivered in a hybrid mode where subject specific lessons are used alongside opportunities to use computers in other subjects.

When the four programmes of study (POS) for ICT are read as a single document, some themes emerge. The most notable theme is the way in which the number of decisions which pupils make about their application of ICT increases as the scale of levels is ascended. In Key Stage 1, we read under the heading *Knowledge, Skills and Understanding*:

Pupils should be taught how to:

a) gather information from a variety of sources [for example, people, books, databases, CD-ROMs, videos and TV]

b) enter and store information in a variety of forms [for example, information in a prepared database, saving work]

c) retrieve information that has been stored [for example, using a CD-ROM, loading saved work]

(DfEE and QCA, 1999a, p.14)

This appears straightforward, ICT is a tool concerned with processing information and this section sets out a three-fold process of gathering, entering and retrieving which is common to almost all human interactions with computer.

By the time Key Stage 4 is reached, the programme of study contained under the heading: *Reviewing, modifying and evaluating work as it progresses*, is recommending the following:

Pupils should be taught to:

a) evaluate the effectiveness of their own and others' uses of information sources and ICT tools, using the results to improve the quality of their work and to inform future judgements

b) reflect critically on the impact of ICT on their own and others' lives, considering the social, economic, political, legal, ethical and moral issues [for example, changes to working practices, the economic impact of e-commerce, the implications of personal information gathered, held and exchanged using ICT]

c) use their initiative to find about and exploit the potential of more advanced or new ICT tools and information sources [for example, new sites on the internet, new or upgraded application software].

(DfEE and QCA, 1999b)

The overall vision of the designers of the National Curriculum becomes apparent when the transition from Key Stage 1 to Key Stage 4 is charted. The lower key stages are concerned with giving pupils the chance to use the technology, grappling with the many ways in which computers can be used to process, store, analyse and represent data. The higher levels, and Key Stage 4 in particular, introduce new themes. These themes can be broadly summarised as the sponsoring of a cautionary approach to the technology and awareness of its inherent limitations, coupled with a requirement for pupils to get to grips with wider import of the new technology. The section of the National Curriculum quoted above, represents a considerable challenge to secondary schools, just as the requirements for Key Stages 1 and 2 hand primary schools an extremely difficult task. The level of sophistication of thought needed to achieve the outcomes above is really rather high. It is self evident that teaching in ICT should not take place in a vacuum devoid of ethical or moral considerations, and pupils should be given opportunities to reflect on the social impact of the technology. But teachers will ask, where will the time to achieve these ends come from? Software continues to increase in complexity, and the range of tasks possible on a computer also continues to rise. Teachers may well feel under pressure to concentrate on equipping pupils with the hard skills to use the computers before they move on to wider philosophical considerations, and the space available for this sort of reflective activity could reduce to the point at which this section of the National Curriculum ceases to have any significant impact upon classroom practice. The inclusion of sections such as this one in the National Curriculum for ICT reveals a truth about the subject. It reminds us that there are still a very real debate about what an ICT curriculum should be like, what it should contain, and what teaching in the subject should look like. In the opening of the newly revised National Curriculum there is a section titled *Values, aims and purposes*, and aim 2 mentions the promotion of pupils' 'spiritual, moral, social and cultural development' (DfEE and QCA, 1999, p.11). Having set out with this lofty goal in mind, when the designers of the curriculum come to ICT they need to ensure that these aims are embedded within it.

When reading the National Curriculum, not only the section about ICT but the entire document, it is often hard to think of any activity designed by a skilful and professionally competent teacher that does not fulfil the NC aims. Indeed most teachers automatically produce teaching and learning whose content fulfils the requirements of the National Curriculum, with their skill and professionalism guiding them towards constantly making decisions about their teaching which give their pupils maximum opportunities to learn. The challenge faced by teachers is to translate what they do in the classroom into the language of the National Curriculum, reworking their documentation about classroom practice into a state where it harmonises with the discourse of the NC. Mastering the National Curriculum means to some extent mastering the language in which it is written, and teachers face considerable challenges when attempting to interpret the document and convert its macro-level recommendations into micro-level educational events in the classroom.

It has been suggested recently that the discourse of IT in education has been dominated by the technical and craft levels (Conlon, 2000). Conlon defines the technical level as embracing questions such as 'how do I?' and 'how can we make this work?' The craft levels of discourse are situated slightly higher and involve questions about how computers can be used to improve the production of work within the classroom. A typical example of craft discourse at work is the question of how word processing can be used to improve students' understanding of the complexities of the writing process, as opposed to merely using the tool as a device to enhance presentation. With discourses from these two areas dominating the debates, Conlon argues that there is a widespread avoidance of the visionary questions which relate to the overall status of ICT within the curriculum, and he seeks an explanation as to why these questions are not asked:

> The explanation could be that the technology is so new, so difficult and absorbing that we can easily exhaust ourselves by working as technicians. Perhaps also we assume that effort is unnecessary. Surely we are already working to a grand plan? Isn't there a document somewhere setting out a vision? (Conlon, 2000, p.110)

Conlon is seeking a grand narrative to justify the inclusion of ICT within the curriculum, and his question about the existence of a document setting out a vision for ICT teaching within schools clearly demonstrates that the

National Curriculum is not this document. Support for Conlon's view is provided by Selwyn (1999) who argues that the discourse of ICT within education has been largely deterministic, and is generated by a view of education and computing where questions about the definition of the subject have already been answered.

The confidence with which the National Curriculum goes about its task of specifying ICT may not seem that deterministic at first glance, but the very existence of the document works to prevent debate amongst teachers about what they should be teaching in ICT. Why should teachers spend valuable time formulating new and exciting definitions of what computer literacy means, and then converting this into curriculum content, when a ready-made and legally binding document sits on the shelf with the answers in black and white? We now find ourselves close to the heart of the operation of the National Curriculum. The process of telling teachers what to teach could be considered an erosion of professional responsibility, but the National Curriculum also presents an attack on professional autonomy, limiting the ways in which teachers can use their knowledge of pupils to redefine curriculum subjects in ways which encourage innovation and the exploration of new ideas. When asked to respond to the Revised National Curriculum for ICT, the Association of Teachers and Lecturers provided this comment:

> Teachers welcome the fact that the drive to raise standards in ICT is implicit in all subjects in the consultation materials. However, the requirements can be both too precise and too vague. (QCA, 1999b)

One of the manifest problems with the National Curriculum is the level at which its discourse operates. The Programmes of Study and associated attainment targets are expressed in a language which prefers the general to the specific, and the specification of broad sets of skills and knowledge rather than fine detail. The discourse which the curriculum makers employ is extremely efficient at specifying what the students should know, but it distinctly lacks any substantive amplification of how exactly schools should go about the rather difficult business of designing content to achieve this knowledge.

It is clear that the National Curriculum works to specify outcomes, not to specify the content of works schemes. This is common across all curriculum areas, but is particularly acute in ICT, where moving down from the lofty levels of the original curriculum specification, it is all too easy to become embroiled in technical details. But it is precisely at this level which schools face the greatest challenges in implementing the National Curriculum for ICT. Complex decisions about hardware specification, operating systems, network architecture, and software purchase all proliferate at this level. As schools move to using computing platforms and software imported from the commercial world, the amount of resources which need to be devoted to achieving these aims increases.

This is clearly seen in Primary schools which are currently using government funding to purchase their first networks of PCs, replacing the stand-alone Acorn machines which were previously used. This dramatic influx of new technology into the primary school may give the impression that schools are moving towards placing ICT at the heart of the curriculum, but what is often masked is very real tensions which this new technology can place on the infrastructure of the school.

Here is a head teacher of a primary school responding to the National Curriculum Review Consultation:

> First of all people need to understand what they mean by ICT, particularly the government. I think ICT can only be taught when you've got large numbers of machines. If you have one stuck on one side of the classroom and incorporate it into History and Geography it does not work. So you need a large amount of hardware. The training implications for my staff are enormous. (QCA, 1999b)

Within the primary school the tensions are most obvious in the areas of staff knowledge, timetabling and physical space. The day-to-day maintenance of these newly installed PC networks requires quite large amounts of technical knowledge. Without regular interventions to restore missing files, adjust settings and monitor the health of the network the integrity of a network of computers is soon degraded. Some machines may well stop operating correctly without regular software maintenance, at other times a whole school network could be brought down if infected by a virus circulating on the Internet. Recent e-mail viruses such as *Melissa* and the *I love you* virus, succeeded in causing major problems for companies with specialist computer support departments, the potential for damage to school networks, which are far more exposed is much higher. In the absence of dedicated PC technicians, teachers will either have to equip themselves with these skills, or resign themselves to the fact that the PC suite will always have problems.

The timetabling of computer use can also be an issue in primary schools. In order to ensure that all pupils have access to the facilities a school-wide timetable along the lines of a secondary timetable may need to be drawn up. They physical space of the primary school can also be the subject of tensions, as the newly installed computer suite competes for room with other areas. Some schools with little free space have had to choose between reducing the size available for the library or the installation of a computer suite. It is noticeable that the DfEE and QCA pronouncements on ICT do make mention of the resourcing issues associated with increasing ICT use, but schools faced with hard decisions about priorities may not find much practical advice abut solving the problems faced.

Harrison (1998), discussing the issue of teaching quality in ICT in the primary school makes the following point:

> The quality of children's work when using computers, as with almost everything else in primary education, depends upon the skills of the class teacher, not in the grandiose plans for management systems, glossy heavyweight policy documents, or the titles and job descriptions of promoted staff. (p.3)

This represents a practical, albeit slightly cynical look at the challenges involved in introducing ICT into the primary school. Harrison argues that individual teachers drive excellence and innovation, and these solitary efforts are neither helped nor hindered by the existence of a National Curriculum.

Both Conlon whose lamentations about the lack of an overall vision for the implementation of ICT, and Harrison who sees excellence in this area as being fuelled by the teacher rather than policy, are sceptical about the merits of a centrally specified curriculum. Conlon argues for the fundamental irrelevance of this type of document because any curriculum for ICT runs the risk of becoming rapidly mired in detail and technical considerations, with an accompanying loss of the visionary quality and articulation of the revolutionary possibilities of ICT in formal education. Harrison makes a similar attack on the curriculum but uses a subtly different argument: for him the individual teacher in the classroom using the technology to support micro-level curriculum design is most likely to make an impact, and this would happen with or without the National Curriculum. What emerges from a study of this area is the distinct lack of commentators who are prepared to endorse the National Curriculum for ICT and assert its effectiveness in guiding schools towards improving their provision of teaching pupils about computing.

The Challenges of Virtual Learning

Much of the current work in educational applications of technology and associated research concerns the most efficient uses of the educational possibilities of the Internet. Virtual learning environments and systems for delivering online educational content are currently the focus of attention. Most of the current innovative work in this area is to be found in the Further and Higher Education sectors, where much of the infrastructure to exploit these possibilities is already in place. Compared with the post-compulsory institutions, schools are decidedly non-virtual places; the routine of school life for most pupils remains stubbornly physical. But if schools remain wedded to a mode of teaching and learning which still relies on the physical technology of classrooms, teachers, timetables and face-to-face contact, elsewhere it is apparent that dramatic changes in the way pupils access information are underway. A survey of home computer use and ownership conducted in 1999 revealed that 77% of lower secondary (11-14 years) have access to a computer at home (Harris, 1999). This figure is surely set to rise sharply as sales of PCs to home users are rising sharply, and may well peak at over 90% saturation. The survey also found that pupils were using the computers for a range of tasks, and activities with links to schoolwork were as likely to occur as games playing or other types of recreational computing.

The development of the National Grid for Learning is an attempt by the government to give pupils, teachers and parents access to the educational possibilities of the Internet. Increasingly pupils can look outside the walls of the school for access to knowledge and opportunities for learning. The NGfL sets out a government led vision where school children can return home, log on to the site and access material and resources. It is paradoxical that a child who seeks to use the Internet for homework may well fulfil many of the requirements of the National Curriculum for ICT and immediately begin scaling the ladder of attainment levels, but in so doing the pupil reduces her reliance on the school as a source of knowledge and learning. Viewed in this way, the ICT orders coupled with the phenomenal growth of educational material on the Internet may actually lead children to view the curriculum imposed at school as increasingly outdated and irrelevant.

The National Curriculum aims to control what happens in school, and gives teachers a clear framework in which they are expected to work. These frameworks are laid down by central government agencies. The paradox is that ICT is not a stable subject and waves of technological innovation are constantly redefining the skills and knowledge which a competent user of the technology needs to possess. The National Curriculum for ICT is framed in a language of such generality that it floats above these contingent details and prefers not to dirty these hands in these debates. Whilst this stance may make for a stable curriculum document which can give a strong impression that the government is taking this area of the curriculum extremely seriously, by not engaging with the more detailed, and ultimately harder questions surrounding ICT as a subject, the document risks becoming irrelevant to teachers struggling to turn curriculum into content. The latest revisions to the National Curriculum for ICT do improve the clarity of the document and in particular the status of ICT as a cross-curricular discipline is enhanced, but despite the revisions many key issues remain unresolved and no doubt we will be debating exactly what we mean by ICT for many years to come.

References

Baron, G.L. and others (1999) *Deliverable a05: Modélisation conceptuelle initiale*. Unpublished report. Available: http://hermes.iacm.forth.gr/html/del_a05.html.

Conlon, T. (2000) Visions of Change: Information Technology, Education and Postmodernism, *British Journal of Education Technology*, 31 (2), 109-116.

Crawford, R. (1997) *Managing Information Technology in Secondary Schools*, London, Routledge.

Davies, M. and Edwards, G. (1999) Will the curriculum caterpillar ever fly? *Cambridge Journal of Education*, 29 (2), pp.265-275.

Department for Education and Employment and the Qualifications and Curriculum Authority (1999a) *The national curriculum: handbook for primary teachers in England*, London, HMSO.

Department for Education and Employment and the Qualifications and Curriculum Authority (1999b) *The national curriculum: handbook for secondary teachers in England*, London, HMSO.

Harris, S. (1999) Secondary school students' use of computers at home, *British Journal of Educational Technology*, 30 (4), pp.331-338.

Harrison, M. (1998) *Coordinating information and communications technology across the primary school*, London, Falmer Press.

Qualifications and Curriculum Authority (1999a) National Curriculum Review Consultation [online]. Available: http://www.qca.gov.uk/ncr/more-flexible-nc-old.htm. Date accessed 1st May 1999.

Qualifications and Curriculum Authority (1999b) Consultation on the review of the national curriculum in England 1999 [online]. Available: http://www.qca.org.uk/ncr/recommendations/mori-chap6.htm. Date accessed 1st May 1999.

Selwyn, N. (1999) Why the computer is not dominating schools: a failure of policy or a failure of practice? *Cambridge Journal of Education*, 29 (1), pp.77-91.

12 Conclusion: Logic, Rationality and the Curriculum

PAUL OLIVER

There are many different ways in which policy makers may seek to justify educational initiatives, and also more than one group to whom justifications may be directed. Pragmatic justifications rest upon arguing essentially that a policy is desirable either because it achieves its goals, or is likely to do so in the future. Of course, simply because a policy is successful in pragmatic terms does not affirm that it was a sound policy in the first place. Schools might be asked for example to change the curriculum so that it consists of 75% sport and games, and 25% academic work in order to improve the physical fitness of pupils. This strategy would no doubt succeed, but whether it was a sensible policy initially is clearly open to question.

One can also seek to justify a curriculum on the grounds that it is popular with consumers. However, education does not simply have one body of consumers. What is popular with pupils may not necessarily be popular with parents. In the case of pupils it would not be too difficult to envisage changes to the curriculum which would probably be very popular in the short term. Usually however, decisions about the curriculum have to take a longer-term view. Those decisions have to be based upon considerations concerning the type of citizens and human beings who may emerge from a particular educational experience. Parents, on the other hand, may well take a longer-term view, but again, popularity with parents does not constitute any absolute justification. A new curriculum may be advocated for example, on the grounds that it prepares young people for a particular area of work which policy makers argue will increase in the future. This type of argument may be popular with parents who are very much pre-occupied with the employability of their children. However, they may be in no position to either support or negate projected employment patterns for a country.

Other forms of justification are essentially *a priori* in character. It may be argued for instance, that young people should be aware of the main historical and political events of the previous century, on the grounds that a civilised and educated human being should know something of the forces which have moulded her or his contemporary world. It is being argued here that it is part of the concept of an educated human being to possess this type of understanding, and hence a historical perspective should be included in the curriculum. It is not easy to subject such arguments to any kind of pragmatic test, since it is difficult to provide a positive correlation between historical understanding and practical success in later life, largely because of the difficulty in eliminating other variables. However, consumers of education, particularly parents, may find it a plausible argument that young people should have a sense of history.

Major policy initiatives in education such as the National Curriculum have important implications for the country and are also resource intensive. It seems therefore very important that there should be clear reasons for proceeding in one way rather than another. There is however, a fundamental difficulty with research into the implementation of curriculum initiatives. This arises because of the typically long period of time between implementation and the possibility of seeing the results of the policy. In the case of a primary school initiative, it may well be twenty years before the relevant cohort of children are fully embedded in the employment market, and one is able to monitor trends. In the meantime of course, a very large number of variables have intervened, making it very difficult to establish clear causal relationships.

There is no doubt that research is required in relation to major initiatives such as the National Curriculum, but it is important that such research should be systematically planned, and that it is clear which issues the research is designed to clarify. If we start at the point of designing the new initiative, it is important that policy makers make it clear in the public domain the value judgements and principles which are the basis of the initiative. These may supplement instrumental considerations, but there are almost certain to be some assumptions made about the concept of education in devising a new curriculum. As Cohen (1983, p.76) argues:

> The liberal concern has been to show that education is an evaluative or normative concept, and that because of this, the analysis of education has practical implications both for the content of the curriculum and for educational methods and procedures.

By placing such assumptions in the public domain, the policy maker is being open with consumers concerning the parameters of the new development.

The other way of justifying a new development is to look backwards in time to a previous initiative and then to research some of the apparent consequences of that development. The assumption of such historically-based research is then that the previous development can inform the present one. The problem with such research designs however, is that the environment and context of the research development will have changed, perhaps significantly. Nevertheless, empirical data gathered in this way provides at least a provisional basis for future developments.

A further research design which may be appropriate for a major initiative such as a National Curriculum, is to engage in a series of research studies to collect empirical data on the effectiveness of the development. Such data can then be used progressively to refine and adapt the initial development to enable it to more closely achieve its original aims. The assumption with this type of research model is that the original initiative was set up in such a way that the possibility and feasibility of amending it, are accepted from the outset. Systematic research and evaluation is thus essential in order to support any major educational initiative, but that research should be formulated and presented in such a way, that its fundamental assumptions are clear and transparent.

Just as value judgements are implicit in the selection of curricular materials, so are values a part of the transmission of the curriculum. Indeed it is very difficult to disentangle the concept of what is taught and how it is taught from the notion of values. Immediately we argue that one particular historical event or process should be studied rather than a different one, we are making value judgements. Such judgements are in effect ethical, because we are arguing that children 'ought' to study one thing rather than another. Part of the problem however with a 'national' or centralised curriculum is that it is easy to forget that such a curriculum is in fact a human creation, and as such reflects the value positions in terms of selectivity of material, of the people who devised it. No matter how much consultation takes place during such a process, there is still a final decision to make to include A and to exclude B.

The question of ethics is also central to the delivery of the curriculum, and this is partly a question of content and partly a question of pedagogy. For example, it would be possible to teach subjects such as science and technology in a completely decontextualised manner, but that would ignore the enormous variety of ways in which such subjects impact on the contemporary world and raise important ethical issues. One could teach genetics in an abstract way, but to ignore the ethical issues implicit in genetic engineering would be to miss the opportunity to discuss a very significant current issue. This is not to say that teachers should take a specific viewpoint on such issues, but rather that they have the opportunity to explore the complexities of such issues with pupils, and hence give them the chance to begin to formulate their own views.

There are some philosophical difficulties when a curriculum seeks to transmit what we might term generic values. These could be values such as 'fairness' or 'tolerance of the views of others'. Taken in isolation these values, and others of a similar nature, appear utterly praiseworthy, and the type of values which presumably most parents would wish to see inculcated in their children. However, once such values are contextualised it can become very difficult to clarify exactly what the teacher is transmitting. Suppose in a classroom discussion on pollution, a pupil asks her teacher whether it is 'fair' that people with cars, and sometimes more than one car, should pollute the atmosphere for everyone else. The discussion inevitably strays into conceptual analysis of the term 'fair'. Questions arise of the nature 'Fair to whom?'; 'Fair in what way?', and 'What do we mean by fairness anyway?'. One pupil might raise the issue of people who live in rural areas and need their own transport. Another might raise a question about the idea of personal liberty, and the extent to which people with the requisite money should be able to select their own means of transport. This pupil might want to know the relationship between personal liberty and fairness, and raise the issue of whether personal liberty was one feature of being fair to oneself. Hence, where a value which is expressed as an abstract concept may seem desirable as part of an educational enterprise, once it is contextualised it may not appear as straightforward.

It is a similar matter with the question of being tolerant of other peoples' views. In a general context this seems a laudable proposition, but once we consider specific viewpoints, we realise that as teachers we may not wish to advocate tolerance for such views. There are surely many viewpoints which in a civilised society (or one which we would like to consider civilised) we would be less than happy if our school pupils tolerated or even accepted, simply because they were held by others. It thus seems rather problematic if we are going to advocate as part of a centralised curriculum, that certain specific values should be transmitted as part of a compulsory educational experience. Rather than being exposed to certain values, our young people should be encouraged to be critical, in the sense of being able to analyse rationally the value positions of others. As Scheffler (1973, p.143) argues:

> We encourage them to ask questions, to look for evidence, to seek and scrutinise alternatives, to be critical of their own ideas as well as those of others. This educational course precludes taking schooling as an instrument for shaping their minds to a preconceived idea.

One argument for a 'national' curriculum is that there is a certain body of knowledge to which all pupils should have access, if they are to be regarded as having participated in an adequate educational process within a certain cultural milieu. Whether or not it is possible to define a body of knowledge appropriate for all pupils can be evaluated within the terms of an argument about relevance and the instrumental uses of education. Pupils may well challenge from time to time, the value of a particular section of the curriculum by implicitly suggesting that it is not relevant to them or to their situation. Now relevance is a very interesting concept in educational practice, partly at least because it is heard of so frequently. Although we may know to whom something is supposed or supposed not to be relevant, it may be less than clear in what context this assertion is made. For example, when a pupil says that something is not relevant, s(he) may be claiming that it is not relevant to his or her development at the time, or to his or her interests, or to the possibility of gaining employment, or to his or her future development; and so on.

Part of the difficulty with the concept of relevance is that school pupils find great difficulty, understandably, in peering in to the future, and hence appreciating what out of the current curricular offerings will be most useful to them. They cannot gaze ahead and see that in ten years time they will be studying accountancy, and that all the maths which they find tedious now, will in fact prove to be very relevant. They cannot imagine that they will eventually become a sports journalist and that all those grammar exercises in English will ultimately prove to be worth their weight in gold. Hence the concept of relevance tends to be applied within the parameters of the present. A part of the curriculum is or is not relevant to pupil interests at this moment, or does not seem relevant to the employment opportunities which are available. Now it is certainly true that school pupils are very individualistic, and clearly have a wide range of different interests. It would seem a very difficult task to mould a curriculum to so many diverse interests.

Hence there is no doubt a tension between the insights of mature educators who can envisage young people working in a future where it is not completely clear which skills will be required, and pupils who may have a very specific idea of the kind of employment which they want. The educator has to take the long-term view and to devise a curriculum which will not close off options for young people in the future. It should be a curriculum which enables young people in principle, to aim for any occupation which interests them. Nevertheless, there is a sense in which this approach can be said to be requiring an acceptance of deferred gratification on the part of pupils. One can imagine the teacher saying to pupils, 'Well, study the Latin poets diligently now, because you never know, you may wish to become a classics teacher in the future.' One has some sympathy with young people who look around their environment in their early teens, identify a job to which they aspire, and then ask themselves the perfectly reasonable question, 'How is my study at school helping me to achieve this goal?' The answer may be that it is rather difficult to envisage how much of the school curriculum helps such a goal in a very direct sense.

To extend this argument slightly, one can also consider the variations in employment prospects in different parts of the country. It may be that children living in inner city areas do not aspire to jobs in agriculture as much as children living in the countryside. This may be simply because they have no experience of such jobs and also no adult role models to follow. Certainly, job opportunities in terms of types of vocation, do vary from one part of the country to another. One wonders therefore whether it would be sensible to include in a national curriculum some degree or possibility of flexibility, to enable young people who so wished, to follow subjects which had more direct relevance to the jobs to which they aspired. This is not to suggest that the curriculum should become so vocationally specialised that children are channelled into certain occupations simply because they predominate in a particular area. Rather that some consideration be given to the potentially positive motivational effect on young people who perceive what they are studying in school to be directly relevant to their career aspirations.

These kinds of arguments about relevance may not be entirely unconnected with the issues of disaffection in school, and of exclusion from school. It is clearly very difficult to establish a direct causal connection between a particular type of curriculum and the level of exclusions from school. There are so many social and economic factors which might operate in such situations. However, what can be reasonably argued is that disaffection from school is linked in some way to what is traditionally termed motivation to study, and which in turn, one may reasonably hypothesise is connected to the perceived relevance of the content of the school day.

Questions of relevance and individual motivation of pupils are very much connected with important philosophical principles such as autonomy and self-determination. We have already discussed many aspects of the position of pupils, and to some extent these are connected to issues of personal rights and in particular the right to self-determination. Pupils certainly do have rights, and the rights which they possess in this regard are perhaps more centrally connected with their rights qua human being, rather than their rights qua citizen. Unfortunately, and in some regards rather sadly, a national curriculum is rather about doing something to pupils, rather than for them or on their behalf. In a legal sense, perhaps school pupils have few direct rights to change this situation, but as human beings they do have rights. Even if they are not in a position to articulate these clearly for themselves, then others are in a position to do so.

Pupils certainly do have rights which result from the general human right to self-determination (Bramall and White, 2000, p.12). They have the right to study and learn about the things which interest them. They have the right to learn the knowledge and skills which will help them start in their chosen occupation (and implicitly they have the right to select that occupation). They also have the right to interesting, well-informed and well-resourced teaching. Naturally, rights bring obligations. Pupils have the obligation to work attentively in schools within the prescribed times of attendance, and to behave in a civilised manner. However, it is a fair supposition that many young people have clearly identified a vocation, and all they seek is a reasonably-structured and interesting preparation for such a vocation. Such pupils actually do wish to make an effective economic contribution to society. The danger of providing them with a school experience which does not satisfy their needs and which ultimately alienates them is that it may result in their disaffection not only with school, but afterwards with the entire prospect of making a positive contribution to society.

The question of self-determination is also a very real issue for teachers. Our school teachers are very well educated to degree level, and then trained as teachers to a very high standard. A great deal of our higher education system is designed to produce autonomous learners. The skills of analysis, synthesis, creativity and innovative thinking are highly prized. When graduates near the end of their degree programme they have to produce a research dissertation, which requires them to collect and analyse data. It can be argued that having successfully completed an intensive course of education and training which particularly prizes qualities of independence of thought, teachers are placed in a situation where they have to transmit the curriculum in a relatively predetermined manner, and with little opportunity to adapt what they teach to the perceived needs of their pupils.

It is possible, of course, to standardise the content and delivery of any curriculum. Ultimately one could devise study packs to be delivered on a distance learning basis, where the learning method essentially involved self-study and individualised learning by the student without any dialogue with the tutor. Assessment would then be by examination. In such cases, the role of the 'teacher' is reduced to the writing of the study packs in order to present the curriculum material in a systematic manner which is easy for the student to absorb without recourse to the advice of the tutor. If courses are offered in this type of model, it is certainly one which involves few resources, once the study packs have been written. However, one does wonder whether this type of approach is in accord with many of the principles which are normally associated with the concept of education.

Clearly the model outlined here is a rather extreme version of a view of education where the opportunities for interaction between teacher and student are reduced to a minimum. The teacher delivering the national curriculum is clearly not in this position, and yet there are considerable constraints on action which result from the notion of a centralised curriculum. Part of the process of dialogue between teacher and pupils occurs when a pupil is interested in a topic and wants to explore this further in a particular direction. This is in a sense the excitement of education. Yet within a centralised curriculum the teacher often feels constrained to bring the discussion back again and again to the set topics. There must on many occasions be circumstances where pupils feel that the opportunities to explore their own interests are being closed off, and that teachers feel that there are artificial limitations being placed on the creativity which they can show in order to interest and motivate their pupils.

There is surely something in the concept of being a teacher which is about engaging in a dialogue with one's pupils and exploring issues together. The teacher is not simply a repository of knowledge, who transmits this knowledge. The educational process must be about something more than that. As Peters (1967, p.6) argues:

> But even this is not enough; for we would be disinclined to call a man who was merely well-informed an educated man. To be educated requires also some understanding of principles, of the 'reason why' of things.

It is arguable that this 'understanding of principles' is the process which takes place when a good teacher is free to follow the interests of pupils and to explore with them some of the underlying ideas of what they are studying. Not only is this more motivating for pupils but it enables teachers to use their own education and creativity to the full.

The chapters in this book then raise, either directly or indirectly a number of important issues about a centralised curriculum. First of all it seems essential that something as crucial to the national future and prosperity as the National Curriculum should be supported by the most detailed research, even if some of the data suggests shortcomings in the process. If indeed such research reveals inadequacies in the manner in which the curriculum has been set up, the research should continue in order to explore ways of improving the situation. The parameters of such research should be made clear, and be available within the public domain. Quite apart from educational issues, the National Curriculum has cost a great deal of money to implement, and there is a need to employ evaluation research strategies to examine whether all of this money appears to have been effectively spent.

Secondly, it is important to recognise that values are an inherent part of any educational process. The curriculum must inevitably be transmitted within a framework of values. It is important that parents and members of the public, as well as school pupils, are aware of the value system which accompanies the curriculum. However, quite apart from making such a value system public, it is perhaps even more important that children are taught logical processes of analysis whereby they can analyse value systems, and make up their own minds about which systems for them have the greater validity.

Thirdly, it is important to remember that any curriculum, and perhaps more importantly a national curriculum, retains much of its significance for pupils, when it prepares them for, and supports, their chosen vocation. One of the most important motivating factors for children at school is the idea that what they are studying is preparing them for the world of work in general, and for a career for themselves in particular. The national curriculum should reflect this important aspiration of children, and provide a mechanism for them to gain a foothold on the path to their desired career.

Finally, it should be remembered that neither teachers nor pupils will achieve their full potential within the educational process, if they are unable to exercise their creativity and pursue lines of enquiry which are meaningful to them within a particular learning context. Education is inevitably a process of negotiation and discussion in which ideas are explored and clarified. It is vital if the excitement and sense of adventure of education are to be nourished that the curriculum is not reduced to a prescribed body of knowledge, but retains a degree of fluidity to enable pupils to follow some of their own interests. This is not to say that society should not define some of the ideas and skills, important in an educated young person, but this process should not go so far that a sense of wonder at the sheer possibilities inherent in learning, are lost to the need to acquire a specified body of knowledge.

References

Bramall, S. and White, J. (2000) *Will the new National Curriculum live up to its aims?* London, Philosophy of Education Society of Great Britain.

Cohen, B. (1983) *Means and Ends in Education*, London, George Allen and Unwin.

Peters, R.S. (1967) What is an educational process?, in Peters R.S. (ed) *The Concept of Education*, London, Routledge and Kegan Paul.

Scheffler, I. (1973) *Reason and Teaching*, London, Routledge and Kegan Paul.